# Patria

*The Complete Cycle*

# Patria
## *The Complete Cycle*

R. Murray Schafer

 COACH HOUSE BOOKS

Published with the assistance of the Canada Council for the Arts
and the Ontario Arts Council.

The Canada Council | Le Conseil des Arts
for the Arts | du Canada

ONTARIO ARTS COUNCIL
CONSEIL DES ARTS DE L'ONTARIO

NATIONAL LIBRARY OF CANADA CATALOGUING IN PUBLICATION DATA

Schafer, R. Murray (Raymond Murray), 1933-
    Patria : the complete cycle / R. Murray Schafer.

Expanded ed. of: Patria and the theatre of confluence.
c1991.
ISBN 1-55245-109-7

    1.Schafer, R. Murray (Raymond Murray), 1933- . Patria.
2.Opera–Canada–20th century. I.Title.

ML410.S25P314 2002        782.1'092        C2002-903223-7

# Contents

# Preface
## *The Labyrinth and the Thread*

THE WORKS DISCUSSED in the following pages represent almost forty years of activity in music theatre. It was soon after completing *Loving* in 1965 that I began to conceive a series of thematically unified works under the generic title of *Patria*. At the outset I envisioned three pieces in the cycle. Eventually this grew to twelve works of varying complexity and requirements. Music is at the centre of all the *Patria* works, but not in an overwhelming sense; none of the works is truly operatic. Had I lived in a country where operas were commissioned and performed, I might have written one or more, but Canada has protected me from such conventionality, so I can honestly say that each of the *Patria* pieces has been shaped by its inner exigency, frequently without regard to how it might be produced. Productions have accordingly been infrequent. Many have cost me money.

Although the works are connected, I never intended that they should be performed sequentially, like Wagner's *Ring* or the *Oresteia*. Each part is complete in itself but gains in richness if the audience is familiar with others in the cycle. Occasionally, whole scenes are replayed from different angles. Many of the same characters reappear, sometimes with new names,[1] as we move from a wilderness lake to ancient Egypt and Crete, medieval Europe, China and then twentieth-century North America before finally returning to the wilderness.

My idea was that two principal characters, a man and a woman, would engage in a search for one another through a labyrinth of different cultures, almost as if they were the split halves of the same being. They might return in various guises, but the quest for unity and the homeland they were seeking would remain elusive until their final encounter.

*Patria* is Latin for homeland – hence 'patriotic.' Throughout my life I have found it difficult to feel patriotic about Canada. Perhaps, as Lawrence Durrell suggested, the duty of every artist is to hate his own country creatively. In these days of restless migration and social instability, many countries, like my own, have lost their sovereignty and their ethnic identity. Others have been invaded, and their original inhabitants murdered or expelled. All countries are rapidly losing contact with nature as well as with history and tradition. *Patria*, then, is not a country, but a state of

---

1  In Appendix I, I give a diagram presenting some of the various names and affiliations of the principal *Patria* characters.

mind, a quest for identity and security – a place to breathe and be inspired. This is what animates the *Patria* cycle.

I have written these articles as a guide to directors and performers. They chronicle my thoughts as the works took shape or were performed. Since performances have been infrequent, there are probably many readers who have never seen a *Patria* piece live. But I have always believed that the works can be appreciated in formats other than physical performance. Several of the scores are quite graphic, with drawings and diagrams; all texts contain glossaries with references to sources from mythology, language and literature. The cross-references and relationships among the individual pieces in the *Patria* cycle are complex and can be understood on many levels. One can find meanings at whatever depth desired. This is why the metaphor for the whole series has been the labyrinth, in which Wolf (Theseus) provides the force and Ariadne the thread leading to the eventual solution.

Although the *Patria* works are not intended to be performed in sequence, there is a natural order in the overall cycle. I have, however, altered it somewhat in the first part of this book, presenting the more conventional works first, with a discussion of *Loving* as a prelude. Three theoretical essays entitled 'The Theatre of Confluence' are inserted at appropriate points to explain the evolution of my thinking about how the units might flow together.

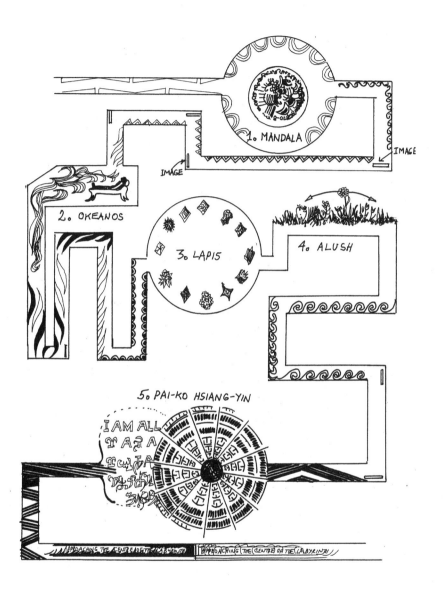

1. MANDALA

IMAGE

IMAGE

2. OKEANOS

3. LAPIS

4. ALUSH

5. PAI-KO HSIANG-YIN

I AM ALL
ΨΑЯΑ

APPROACHING THE CENTRE OF THE LABYRINTH    APPROACHING THE CENTRE OF THE LABYRINTH

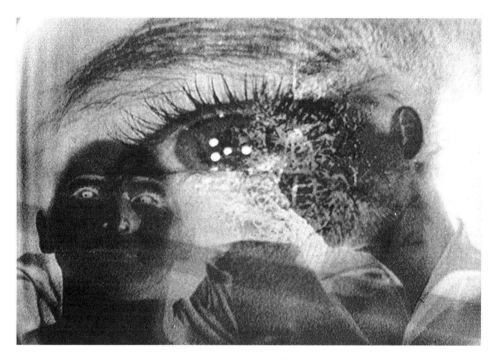

Scene from the television version of *Loving*, producer Pierre Mercure, Radio Canada, Montreal, 1966.

# My First Stage Work:
## Loving

*Composed:* 1963-65, St. John's, Newfoundland.

*Cast:* Two actors, four female singers, dancers optional.

*Orchestra:* String quartet, harp, piano (harpsichord, celesta), guitar (Spanish, electric, banjo), mandolin, accordion, percussion (six players).

*Duration:* 70 minutes.

*First Performance:* CBC-TV (French Network) February 3, 1966.

*Note: Loving* was composed 1963–65, mostly in St. John's, Newfoundland, where I was then living. The following essay was given as a lecture for the Humanities Association of Memorial University of Newfoundland on January 8, 1965. I still have a vivid memory of the little crowd who came out that cold, snowy night to hear the young composer discuss his first work for the stage. The minutes of the meeting spoke of the puzzlement of the audience:

> A previously recorded excerpt of the sound was played back to a somewhat startled audience of about fifty members and friends who had not all understood that to appreciate the jangles and screeches, the clangings and the swishes, it is necessary to divest oneself of all prejudice....

Only one aria, 'The Geography of Eros,' had been performed at the time and I had played a tape recording of it as an illustration.

Sometime after the lecture, Pierre Mercure proposed to me that Radio Canada (CBC) should commission *Loving* for television. This was audacious, for not only was I quite unknown, but the work was being written in the 'fatal' language of English. The final version was bilingual, with each of the actors speaking one of the two languages which have kept Canada intimately divided for 300 years: the Man, French, and the Woman, English. Between their several conversations, four female singers extended romantic fantasies in the mellifluous balloons of their arias.

Pierre, Gabriel Charpentier and I worked together closely in Montreal for several months. I flew in from St. John's for several days at a time. I recall that the French title gave us some trouble. Pierre favoured *Les Labyrinthes de l'amour*, but I thought that too long. Eventually we settled on *Toi*; then the work became known as *Toi/Loving*, which is really rather absurd.

Our collaboration was not regarded without suspicion by Pierre's administrators. I recall I was once asked to refund $1.21 of my per diem money because I was taking a flight back home an hour earlier than expected. On another occasion I recall a supervisor coming across the word 'putain' in the libretto. For a moment his puréed face clipped to attention. Gabriel was instructed to find a euphemism, 'dévergonde.'

The problems were subsequently more complex. I won't discuss them here, except to say that Pierre's sudden death prevented the proper completion of the work. Much of the music was left out and the final editing was done in haste. Since the work was not presented on the stage until 1978, and even today has not been given a complete stage production, many people assumed that *Loving* was a television opera and that its non-linear development meant that it could not be effectively staged. But, as this essay demonstrates, I had originally planned the work for the stage and consider that it will finally assume its destiny in this form. If I were to stage it now I would keep the *mise en scène* very simple, retaining the projections and lumatic effects, particularly for the musical sections, with the actors in the foreground and the musicians behind a scrim.

*Loving* is still one of my favourite works. Structural techniques were tried out here that were later developed in *Patria 1* and 2. But the music is purely lyrical and subscribes to no system. I also consider the work curiously Canadian – the description of a romance in two languages whose only purpose is to mystify, deceive and enchant.

THE WORK FOR THE STAGE on which I am engaged at present is titled *Loving*. It employs an orchestra, singers, actors, projections, lumia (mobile lighting effects) and electronic sounds; it lasts approximately one hour and a half without intermission. I do not call *Loving* an opera, though it may seem closest to this genre. It is really an audio-visual poem, related, in my mind at least, to the medieval chant-fable of which *Aucassin et Nicolette* is perhaps the best-known example.[1]

For some time I had been considering a work for the stage. At first my thoughts ran to a work of social protest,[2] but eventually I set this aside for the present theme. As little of the work exists at present in completed form, it will be understood that everything I say about it now is tentative.

I always welcome an opportunity to speak about a work while it is being composed. It helps me to focus my thoughts. Once it is completed I can say nothing more; I have lost interest in it. It has left me to go out and live an existence of its own, quite independent of my will.

---

1  *Aucassin et Nicolette* was well known to me while I was writing *Loving* since I had organized a production of it in Toronto on Ten Centuries Concerts in 1962.
2  Subsequently *Patria 1*.

*Loving* is a synaesthetic work. It employs a number of arts in extremely close, frequently interpenetrating relationship. This does not mean that it indulges in a pileup of as many arts as possible (Wagner, Hollywood) in order to smack all the senses at once. *Loving* is more concerned with counterpointing the various arts or locating the precise points where their nerve-endings touch than with creating fat parallel structures. Nevertheless it would be useless to deny that music is the foundation of my plan.

*Loving* does not have a plot. It does not move from A to B in the narrative sense. It inhabits an unreal space-time in which distances vanish, in which events may be completed before they are begun, or in which questions may be answered before they are asked. *Loving* is any time and any place or all times and all places or any number of times and places.

Nor does *Loving* have characters, if by characters we mean well-rounded and independent human beings with clear motivations. The personages of *Loving* are not fixed in social settings like those encountered in the works of bourgeois playwrights (Ibsen) or boudoir dramatists (Schnitzler). Here everything is stripped away to study directly the effects of confrontation between the male and female psyches. In fact, it is definitely part of my purpose to keep the identity of the personages on stage a mystery or at least in a constant state of flux.

The listener may wonder: is there only one man and one woman, or are there several men and women here? Are they meeting for the first time or last time? Have they ever met? Which are honest actions, and which are fictions, myths, masks? How much is dream and how much is reality? These questions cannot be answered, for to answer them would be to give the work a development, a place in time and space.

I once came across a remark of Nathaniel Hawthorne that seems to describe what I am attempting:

> In writing a romance a man is always – or always ought to be – careening on the utmost verge of a precipitous absurdity, and the skill lies in coming as close as possible, without actually tumbling over.

I have created no characters, then, but what we might call 'attitudes,' that is, symbolic presences somewhat in the manner in which the figures surrounding the Rose in *Roman de la Rose* are symbolic. For what are *Bel Accueil* (Courtesy), *Male Bouche* (Slander) and the others but anthropomorphic representations of the lady's impulses, or the other influences at work on her mind?

Supposing we assume a dominant female attitude to be vanity, the desire to be and remain attractive to the male. An interesting specimen in the literature of vain women (or at least one that has influenced my own conception of Vanity) is encountered in Mallarmé's poem 'Hérodias.' Here excessive vanity has transformed a beautiful woman into a morbid narcissist who will not even let her handmaiden come near her. She must remain totally inviolate, an ambition pursued with such desperation that she becomes almost savage. Hérodias has been perverted by her own obsession with remaining attractive into a turbine of unhealthy desires and fantasies.

Ortega y Gasset has something revealing to say about Salomé's persistence in maintaining her virginity.

> It becomes clear how, in a woman's extreme physical virginity, an immoderate preoccupation with prolonging the state of maidenhood, usually appears in conjunction with a masculine nature.... Her flesh, firm and flexible, with fine acrobatic muscles – Salome was a dancer – covered with the glitter of her gems and precious metals, gave the impression when in movement, of an 'inviolate reptile.'[3]

A second feminine attitude in *Loving*, which I have called Modesty, is a figure personifying girlish innocence. But forces and counterforces rage within her; a desire for abandonment is countered by a fear of violation. And yet this event could bring a new depth to her personality, even if it were to lead to new spiritual anguish. Such was the case, for example, with the Portuguese nun Mariana Alcoforando, who wrote to her faithless seducer (words which I have borrowed for the Modesty Aria): 'I thank you from the bottom of my heart for the desperation you cause me, and I detest the tranquillity in which I lived before I met you.'[4]

In both Vanity and Modesty restraint overrides freedom. But at some point the feminine psyche must be freed from its inhibitions to burst out in a crescendo of passion. For, as Ortega observes of woman,

---

3   Ortega y Gasset, *On Love*, Cleveland, 1957, p. 162
4   Ibid. p. 11.

... her soul lives as if its back were turned to the outside world, hiding its inner passionate fermentation.... The woman... lives in perpetual confusion because she lives in perpetual self-concealment.... Normally the first impression of a woman excludes the possibility that that delicate, playful, ethereal figure, all disdain and subterfuge, is capable of passion.... And yet, the truth is exactly the opposite: that almost unreal figure is merely awaiting the opportunity to throw herself – with such impetus, decisiveness, courage and unconcern for painful consequences – into an impassioned whirlwind, that she outdoes the most resolute man, who sheepishly discovers himself to be of a practical, calculating, and vacillating temperament.[5]

To the attitude which personifies this explosion of passion I have given the name Ishtar, the Mesopotamian goddess of war and sexual love. Ishtar is a furiously attractive creature, but in her sex appeal lurks the danger of destruction to both herself and her lover. Ishtar is particularly feared by what we might call the Don Juan type of masculine attitude. It will be remembered that Don Juan is attracted by the most modest and outwardly tranquil of women. It is the nun that Don Juan seduces; passionately hysterical women merely frighten him off. Let us refrain from thinking of Don Juan as the disturbing and complex idealist E.T.A. Hoffmann made of him. In his original incarnation as *El Burlador* he was a career philanderer, a jester and deceiver, pure and simple. For him there is nothing so pleasant or important in life as deceiving women and it is this project which occupies his finest energies as he patiently schemes his way from one affair to another.

There is, of course, a more instinctive and less calculating male attitude which we might refer to as the Warrior. The Warrior is brute masculine force, the 'great performer,' whose virility is exercised almost without regard for the attractive object before it which has aroused and excited it so unaccountably.

---

5   Ibid. pp. 134-36. Prudentius gives us an example of this passionate resolution in his description of the martyrdom of the virgin Agnes. When her executioner arrives she cries: 'I rejoice that there comes a man like this, a savage, cruel, wild man-at-arms, rather than a listless, soft, womanish youth bathed in perfume, coming to destroy me with the death of my honour. This lover, this one at last, I confess it, pleases me. I shall meet his eager steps half-way and not put off his hot desires. I shall welcome the whole length of his blade into my bosom, drawing the sword-blow to the depth of my breast.' (*Crowns of Martyrdom*, XIV)

At the opposite extreme is the male attitude which I have called the Poet. The Poet idealizes his beloved and through his art he practises a continual act of worship before this ideal. In extreme cases the Poet may even renounce all physical contact with the beloved (as Petrarch did for Laura) in order to adore her from a distance. In *Loving*, the Poet will be especially important since it is he who is writing the work. It is he who has gathered up all the memories and fused them in an act of creation.

THE POET:      Listen...

When I press my ear below the mirror of the sea,
I hear your voice.

Listen...
When I touch the air,
I hear your voice.

Listen...
In the shadows of this strange room,
I hear your voice.

And I listen,
often without understanding.

It was in the open air that we met for the first time,
do you remember?
And I listened to the wing of your sigh.

'Wait for me.'

I wait for you on the strand, among the million
grains of sand,
and I think:
I will not engage your mouth,
I wish it to remain free.

And then I saw you for the first time,
supine and luxuriant in the azure darkness,
and your body told me there was love between us.

And I listened to your voice –
do you understand, little fox girl –
To love another is to reveal the contours
of your own heart.
The shells and seaweed of your own deepest nature
are the shape and the presence of the beloved.

My work: you.
And as my work turns endlessly in the night
I go on speaking, speaking, speaking...

I do not claim that the various male and female attitudes I have discussed
here are comprehensive, but for my purposes they offer potential enough
and it is around them that *Loving* will be fashioned.[6]

Different instrumental groups will colour and characterize the various
attitudes. For instance, to emphasize the reptilian qualities of Vanity I
employ a battery of plucked instruments (mandolin, guitar, banjo, harp,
harpsichord and plucked violin and cello). Here we have sounds which are
abrupt in attack and brief in duration; in the higher registers they possess a
dazzling quality that will be useful to underscore Vanity's frigidity.

During her aria Vanity is beautifying her face and body. The text of her
aria is largely in the form of a dialogue, for her charms speak back to her.

VANITY SINGING: I pour the perfumes into my bath –
Pink, burning contact –
Hot against my thighs –
ecstatic –
nerve-tingling liquid –
Embrace the watery lover –
Water flowing through my hair –
The torrent of my hair –
bathes my solitary body –
I comb sumptuously
with a grand, quaint, carven comb –

---

6   *Afternote*: As the work took shape, the male attitudes of Don Juan and the Warrior
were fused in the Man, while the Poet became his pre-recorded voice. The feminine attitudes were Modesty, Vanity, Ishtar and Eros, the last of whom fuses the
qualities of the previous three in the final and most lyrical aria of the work. The
Man and the Poet spoke French; the Woman spoke English, while the arias of the
feminine attitudes were in both languages.

| | |
|---|---|
| RECORDED VOICES | I am your eyes, languid – |
| OF VANITY'S | Do not forget, darling, your lips – |
| CHARMS SINGING: | I am your breasts, snow white – |
| | Flash of emerald eye – |

I wanted also to find a visual equivalent for this fragmentation of the voice, and eventually it occurred to me that the answer lay in the mirror of the vanity table. It could be shattered. Vanity sings her aria from behind a constellation of mirror fragments which are suspended, mobile fashion, so that they slowly rotate, reflecting portions of her body, an eye here, a hand there, a swirl of hair somewhere else. The more Vanity worships her own charms, the more brittle the music becomes, ending in icy splendour.

| | |
|---|---|
| VANITY: | I died for burning chastity – |
| VANITY'S CHARMS: | Cold – |
| | Cold – |
| | Cold – |
| | Cold – |
| | |
| VANITY: | Close the azure shutters, my darling, |
| | and observe me – |
| | |
| VANITY'S CHARMS: | Darling, you have a tear in your eye – |
| | |
| VANITY: | A tear? |
| | |
| | No! |
| | |
| | I am rich, puissante, lovely – |
| | and I lie luxuriant in the azure light, |
| | and I remember how it was |
| | when you came to me. |

Each of the arias has its own orchestral colour: Modesty, strings and accordion; Ishtar, double bass and drums (a disco scene is suggested) and Eros, harp, piano and bells. I want to employ the singers' pre-recorded voices a great deal and also some electronic sounds, especially in the dream-like sections, but I don't want any of these effects to intrude or become conspicuous.

Everything in *Loving* must flow, even the décor. This is why, when constructional divisions are necessary, I am using the term 'editing unit' rather than scene. An editing unit is a rhythmic measurement and may be a few seconds or many minutes long. For instance, a two-second projection on a screen could be a finished action, therefore a complete editing unit. On the other hand, so could a fifteen-minute aria. The audience is never aware of what constitutes an editing unit but merely of the fact that the work consists of a series of rhythmic stresses and impulses without the benefit of a curtain or intermission to articulate them.

Time is introduced into the décor of *Loving* by means of lumia, or mobile lighting effects. The whole or part of the décor can become a scrim for the abstract play of lights, which are never static but are soft or bright and brassy as required. In this way the entire set will begin to approach the fluid condition of music.[7]

Film might also at times be used, that is, certain sections of the work could be pre-filmed and played back in counterpoint with the live action. It is conceivable that the so-called 'magic lantern' technique, in which actors appear to step directly out of the film and onto the stage or vice versa, could also be used, but care would have to be taken to eliminate the hard, rectangular frame of the film screen. There must be no unbendable shapes in the décor of *Loving*.

It remains to justify the use of film in the first place. Many film commentators have mentioned the similarity between certain film techniques and dreams. The film can distend or compress the tempo of the action. By means of the editor's scissors it can abolish time and space. Objects can be distorted or their 'emotional climate' altered by means of lighting or a change of context, and all these techniques tend to put film in the dream mode. Moreover, there is a precedent for using films to portray dream sequences in stage productions. Some of Ernst Toller's earliest plays, such as *Die Wandlung* (1919), employ film in this way.

Still projections are also employed in *Loving*, programmed in a desired sequence using animation techniques. Usually the animation artist starts with the music and synchronizes his shots to fit it. I have attempted a

---

7   *Afternote*: Lumia is a word employed by Thomas Wilfred to describe his colour organ. Although I had never seen it, I imagined that something like it could be used in *Loving*. Through reading I had also become familiar with Père Castel's 'clavecin en couleur' and was also familiar with Adolphe Appia's theories concerning the plasticity of light and its relationship to music.

departure from this technique. A series of about one hundred still photographs of the female attitudes, in characteristic poses or situations taken
from the live work, is programmed in an animated sequence lasting about
five minutes. The rhythm of these shots (some of which are repeated) is
graded from very slow to very fast, even subliminal. The singers take their
cues from the shots as they appear so that they are literally 'conducted' by
them in a phantasmal quartet composed of fragments of their individual
arias.

*Loving* is composed over a neutral foundation of darkness and silence.
There are scarcely any points in the work where the stage is brilliantly lit.
Working away to the edges, silence and darkness predominate. Two things
in particular attract me about these conditions. First of all, since nothing is
happening in silence and darkness, anything can happen. The more sound
and light introduced, the less that can happen to intensify a given effect.
Absolute surprises can only happen in a vacuum. Secondly, the absence of
acoustic or visual stimuli encourages greater intimacy. The effect of a
pianissimo has always been to draw one in. If I let the work begin with the
sound of whispering voices it is because a whisper is a secret, and if I let the
voice of the Poet be heard in darkness it is because I know that this is the
way we will come to know him best.

*Loving* is not a narrative but a web. The enigmas posed by the work –
the contradictions between reality and dreams, the impossibility of sorting
out the past from the future or the conscious from the unconscious – allow
*Loving* to unfold along many different lines simultaneously.

I once saw a sketch for a new type of theatre building that impressed
me very much. It was by Weininger, a student at the Bauhaus during the
great days of that institution. Weininger's theatre was to be egg-shaped
with a spiral catwalk down the centre. The audience was to sit on the
inside of the eggshell and the drama would develop up and down the
catwalk, all scenes developing simultaneously. Such a theatre would, of
course, call for an entirely new dramatic repertoire – but why not? Even
though *Loving* is intended for the traditional theatre, Weininger's concept
has influenced me considerably in building the dramatic structure of the
work.

Often the action or dialogues are interrupted, frozen as it were, while
material from a comparative scene is inserted. Sometimes events loop back
on themselves to discover richer meanings, sometimes they become
inverted and lose sense altogether. The work is a constellation of sugges-

tive relationships and cross-references. Thus the form of *Loving* becomes its texture just as the texture of Joyce's *Finnegans Wake* is also its form, reaching back on itself to make a circle.

The text of *Loving* is also its music. It has been deliberately limited so that certain words or phrases are used repeatedly like musical leitmotifs. In certain vocal sections of the work I collected words and phrases that seemed to be suitable and put them on cards. Then I shuffled the cards and turned them up. If the words were appropriate I set them, if not, I put the card at the bottom of the pack and turned up the next. 'The Geography of Eros' was completely composed this way. Perhaps this sounds more random than it really is, for I usually have a very strong feeling for the shape of the music before I begin. Then it is really just a matter of locating *le mot juste* to fit a melodic curve.

The perfect wedding of poetry and music is not easy to attain. In fact, the evidence for a balanced relationship between sense and song is actually quite exceptional: plainsong, the songs of the troubadours, German *Lieder*, and a few other instances. More often the demands of one art overpower the other, as for example in the ballad, where a few basic chords are whacked with the insistence of trackends on a railway journey while the balladeer expectorates his story. On the other hand, hyperactive composers like Wagner drown the words under the waves of an orchestral ocean, leaving the singers quite incapable of communicating any articulate message whatever. If Wagner had been introduced to the art of semaphore it might have helped him out.

To be set to music, a poem must be versatile, for song attenuates it and blunts its articulation and imagery. Song imposes simplicity. Complex ideas, uncommon words, homophones, etc., cause trouble. Even the most deliberately 'musical' devices of poetry such as rhyme and metre are largely obliterated by a complex musical setting. Music establishes new time laws for language. Contemporary music, in attempting to obtain a new vocal ecstasy, often distorts the text to a point where it cannot be understood at all.

But one should have a conscience about words, both as sound and as sense. In *Loving* I have used a great many types of vocal presentation from one extreme right through to the other. These can be shown in tabular form:

SENSE   1) Stage speech – deliberate, articulate, projected;

2) Domestic speech – could include slang or sloppy enunciation;

3) Parlando – slightly intoned speech (sometimes used by clergymen);

4) Sung-speech – (*Sprechgesang*) in which the moving curve of pitch, duration and intensity can be indicated by means of musical notation;

5) Syllabic song – with one note to each syllable, notated musically;

6) Melismatic song – with more than one note to each syllable. Sometimes one vowel will be protracted over a whole musical phrase;

7) Vocalism – including many forms of voice play involving invented languages, vocal mannerisms, humming, whistling, screaming, etc. (Dadaist poetry);

SOUND   8) Electronic transformation – may transform or distort words completely (*musique concrète*).

At each stage we observe a higher intensification of music or pure sound and less emphasis on meaning and sense. But the true bridge between music and poetry cannot be said to exist in any of these forms exclusively; rather it is in the imaginative use of many or all of them that a rich interplay of possibilities opens up.[8]

There is another feature of vocal sound production which should be mentioned. When broadcasting and recording were invented it became possible for the sound of the human voice to be dislocated and to appear from any place desired or all places at once. It is no longer tied to a hole in the head but can be liberated to embellish the live voice or dialogue with it, as was the case in the Vanity aria. I have used pre-recorded vocal sound in Eros's aria as well. Eros is scored for soprano and a large battery of percussion instruments, consisting almost exclusively of idiophones, i.e., instruments made from solid, sonorous materials, such as gongs and bells, to which I have added a harp and a piano. At times the taped voice of the singer is heard as an echo but at other times it achieves equal emphasis with that of the live vocalist. The text consists of fragments of some of my own rather youthful love poems.

---

8   I might mention here that the decision to make *Loving* a bilingual work added to this richness since anyone not perfectly fluent in both languages was forced to listen to one of them as pure music.

I saw Eros as a consummation of all the attitudes of the feminine psyche, which is the reason her aria comes last. A little later the Man and the Woman reappear for their last brief dialogue.

SHE:        Yes, I have a name.

HE:         I asked you your name, your real name...

SHE:        When will your work be finished?
            I hope you will let me see it. When I
            think about it I am reminded so much of
            Botticelli....

            (They freeze)

THE POET:   ...then I remembered who you were.
            You were...

SHE:        Primavera? Yes, Botticelli has always been
            one of my favourites. His mystery...

            (Her voice trails off)

THE POET:   We have spoken so much, spoken as if to
            avoid saying something. And every word
            you spoke complicated the mystery of you.
            And now, once again, I've forgotten your
            name.

SHE:        Are you coming?

HE:         Will you come?

            (They move off in different directions)

The work has turned full circle on itself to produce 'the work.' The meeting has become the parting, both for the Man and the Woman and for the composer and his muse. The chorus sings softly as the lights fade out. The neutrality of darkness and silence returns.

First published in Open Letter, 'R. Murray Schafer: A Collection,' Fourth Series, 4 & 5, Fall 1979, pp. 30-47.

# The Theatre of Confluence I

Note (1972): This essay was written in 1966 after I had completed *Loving* and was considering new works for the stage. This was the beginning of *Patria*. I composed the complete libretto for *Patria 1: Wolfman* and *Patria 2: Requiems for the Party Girl* and completed a substantial portion of the music, particularly for *Patria 2*. Then it dimmed; I realized that not only was there no company in Canada interested in taking it on, but there was no stage adequate to the demands I was making – for the two parts were to be executed simultaneously with two complete casts on two stages but in the same theatre. These difficulties discouraged me, and gradually the work moved to the back of my mind as more urgent matters came forward.

25

It is now January of 1972. I am travelling across Canada on the train. The old voices have begun to speak to me in their strange dialects once again, and I have taken out the lecture-essay I once hoped to give to a Humanities Association meeting, but was never invited to do so. The original was in the form of a trialogue with the three speakers (by some form of legerdemain I had intended that they should all be myself) occupying three points on a stage before the audience, while additional comments and pictures were projected on screens above their heads. I have reduced the three voices to a solo statement, for a less restless format seems in order. But I have not altered the 1966 thoughts, for even though I now begin to think of more radical works, the basic conclusions of 'The Theatre of Confluence' still appear capable of embracing them.

I AM USING this discussion to wrestle with some ideas in my mind concerning theatre, in an attempt to clarify them before embarking on the work *Patria*.

My interest in the theatre dates back to about 1964, to the time when I began to contemplate the work *Loving*. In 1966 it was produced on television, where for many reasons, now unimportant, it received its inadequate première. It has yet to be produced on the stage, the place where, I believe, it will have whatever destiny it deserves.[1] Many people viewing the television version thought it didn't work. I am inclined to think that was because *they* didn't work.[2] Television encourages slovenliness. An artist can't be concerned about an audience that doesn't bring its brains to work. *Loving* is not a work which falls into the laps of its audience. For one thing it is bilingual (in French and English) and a good many people said they

---

1    Note (2002): *Loving* was given its first semi-staged production by New Music Concerts of Toronto in 1978. The production toured to Ottawa, Montreal and Halifax.
2    One is reminded of Joyce's remark: 'Demands? I only make one demand of my readers: that they should devote their lives to the study of my works.'

didn't understand half the words. It was unusual in other ways as well: plotless, essentially characterless, it was a spell rather than a story, a tone poem in the undefaced sense of that genre. I think I may have broken some new ground with it, but so long as the porcine managers of opera companies refuse to give audiences a proper chance to make its acquaintance, I shall remain a minority of one.

At about the time I completed *Loving* I began conceiving a second, bolder work. I still think about it almost every day. But I am unable to begin it. It hasn't crystallized sufficiently in my mind. It is to help myself crystallize this work that I am composing this piece as a sort of prognostication of the kind of theatre I want one day to see and to help bring into being. *Ideally what I want is a kind of theatre in which all the arts may meet, court and make love. Love implies a sharing of experience; it should never mean the negation of personalities. This is the first task: to fashion a theatre in which all the arts are fused together, but without negating the strong and healthy character of each.*

I am calling this the Theatre of Confluence, because confluence means a flowing together that is not forced, but is nevertheless inevitable – like the tributaries of a river at the precise moment of their joining. In choosing this title I am rejecting two terms that are current and imply something possibly close to what I am suggesting: *total theatre* and *absolute theatre*. These terms have been made too ambiguous to be acceptable.

'Absolute theatre' has an apocalyptic ring, and who are we to presume that the apocalypse should come in our time? Greek theatre, Shakespearean theatre, Wagnerian theatre – each was in its own way absolute because it climaxed trending that had been in progress for some time. We respect these as absolute expressions of cultural fulfilment and we may draw inspiration from them. But we must seek the operative forces of our own times and give them precisioned and cogent expression. We aspire towards our own absolute theatre, but without preliminary assumptions as to the success our endeavours may bring.

'Total theatre' is rejected for another reason. As the word is used today, it has become associated with the messy excretions of *mixed media*, a style of expression not always synonymous with mindless slopping, though it happens frequently enough to keep us in suspense.

It is always desirable to experiment with new modes of perception. But the incoherence of most mixed-media activities today results in a glutting of the senses to a point where discrete acts of discernment are no longer possible. Sensory overload may produce states of consciousness that are useful to the artist, but an intrapsychic 'trip' is no more a work of art than a trip to the dentist is. Such activities will leave no conclusive theatrical evidence.[3]

The term *theatre of confluence* has the virtue of being pure; for so far no works have been composed for it. Parenthetically I feel compelled to add, however, that *Loving* (in its original stage version) was an attempt in this direction.

Confluent theatre has not been possible in the past because of the hierarchical nature of all combined art forms. In traditional drama, for instance, the arts have been forced into an arrangement in which the spoken word comes first, then action, and finally décor and music. In opera, on the other hand, music is the central force to which all the other arts are made to relate, often requiring them to behave in ridiculous ways. The traditional forms solicit contributions from various artists but in a way which is progressively restrictive. Thus, a composer has an idea for an opera, finds a librettist to write him a text (which he then smothers with his music) then a producer to put it on stage, then a *metteur en scène*, a conductor, soloists, a choreographer, and so forth. These I would call rank-order creations.

The works of the future will be distinguished from rank-order creations by being conceived on all levels simultaneously. All the parameters of these new works *must* be elaborated coevally. It matters little whether this is accomplished singly or collectively.

Wagner had the right spirit here, at least during the earlier part of his life when he wrote his theoretical work *Opera and Drama*. He felt that all the arts had to undergo adaptation so that each would co-operate with the purpose of the *Gesamtkunstwerk*. Later, after he had assimilated Schopenhauer's philosophy, it was music that took on the dominant role and it was towards the spirit of music that all the other arts were made to aspire. We need not feel betrayed by Wagner. An artist hunts for philosophies which reinforce his natural inclinations; and Wagner was above all a composer and only secondarily a librettist and stage director.

Throughout the twentieth century the arts have demonstrated a strong susceptibility to fusion or at least reciprocity. We have stereophonic music

---

3   Note (1972): There is no reason to retract this assertion, despite the recent growth of picture books in which various experiments in (particularly the American) total theatre are presented as if they were substantive or repeatable contributions to art. They are documents only, smoothed down photographically and multiplied in quantity to give the contemporary public – which prefers illusions – the impression that something important has happened. But the essence of a 'happening' – like the essence of any newspaper story – is its nonrepeatability; hence it is at variance with the fact of art – i.e., the artifact.

(music in space) and kinetic sculpture (art in time) to mention only a couple of the more recent manifestations of this desire to discover the precise points where the nervous systems of the different sensorial experiences touch. Now we have mixed-media forms. We are definitely propelled in a certain direction. We do not understand exactly how to handle the problems posed by the interpenetration of the arts, but the activity is before us and its potentials are exciting.

These propositions call for a clear commitment of purpose. I state my position. The danger of uncontrolled synaesthetic exercises is that an overindulgent piling up of resources merely brings about a confusion of the senses rather than an acuity of sensorial experience. I prefer to start with the most elementary gestures of each art form, those that possess in their very simplicity cosmogenic importance. The extended study that Kandinsky, Klee and others at the Bauhaus gave to the basic elements of the graphic arts (Kandinsky, for example, spends almost forty pages discussing the significance of the dot in his book *Point and Line to Plane*) needs to be duplicated in the other arts – in music, for example, by a prolonged study of the single tone. Only when the matrix elements are purified and clearly apprehended is it possible to create a basic vocabulary for each art form. From this a contrapuntal grammar will be fashioned, making it possible to employ tested effects for specific synaesthetic purposes. Gradually more and more complex relationships can then be observed and studied until finally each art form will emerge in all its richness as contiguous with each of the others and artistry will then become an activity involving the total sensorium, just as living is an activity in which all the senses corroborate and counterpoint one another.

The various senses are bound together by the biological and neural rhythms of the human anatomy. The real meeting place of all the arts is therefore *rhythm*, particularly in those basic rhythms which condition the resolving powers of the senses, and of the body (heart, breath, motor rhythms, sleep, etc.).

This need not simply mean the rhythmic synchronization of the arts. In the past whenever the arts were drawn together, a fatal mistake was made. It was thought that the total experience would be strengthened by having all the arts proceed in parallel motion; that is to say, whatever happened in one art had to be duplicated at the same instant in all the others. But this technique of synchronization results in an art form that crushes more than it exalts, as André Gide has aptly noted of Wagner.

This has never been true in the East, in the art of Japan, for instance. So far as I know, Sergei Eisenstein was the first artist in the West to grasp the contrapuntal nature of Japanese theatre, when he attended performances given by a touring Kabuki troupe in Russia in 1928. (See his essay entitled 'The Unexpected' in *Film Form*, London, 1963.) In discussing the prospect of the sound film he noted (also in 1928): 'Only a contrapuntal use of sound in relation to the visual montage piece will afford a new potentiality of montage development and perfection. The first experimental work with sound must be directed along the line of its distinct non-synchronization with the visual images.'[4]

29

We have discovered at least the potentials of counterpointing the various arts one against the other. The rhythm of one medium may extend that of another medium or it may contravene it. It is this rhythmic relationship that we will have to study.

Our interest in counterpoint between the senses has been strongly influenced by our discovery that to plot a sensorial experience accurately, the use of two senses is necessary. Thus if we wish intentionally to create ambivalence or to confuse the observer we employ the contradiction of sensorial counterpoint. The montage technique in film takes two known quantities (two pieces of film) and produces a third experience which is neither of the two. We can create fresh experiences in the same way. *Life itself is the original multi-media experience.* Single art forms amputate all of the senses except one. If we look for examples of ritualized multi-channel experiences we will find them in unusual places. Thus, the Roman Catholic mass is (or was) such an experience. All the senses are summoned up: vision – the architecture of the church, the colour of the *vitraux*; hearing – the music of the choir and instruments, the ringing of bells; taste – the transubstantiation of the bread and wine; smell – the incense; touch – devotion on the knee (which at times even took the form of elaborate peregrinations about the church), prayer beads in the hand, etc. What strikes us here is that at no time are the senses bombarded aimlessly; everything is neatly integrated. In the Catholic mass there is no sensory overload. It could serve as a useful model for study. The wine-tasting ceremony is another example of a mixed-media ritual. The glasses are beauti-

---

4   *Film Form*, p. 258. Eisenstein did not, however, stick to his credo and, as his discussions in *The Film Sense* show, his work with Prokofiev was directed along the very lines he wished to avoid. The first film composer to seize this concept and put it into practice was Hans Eisler who applied Brecht's 'alienation effect' to film by counterpointing visual and aural images in a series of socialist documentaries. (See: *Composing for the Films*, London, 1951.) Hollywood, of course, resisted the idea up to the time of its death.

ful, the wine is lustrous and colourful, one smells the wine, one tastes the wine. The touching of glasses provides a delicate ring to the ear, for it has no other function than to bring forward this sensation.

I am not going to elaborate further on this theme at the moment. I mention only incidental examples, but they may serve as useful objects of study in our attempts to reintegrate life and art.

An equally important discovery for art was that of chance. Chance is a liberating force and a means whereby unforeseeable configurations of information can be brought into existence. Chance promotes new modes of perceiving. Delight in the unexpected – you asked me what path he followed, I'd say into the ... But total chance? The pleasant serendipity that chance brings to over-organization ends in boring chaos when protracted indefinitely.

There may be a characteristic tendency for entropy to increase in the world; the scientist will tell us that, and that 'all closed systems in the universe tend to deteriorate and lose their distinctiveness, to move from the least to the most probable state, from a state of organization and differentiation in which distinction and forms exist, to a state of chaos and sameness.'[5] But the human being is ill-adapted to withstand the colossal boredom of chance. For as Norbert Wiener puts it: '... while the universe as a whole ... tends to run down, there ... is a limited and temporary tendency for organization to increase. Life finds its home in these enclaves.' Since the exercise of living is one of organizing experience, human beings may be considered fundamentally anti-entropic. Thus the prospect of an art of total chance that is macroscopic and beyond all human intervention or control is a contemptuously inhuman thought, though it has been proposed by some.

The artist may use both chance and controlled operations to give his work a new richness and versatility. At times chance will stimulate his imagination and confound his intellect; then as he comprehends more clearly what he is doing, chance operations will cease – at least until the academics destroy art with their tiresome restrictions, and some surprises will again be necessary. It takes courage to break down a system. It is merely foolish to perpetrate hazardous operations at the site of a destruction.

Today we are living in an *entr'acte*. Our civilization is being attacked. It has not yet been destroyed. There is a temptation to throw out all tradition and surrender ourselves to oneiric and mindless doodling. This is particu-

---

5 Norbert Wiener, *The Human Use of Human Beings*, New York, 1954, p. 12.

larly true among the North American young today. Because of a reckless approach to education, they fear that a skill learned will have to be unlearned later; they therefore come to art possessing no craft or métier, but merely the playful instinct. This playfulness is also encouraged by the artistic media and materials which seemingly reduce all need for skill, or emphasize the ephemeral nature of creation. When specific sensorial acuities have not been trained, there is a great temptation to titillate the senses with whatever gimmickry is at hand, mistaking this for artistic celebration. Thus a theatre of the senses – to give it a name – is supposed to involve its participants in new explorations of awareness, even altered states of consciousness similar to experiences with drugs. All art should lead to altered states of consciousness; but it also insists on complex acts of discernment. Art may be an extension of reality, but it is a ten-fingered grasp of this new state. It is never ceremonial drugging. One understands nothing when one is 'totally involved.' By all means let us keep an open mind on the new means for producing artistic effects, but let us not lose our brains in the process.

It has been suggested that the art of mixed means is new in our time. It is not. The Dadaist Kurt Schwitters had something very close in mind with his Merz stage. In an account of it he says some very revealing things:

> The Merz drama is an abstract work of art. The drama and the opera grow, as a rule, out of the form of the written text, which is a well rounded work in itself, without the stage. Stage-set, music and performance serve only to illustrate this text, which is itself an illustration of the action. In contrast to the drama or the opera, all parts of the Merz stage-work are inseparably bound up together; it cannot be written, read or listened to, it can only be produced in the theatre. Up to now a distinction was made between stage-set, text and score in theatrical performances. Each factor was separately enjoyed. The Merz stage knows only the fusing of all factors into a composite work.'[6]

This destruction of the identities of individual art forms was but one of the exciting but largely unrealized dreams first envisaged by the Dadaists during the 1920s. The materials for the Merz stage were to be '… all solid, liquid and gaseous bodies, such as white wall, man, barbed wire entanglement, blue distance, light cone.'

Schwitters' conception of theatre was something between a happening

31

---

6   *The Dada Painters and Poets*, New York, 1951, pp. 62-3.

and a mixed-media bath. It was never realized. Schwitters concludes regret-
fully: 'At some future date perhaps we shall witness the birth of the Merz
composite work of art. We cannot create it, for we ourselves would only be
parts of it, in fact, we would be mere material.'

This last phrase is significant. Schwitters' helplessness before some higher
force – I suppose he means chance – was probably just a means of dodging
work. But the vision is valuable.

I have rejected chance as the guiding force behind the Theatre of
Confluence. I have also concluded that the artistic experience is different
from the psychedelic experience and that the simulation of the latter in
mixed-media exercises does not lead to an understanding of the former. I am
dealing here with contemporary confusions which threaten to deflect art
from its true purpose. Among these is a theory that the audience should
somehow be self-actualized to contribute more vigorously to the drama.
'Participation' and 'involvement' are the slogans.

'Let's have the whole audience come up on stage!' said a student during an
experimental drama session. 'What will they do there?' asked the director. 'I
haven't thought of that yet,' replied the student.

Experiments have been attempted in Europe in which the audience is
given a number of key words which they may cry out whenever they wish,
and the actors transform the drama accordingly. At Expo 67 a film gave the
audience the option of choosing from among a variety of endings by pushing
buttons on their sets. Such theatrical experiments reflect a contemporary
interest in feedback and the science of self-regulating systems. In a cyber-
nated theatre the steering device is the audience and the mechanism to be
controlled is the drama.

This is indeed a new state of affairs. The assumption that the audience
knows best what it wants is always questionable. The blurring of the distinctions between the giving and receiving of art can be tragic. Everywhere in the
West one notices this frightful descent into homogeneity, blurring distinctions, obliterating the idiosyncratic, dragging the leaders down and the led up
onto some middle ground of fulcrumed banality. Both communism and
democracy are systems dedicated to smoothing out differences between
men. Of course you *can* make a congenital dunce into a prime minister but
this is no guarantee of improvement in the state. Those who are prepared to
pass the responsibilities of the artist to the audience will merely be rewarded
in the same way as the liberals who first prepared the revolution of democracy: their heads were the first to fall when mass-man took over.

There is no reason why an audience, prepared to be an audience, should be expected to be anything but an audience. Is it undignified to receive gifts carefully prepared with affection and hard work? As long as the theatre consists of stages and chairs there will be distinctions between entertainers and the entertained.

The theatre in this form is a mirror. The audience do not have to inhabit the drama; they are reflected in it. When they can no longer see themselves reflected, they adopt the best action available: they stay away. Thus the theatre which presented Daphné and Orpheus passed away with the decline of the Renaissance aristocracy, just as that which presented Caesar and Jupiter passed when the absolute monarchs of the seventeenth and eighteenth centuries had their power curtailed. (The systematic delirium of Puccini is still with us only because the middle class still enjoys being slobbered over.)

It may indeed be possible to produce an art form without an audience at all. All one has to do is remove the chairs. One looks in vain for the audience when the Elizabethans gathered to sing madrigals. Then there were only performers, and the satisfaction of art was in the making of it. But such art presupposes that larger numbers of people would be willing to undergo rigorous training, and I do not think this is so.[7]

A more important issue would seem to be how to get our theatre into contact with larger audiences – those who resist or ignore our work, the smug and the slovenly, the enemy audiences who look at us through 'God knows what chink in the mind' and blink at our agitation. This is a particularly necessary question for all art which would serve as a tribunal for social provocation.

The Theatre of Confluence should not be closed to the possibility that at certain points the audience might be required to participate in uncommon ways or to play an unusually influential role, just as chance is accepted as a conditional resource to bring about special artistic effects; but it rejects the idea that theatre should fall victim to collective or herdesque whims. To contemplate such a theatre at the present time would be to transform it merely into an amusement park.

The Theatre of Confluence may be produced by one individual or by a group of individuals of like temperament. We might call this co-opera. Film is a co-opera. Many talents are required for its successful completion. But a co-opera is not a leaderless undertaking.

---

7   Note (1972): I still don't, though I am now more interested in precipitating such action. *In Search of Zoroaster* is a work intended for 180 choristers, without any audience, and is to be performed as a kind of initiation ceremony to this new ritual of art.

The more directionless society becomes, the more urgent is the need for strong-willed artistic undertakings. This is the lesson taught by the Russian Revolution. The Russians might have produced democratically co-operative work after the Revolution, but precisely the opposite occurred. Their theatre produced a fleet of highly dictatorial producers: Stanislavsky, Meyerhold, Tairoff. In Germany too, the socialists produced theatre dictators: Piscator and Brecht. These men extended the position of the director to one of unprecedented power in order to impose a point of view.

Our situation is little different today. Next to the squalor produced by the masses in their materialistic greed, anarchy is our biggest social threat. The greater this chaos becomes, the more necessary is the need for strong-willed art. We have not yet reached that point in the geological future of time which Teilhard de Chardin calls the Omega Point of human development, a point where all men live together in harmony and humanity of purpose. It is a cloudy vision. It sounds like the schematic for an ant hill. Of course there are those who think the Omega Point can be produced at once by playing patty cake with paints in the general vicinity of electric guitars. In the meantime the real work begins in more humble ways. First a co-opera of two or three people is effected; a few others may wish to come and look over our shoulders. We let them, teach them what we can, ask them to invite their friends. That is all. It is a valuable start. I leave this matter now and pass to the question of the form of the Theatre of Confluence.

## The Form of the Theatre of Confluence

In the original Greek theatre the action takes place in the orchestra, a flattened pit in the centre of an amphitheatre. Here the actor is exposed on all sides to his audience. He hides nothing; similarly his mind hides nothing. The circumference of his thought is a known quantity, and he therefore has no reason to deceive the audience with his behaviour. With the introduction of the *skene* and later the *paraskenia* (the rudimentary backdrop and sides of the later proscenium theatre) the actors were permitted to retreat out of focus. In the classical drama of Western Europe the fact that at any given moment only 50 percent of the actor's body is visible is matched by an invidiousness of mind and temperament.

When Wagner wished to emphasize this to create additional distance between the action and the audience, he constructed at Bayreuth a second proscenium behind the first. For Wagner it was a privilege for the audience to be permitted to witness the action on stage through the fourth wall of the set and it had to be impressed on them that a 'mystic gulf' (his words) separated the supernatural happenings there from themselves.

The twentieth century has returned to the open, more direct concept of the Greeks. I have documented the background to this development elsewhere.[8] The question now is which type of theatre is best suited to the Theatre of Confluence? Do we want a form which invites the audience into the drama, or one which places it outside?

The answer is *both*. It is not really a matter of form at all, but rather of repertoire. First one decides on the work to be written or produced, and then one hunts for the theatre which will best suit its expressive potentials. To have it any other way is to suffer an immediate limitation. There is a current antagonism against the proscenium. However, there are ways to take advantage of the true function of the proscenium without throwing up three walls. For one thing we could give the actors secrets or permit them to express themselves in enigmatic ways. Their withdrawal from the audience can also be made credible by the use of lights and darkness, as the productions of Appia brilliantly demonstrate.

The moment an architect encloses space in the form of a building he makes a social comment about the people who are to inhabit that space. The traditional theatres of Europe reflect the class system. As Piscator wrote: 'The theatrical form which our age has inherited is the outworn form of absolutism – the court theatre. With its division into Parquet, Loges, Balcony and Gallery it mirrors the social class system of feudal times.'[9]

When Gropius designed his Total Theater for Piscator he aimed to provide 1) a circus theatre 2) an amphitheatre and 3) a proscenium, all in one concept, allowing any one of these areas to be employed or all at once. Gropius's Total Theater was never built and while it may have been one of the most influential unrealized designs of the century, we are still by no means getting versatile spaces created in enough quantity to accommodate adventuresome new repertoire.

Now it will depend totally on what one intends to do in a theatre: whether the space enclosed there is considered harmonious with the human scale or something beyond human influence. For instance, the spaces of a cathedral are enormous and man can only perform there as part of some transcendental or suprahuman activity. It is impossible to be at the

---

8 'The Philosophy of Stereophony,' *West Coast Review*, vol. I, no. 3, pp. 4-19.
9 Erwin Piscator, *Das Politische Theater*, Hamburg, 1963, p. 125.

centre of a Gothic cathedral. It is impossible to dominate its space. Palladio was the first architect to conceive of a 'humanized' theatre, that is a space which man himself could dominate. More than that, through the use of perspective scenery he created a 'point of view' for the spectators. Let us put that question again: is man to surrender himself to the abstract space of the stage, or is the stage to conform to him?

This is the issue that was fought out by the two Russian producers, Stanislavsky and Meyerhold, and was presented theoretically as a problem by Oskar Schlemmer at the Bauhaus. Schlemmer's geometric dissection of the stage suggests that the actors must animate an enclosed area of space much as acrobats animate the dome of the circus tent. By pointing out geometrically that the area to be animated is three-dimensional, Schlemmer immediately demonstrates a limitation of conventional theatres, in which the stage is flat and two-dimensional. Some of the constructivist sets of the Russians attempted to give elevation to the stage also, and Meyerhold's acrobatic training for actors prepared them for a three-dimensional theatre. But on the whole we may say that traditional drama remains an essentially flat exercise. The acting surface of traditional drama is a terrestrial confine because it is the expression of pre–space age man. It is not merely historical coincidence that Schlemmer's and Meyerhold's theatres came into existence shortly after the invention of aviation.

*Realism versus illusion is another matter under continual discussion.* Meyerhold demanded that in a theatrical performance the audience should not for a moment forget that they were in the theatre. Stanislavsky demanded, on the other hand, that an illusion should be created so that the audience should forget where they were. He wanted them to inhabit the actual milieu of the drama and its characters. If we ask which of these approaches to the theatrical experience should be adopted for the Theatre of Confluence, the reply can be immediate and uncompromising: Meyerhold's concept must be adopted. The misfortune of opera is that it attempts to be realistic when nothing could be more unrealistic than that the whole world should stop talking and start to sing. Illusions may be created in the Theatre of Confluence to achieve special effects, but they will be illusions, and they will serve ironical intentions.

Returning to the question of the shape of the theatre, we might ask whether it should be limited to one room only. Could it not take place in several rooms simultaneously? Could it not be mobile and processional?

In both antique and renaissance times, moving processions gradually developed into static theatre – that is, the mobility of action was gradually localized. There have been sporadic attempts during the twentieth century to break drama out of the theatre again and spread it abroad. The 'agit-prop' movement is an example; a more recent example is the 'happening.' One of my colleagues recently conceived of what he calls a 'cinemetropolis' that would be projected on the walls of different buildings throughout the city at different times.

Such ideas are atavistic. The mystery plays of the Middle Ages used multiple stages, sometimes placing the scenes on wagons which passed before the spectators at different times. The Passion of Christ is itself the original outdoor drama, and it is still sometimes performed in this way. This outdoor drama was internalized in the medieval cathedral. The Donaueschingen stage consisted of nineteen different acting areas around the church, allowing the drama to circle from Hell to the Gates of Gethsemane, to the Mount of Olives, etc. The audience was itinerant about the abundant abstract space of the cathedral.

Such concepts of the theatre must be reflected on carefully with regard to their applicability to the Theatre of Confluence. For example, a mobile for theatre could be created in this way so that material from the drama could be presented from several different areas simultaneously or successively. If music were to be an important component in the production, however, the complex acoustic problems created by such a disposition of resources might prove insurmountable. It is also doubtful whether an itinerant audience would be as quiet as one which is comfortably seated. Furthermore, there would be the practical consideration of performers' stamina if they were forced to repeat their parts several times over to accommodate a continuously processing audience. However, if it could be realized, there is no doubt that such a mobile theatre could again involve an audience in an ancient and honourable fashion.

We would have to decide on spaces or zones for each section of the action to be played in. Each action might have its own time and space, and would develop within these with a certain improvisatory character, though always aware of integration with other time and space zones. The levels of intensity would also be worked out with these time and space zones in mind. What we would have then is a transformable environment like a circus. Such an arrangement would bring about a theatrical form which was more fluid and itself more confluent, though by no means formless.

I would like to call such an arrangement *a form of possibilities*. By rearranging some of the time and space zoning, by allowing improvised blocks to modulate within a highly organized whole, a theatre would be created that would be truly a 'theatre of first nights only.' But these are matters to be dealt with in the actual production of a repertoire, and as I stated at the beginning the repertoire of the Theatre of Confluence still needs to be created.

## The Senses and the Theatre of Confluence

In combinatorial art forms of the past, theorists have spoken of harmonizing the various arts. It would be better to consider the senses first. Art forms are complex media of expression in which one or another sense may predominate, though others will still be present. Thus dance, opera and drama all involve the kinaesthetic, aural and visual senses to varying degrees, with various weightings. We seek to purify, to refine down to essentials. It would be more essential to consider the various senses as discrete information-bearing channels before indulging in the luxury of aesthetics. Unfortunately a thorough investigation of this sort would carry us beyond the scope of this essay. Let us simply observe that while the kinaesthetic, aural and visual senses are the most employed in the arts today the others are by no means absent, even though they have often made their way mischievously into the artistic experience. Movie audiences long ago brought their eating habits into the cinema – a clear sign that something was missing in the film. To an extent all theatrical art forms share the same culinary tendency, though the producers of art have been slow to take advantage of this fact. Similarly, the well-dressed ladies of the opera-house have tried to enlarge the art by means of the perfume pump. Actually, the senses of taste and smell have not failed to become bona fide art forms for want of trying, but rather because the descriptive vocabulary by which they might be codified and repeated has never been adequately developed.

The question is: which of the senses lies closest to the base of the Theatre of Confluence? Obviously this depends again on the specific character of the work to be created. Any sense may serve as the keel-line of a work depending on the message to be expressed.

I must here limit myself to describing why I have selected the sense of hearing as the main information-bearing channel in *Patria*, just as it was in *Loving*.

It is not only because I am a composer that I decided to give both these works a phonaesthetic basis. The themes of *Patria* and *Loving* impose this consideration. If the sense of touch is the most intimate of the senses, then the sense of hearing, it appears, is the next best approximation of this intimacy. Hearing is like touching at a distance. This is a physiological fact, for not only does hearing, like touching, consist of the perception of physical vibrations – in this case on the tympanic membrane of the ear – but the two sensations actually fuse at the lower extremity of the hearing range, in the area called infrasonic.

*Loving* was a lyrical work and sound poem. Perhaps there were two lovers; perhaps more than two; perhaps only one with his dreams. Two languages were employed: 'He' spoke French while 'She' spoke English. I wanted the audience to listen to the sound of the 'other' language as they would listen to music, as constructions of beautiful and arresting vocables. Of course, there was a certain social provocation involved here also, for *Loving* was an allegory of the ambivalence of the two native peoples of my own country, each of whom detests the language of the other. But *Loving* was ultimately an intimately lyrical expression. To achieve this reverie, music – the most quintessentially abstract of the phonaesthetic arts – extended like a thread throughout the dialogue and monologues, proceeding directly out of the words – themselves often abstractions, full of leitmotifs, non sequiturs and syntactical liberties.

There were practically no sets; just lumatic effects and often darkness. *Loving* could not have achieved intimacy had elaborate visual effects been employed. The audience would have spent too much time investigating the cracks in the scenery, for the work was essentially calm, with little action. I wanted the work to be performed on a neutral foundation of darkness; but television is a *light* medium and totally unsuited to the creation of mystery and the nocturne.

As I see *Patria* now, it too is to be a drama concerned with interpersonal communication. It is typical that man only becomes interested in communication studies when he loses the ability to communicate. *Anomie* is the word Durkheim invented to express the alienation of modern life. *Schizophrenia* is the word modern man, generalizing somewhat, uses to refer to the inability some poor unfortunates experience, because they cannot or will not communicate with the rest of mankind – even though what we do call effective communication is often nothing more than trivial decorum designed to keep us from punching one another in the face.

These are the themes of *Patria*. I do not propose to allow the aural sense to predominate in *Patria*, for I need to make a larger invasion into the emotional resources of my audience. There will be fewer arias, briefer in duration, and more electronic music. But I do propose to employ as many acoustic means as possible in plotting the psychographic curve of the total work.

For instance, the work will employ about forty languages. In this way a structure will be created on many levels with an almost mathematical delicacy; but not for this purpose alone; for it is part of the plan that each member of the audience will be enabled to draw a different conclusion from the action. Only the protagonists will speak the *lingua materna*, i.e. the language of the country in which the work is being produced.

All other characters will speak either foreign languages, or synthetic languages, or gibberish. The audience should find no difficulty in sympathizing with the protagonists' alienation – the central theme of the total work.

I am proposing also to employ several choruses, and they will actually play a more significant role than the orchestra. The texts they sing will be those of extinct or distant languages: Babylonian, Sanskrit, Tibetan, Latin and medieval Italian. The words do not matter here, but the shapes of this chanting will help to provide some coherence to the whole, for the choir will function as an articulate spectator, sympathizing with or resisting the action on stage – the same function often given to the chorus by Aeschylus and the other Greek tragedians in their dramas. At times the chorus may also become a hostile or inimical presence, but this will be a secondary function. Basically they will humanize what might be otherwise an incomprehensible drama, much as the choruses in Bach's Passions and Cantatas humanize those works by registering the emotions of the audience in a vicarious but unmistakable manner.

A final question arises. In view of the dependence of my works on music why have I refused to speak of them as operas? Why have I taken so much trouble to defend them from this epithet by elaborating a new genre, the Theatre of Confluence, into which I wish to see them placed?

Many of the reasons should already be clear from an attentive reading of this essay, together with an intensive study of the works themselves. Beyond this I could say that I do not wish to reform the bad habits opera has developed, which now seem incorrigible. Bertolt Brecht and Kurt Weill were the last to question the function of opera seriously, and in *Mahagonny* they attempted to renovate it 'up to the technical level of the modern theatre' (which for them was the epic theatre). Brecht made elaborate tables (which are published[10]) showing the change of emphasis of the new opera. They got so far as to bring about a radical separation of the elements

---

10   See 'Aufstieg und Fall der Stadt Mahagonny' in *Brecht on Theatre*, trans., John Willett, London, 1964.

constituting opera. This work was necessary but it left the job incomplete. As Brecht explains: 'The great struggle for supremacy between words, music and production – which always brings up the question, "which is the pretext for what?" – can simply be bypassed by radically separating the elements.' Brecht did not attempt to break down the 'culinary' aspect of opera. *Mahagonny* paid conscious tribute to the senselessness of the operatic form. The irrationality of opera lies in the fact that rational elements are employed, solid reality is aimed at, but at the same time it is all 'washed out by music.'

Brecht: 'So long as the expression *Gesamtkunstwerk* (or integrated work of art) means that the integration is a muddle, so long as the arts are supposed to be "fused" together, the various elements will all be equally degraded, and each will act as a mere "feed" for the rest.'

Opera is defined by its repertoire. This makes it irretrievable. Perhaps its obesity distresses us the most, for we want lean, athletic art. The waste of capital is more conspicuous in opera than in any of the other arts.[11] It is also the art form most seriously hampered by the Hollywood star system. And it has taken upon itself the task of perpetuating a good many works for their musical values alone, regardless of the fact that dramatically, and in other ways, they no longer excite.[12]

Yet there it stands in the midst of society with the appetite of a dinosaur, fed by blowzy socialites. The soft carpets and the red velvet are still there, the chandeliers with their thousand tiny drops of glittering light still spill down on the jewelled necklaces. Who are we to presume that such a bastion will fall in our time? Let us circumnavigate it.

---

11  Theatre can also be costly, often more costly than it need be. One cannot resist pointing out the irony of Piscator and the other advocates of epic theatre, who attempted to reach the proletariat with costly and prestigious productions which only the other end of society could afford; even though, as has been said, one of the techniques of Marxism is to use the tools of capitalism to bring about its downfall.

12  Note (1972): In 1966 I conceived an idea for an antidote to opera: the pocket opera. It is realistic to think of such things in a country as spread out as Canada. Succinctly, the idea was to create a tiny company, consisting of no more than six or ten people (including stage crew) with a décor that could fit into a small truck with a repertoire specially created or adapted for it, and transport it across the country – just as the theatre of Europe developed agit-prop drama and took it into the streets and factories. I wanted an aggressive, present-tense opera. Swift, direct, agitational. Not a palliative. Not ceremonial drugging. Not prettifying.

D. P. (Wolf) gently replaces the head of the immigration officer H. Showell Stools in the opening scene of *Patria 1: Wolfman*. Canadian Opera Company production, 1987.

# Patria 1:
# *Wolfman*

*Composed*: 1966-74, Vancouver.

*Cast*: 31 actors and solo singers and a 32-voice choir.

*Orchestra*: Flute (piccolo), oboe, clarinet, saxophone, bassoon, 3 trumpets, 2 horns, 2 trombones, tuba, string quartet, electric guitar, electric organ, accordion, percussion (3 players), electronic sounds on tape.

*Duration*: 1 hour 30 minutes.

*First Performance*: Canadian Opera Company, November 21, 1987.

*Note*: Ideas for *Patria 1* were circling in my head even before I wrote *Loving*, though the work was not completed until 1974, that is, after *Patria 2*. *The Princess of the Stars*, which was eventually to function as the prelude to the whole cycle, was not written until five years later.

The successful production of *Patria 2* at the Stratford Festival in 1972 provided the impetus to complete *Patria 1*. Copies of the printed score were sent out to several potential producers, including the National Arts Centre and the Canadian Opera Company. Hamilton Southam, then director general of NAC invited me to lunch and tried to persuade me, as we both puffed on Havana cigars, to write an opera based on George Orwell's *Nineteen Eighty-four,* but absolutely refused to consider *Patria 1* as a work of equal relevance.

The original title of *Patria 1* was *The Characteristics Man* but *Wolfman* is now more appropriate, since Wolf is the original form of the protagonist of the *Patria* cycle and the form to which he ultimately returns.

The following article was written in 1988, just after the production of the work by the Canadian Opera Company.

FOLLOWING THE ATAVISTIC RITUAL of *The Princess of the Stars, Patria 1: Wolfman* plunges immediately into the modern metropolis – that is, the metropolis of 1975, when the work was completed – where we find Wolf on one of his most alarming and futile expeditions in search of the Princess. In the text he is known by the initials D.P., though he is sometimes referred to as Wolfman, Beast or Wolfie; the Princess too has assumed the earthly name of Ariadne and is evidently already well advanced in her wanderings. Condemned to a life on earth, Ariadne will

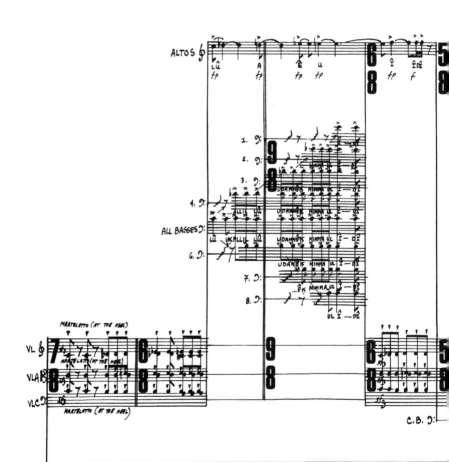

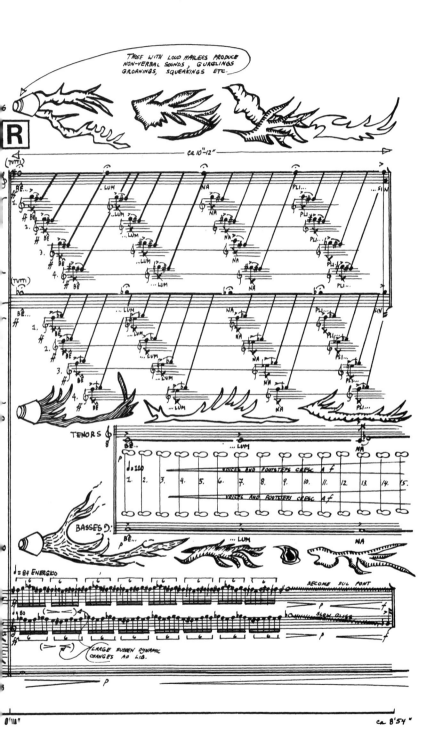

THOSE WITH LOUD HAILERS PRODUCE
NON-VERBAL SOUNDS, GURGLINGS
GROANINGS, SQUEAKINGS ETC.

appear in each of the *Patria* works, extending the thread of potential salvation to the hero.

*Patria 1* is the first of two studies on the theme of alienation. In *Wolfman* the immigrant D.P. arrives in a new country understanding neither the language nor the social customs. He seems to be a sensitive, shy man, lean and ductile, with a Chaplinesque ability to show by limb and eye what he is experiencing. He does not arrive alone but rather with a horde of disenfranchised fugitives seeking asylum and a chance to change their old colours for new opportunities. Absurdly, he sports the numeral 1 on his jersey, advertising that he is both the protagonist and the figure closest to a cipher.

Operating on the principles of self-interest and pleasure, the new land presents no insurmountable impediments to the vast majority of newcomers, whose past lives appear to have been short on opportunity in these areas; but D.P.'s quest is of another order making adjustment more difficult, with the result that he is abused and humiliated as he is tossed from one absurd experience to another in a manner that should keep the audience transiently provoked and flustered. In fact, he is so baffled by his new surroundings that throughout the work he speaks not a single word. What we discover about his thoughts or his past is transmitted by a schizophonic voice on a loudspeaker, the voice of 'an acquaintance ... or perhaps merely someone investigating the story.'

The work unfolds in a series of thirty-three episodes or editing units, played without intermission, culminating in D.P.'s mental collapse and suicide. The pace is fast and none of the episodes is developed to any great depth; the effect is cumulative.

As in Greek drama, the audience knows of the impending tragedy right from the start. The first image is a prescient flash of the final scene and we are further reminded of this by frequent news clips on television monitors throughout the performance. The important thing, however, is that although the audience knows the conclusion, they must be constantly distracted from it until the final scene suddenly explodes on them with calamitous realism. Up to that point *Wolfman* has been a grim comedy of errors. Now it becomes a thriller in which the viewer discovers that he is also a victim.

The story begins at the disembarkation point where the refugees are being processed. The immigration officer H. Showell Stools[1] wears a gas

46

---

1   A paragraph could be written about names in the *Patria* cycle, but I won't write it. Suffice to say that all the names in *Patria 1* are either eczematous purebred or leprous hybrid.

mask in order not to be contaminated by the mephitic atmosphere and speaks an unintelligible language, which is really a letter-reversal of the *lingua materna* of the country in which the work is produced. Doctors (also masked) inoculate the immigrants with an enormous hypodermic needle, then pass them on to have their photographs taken; they are given lollipops, perhaps in return for swearing allegiance to some phony flag. While the dwarf Arturo Schitzlip follows D.P. around with a pointed sign reading 'THE VICTIM,' another arrival in the new land, the famous opera singer Mimi Mippipopolous is greeted by the immigration officials with exaggerated respect for which they are rewarded with a few roulades from her repertoire of gilded spaghetti. While happy relatives (who may be members of the audience) wave welcomingly to the new arrivals, a vocal chorus sings a different tune: 'Abandon hope, all ye who enter here,' the famous inscription over Dante's *Inferno*, accompanied very brutally by the orchestra and tape in which a number of additional and contradictory messages are enciphered in the rhythms of Morse code (see notes at the end of the score).

The tragicomic atmosphere struck at the opening of *Patria 1* attends the entire work from start to finish. This is not the only work I have written in which the audience is deliberately suspended between laughter and tears – parts of *Patria 3* are balanced in the same way – but it is the most sustained and unrelenting. This is the tone the director must find, that of a thousand laughs stabbed in the back.

The focus narrows to D.P. – the mote in the light – as he is interrogated by the employer Henry Judah Treece, the psychiatrist Ovid Klein and the intern Rodney Livermash Bashford, whose questions are drawn from the admission papers to a mental hospital. The photographer Cecil Blish takes his picture. When the bulb flashes, all the lights go out and a passport photograph of D.P. appears on the screen. It is a portrait of Franz Kafka, whom we now realize D.P. reminded us of all along.[2] The first of the monologues is heard over the loudspeaker to the accompaniment of an accordion – D.P.'s instrument – suggesting his eastern or southern European

---

2  I cannot say whether there is *Heimweh* in D.P., but that homesickness exists in the modern world to an extent never before dreamed of, I have no doubt. Once it was the Swiss mercenaries who felt it whenever they heard the *ranz des vaches* and it was also treated as an organic malady among Second World War soldiers, and still is among students in university medical clinics, where it is as common as flu and hepatitis. But how can we measure the homesickness of immigrants for whom return to their native lands is impossible, except by the dark and mirthless faces they present on subway trains in spite of the gorgeous prospect of a full meal and a bathtub awaiting them at home?

origin. While the voice speaks of loneliness, D.P. crawls into a hovel, which may be one of several hovels he is destined to inhabit at various times when he is let free and which are always, like basements in rooming houses, below the level of the raised audience.



His solitude does not last long. Soon the workers Glenn Frever, Sass Boomga and Ron Muck arrive to haul him off to a job in a factory.[3] I envisioned the factory as an abattoir. Objects resembling animal carcasses proceed across the stage, suspended from the ceiling on a conveyor belt. But the work done by one worker seems to be undone by the next, so that the carcasses are dismembered and 're-membered'. An ominous chanting accompanies the work, a polyglot chanting of the Lord's Prayer in eleven languages.

In his book *Mechanization Takes Command*[4] Siegfried Giedion provides numerous illustrations of patents taken out in an effort to discover the most effective method of slaughtering animals. 'This was the first time complex organic substance and mechanization came directly together.' But the patents didn't work and the engineers didn't emerge victorious. To kill decisively takes the human touch. Whether or not the abattoir setting is preserved or is transformed into some equally repellent absurdity fit only for halfwits or immigrants,[5] Giedion's description of the scene remains a useful guide.

> Everything in the slaughterhouse must be precise. Exact, disciplined movements are required, as the foreman keeps pointing out to the workers. They are economic atoms in an equation which no one expects them to understand. 'You stand here, you place your legs 11 inches apart, your arms will move x inches in a course of y radius and the time of the movement will be .000 minutes. (p. 216)

---

3 Ron Muck, like several of the characters in *Patria 1*, is a real person. When I lived in Coquitlam, British Columbia, I was continually harassed by the nightly operations of a bulldozer a few lots from my house. I went to complain, but before I could open my mouth a thickset and very red-necked primate in the driver's seat called down: 'Hi! My name's Ron Muck and this's going to be my new home.'

4 Oxford University Press, New York, 1943, pp. 209-46.

5 A Hungarian immigrant told me that his first job in Canada was to remove the blood-soaked sheets that came down the chute from the operating room in a hospital and put them in a washing machine. After a year he was promoted to folding the clean sheets that came out of the washing machine and sending them back up to the operating room.

*Arbeit macht frei*, and so with the dismissal bell all the workers break free to line up for their pay from the factory owner Henry Judah Treece. Their payment is in inflatable toy cars, which they drive about in a state of euphoria, affectionately bumping into one another – that is, all except D.P. who is left to dodge about on foot. The accompanying music undergoes a series of metamorphoses from a soft, *Gymnopédie*-like beginning to a light-hearted bossa nova and finally to big-band swing as the workers are joined by their fat little wives, clutching their own share of hot-air trash.[6]

The disc jockey Eddie le Chasseur in *Patria 1: Wolfman*. Canadian Opera Company production, 1987.

A ring of light bulbs begins flashing around Eddie le Chasseur, disc jockey of the station SLAM, whose prestissimo speech and battery of sound effects dazzles momentarily, but is soon put into competition with other forms of equally persuasive demagoguery. The general, Amadeus Nagy-Toth Toth, vibrating with sforzando ribbons from sternum to axilla,

6  The inspiration for this scene was a visit I paid to the Canadian Consulate in Hamburg in 1957, where I heard an officer describing my homeland to a family of prospective emigrants with the oily glibness one expects from the diplomatic corps. But who would recognize the *pays des chimères* he was describing? He painted it like a colour spread in the *National Geographic*: streets of gold, money on trees, fantastic jobs even for the illiterate and feeble-minded (though not for the tubercular or crippled). Europeans today would scoff at such nonsense, but many people in other parts of the world can still be persuaded to believe it.

captures part of the crowd while elsewhere the psychiatrist Ovid Klein delivers a homily on the downward convergence of the human race; but the real accolades are won by Mimi Mippipopolous when she sings an aria from Gounod's *Faust* to the gaping multitude, who follow her out sycophantically bearing the eighty-metre train of her gown.

D.P. is hauled from another of his hovels by the Frever-Boomga-Muck gang who pound him into a pulp and exit waving at the pretty girls in the audience. Another monologue follows, Ariadne's name is mentioned and her voice, like a silver thread, is heard off-stage.

Two deaf mutes enter and ask in sign language for directions to the Garden of Eden. D.P. points in various directions and the couple moves off in the one direction he has not indicated. He smiles, glad to have been of service. Perhaps this is the only time we see D.P. smile in the entire work, that is really smile with his heart, as distinct from the slight concave smirk he often produces as a survival tactic.

The ubiquitous hard-hat boys again enter and grab D.P., this time conducting him to a night school where English grammar and pronunciation are being taught by Professor Hieronymus Knicker in an accent permanently manacled to Luther and the Brothers Grimm. The nightschool students, dutiful at first, gradually gain confidence after mastering a few 'hit' words and curtail the lesson by attacking the teacher.

At this point the second of the three large choruses begins: the Assyrian Penitential Psalm. Since this spreads over several units, sometimes endorsing and sometimes counterpointing the action, a word about the function of the chorus may be useful. This thirty-two-voice ensemble bears much of the musical accompaniment throughout *Patria 1*. Like a Greek chorus, like the chorus of Bach's Passions, its function is to behave like an articulate spectator reacting to the action. But it also exerts an inimical pressure, directed against D.P. primarily but all the actors in general, whom it regards with suspicion or hostility. The archaic languages it speaks (medieval Italian, Assyrian and, in the final chorus, Sanskrit) suggest the ossification of the old regime, wise perhaps but also encrusted with prejudice. Like any establishment, they view the world from above and selectively; it is as if they regard what is to be seen in the bus terminals and shantytowns of the empire as so many optical illusions requiring the corrective of good moral scripture. That neither the immigrants nor the audience – whom we presume for the most part to be at a halfway station – understand anything they are saying is of no consequence. The drift of their chanting and its emotional curve, projected over the floor from the gilded halls of the

Tabernacle and the Empire Club, is not intended to have practical significance though its forcefulness can never be denied.

To return to the story: old Professor Knicker hangs himself in despair. When D.P. cuts him down he turns on him angrily, accusing him of being an informer, and stomps off. The stage begins to become repopulated; a political rally is in the making. General Amadeus Nagy-Toth Toth, his uniform gleaming and jingling, steps up to address the crowd but finds himself in competition with Glenn Frever, the union leader, and the disc jockey Eddie le Chasseur. All three proclaim the same message, each in his own language: in the age of the masses the individual counts for nothing. The mob goose-steps around approvingly but scatters when police officers Maurice Ayoub and Sappho Silikens arrive on a tandem bicycle. D.P., alone and still waving the partisan flag someone has given him, becomes the object of their attention. With delicate sensuousness they move around him, flicking at his face or waving remonstrating fingers at him before finally leading him off to a rack where they handcuff him in a mock crucifixion. The child Ariadne passes beneath D.P.'s cross carrying a candle, which she gives to the woman Ariadne, who enters from the opposite side. (The relationship between the child and the woman both bearing the same name is taken up again in *Patria 2*.)

Eddie le Chasseur announces a party and the full cast reappears: streamers and balloons, champagne and laughter, Columbines and Pierrots, dancers lip to lip and hip to hip. A rock band plays as Primavera Nicolson belts a popular song in a topless dress; the Sunday poet Mercedes Jardine recites poems in the style of Mayakovsky; Mimi Mippipopolous warbles from *Faust*; the police officers return and dance provocatively.

Unnoticed, Ariadne has entered this frenzy with a pistol. D.P. alone sees it. He tries to reach her but cannot find a path through the crowd. Ariadne disappears in a whirl of dancers and when they clear she is on the floor, presumably shot.

The final chorus is a setting of a portion of the *Bhagavad Gita* concerning the attainment of serenity. Over the choir the brass punctuates startlingly, as if the desired state is falling awkwardly short of fulfilment. It is over this continuous music that the final scene is played.

Alone and disillusioned, D.P. has wandered away from the party. The girl Ariadne enters and begins talking to him. For once someone displays some sweetness and humanity, but it is too late; D.P. seizes the child and holds her at knifepoint. Around them the scene converges just as we saw it at the beginning of the work and have seen it from a repletion of TV angles

SANSKRIT: saṅgas teṣū 'pajāyate saṅgāt sam̐
ENGLISH: ...attachment' to them is produced. From

VOICES RANDOMLY SPEAK
THE WORDS GIVEN ; FIRST
LOUDLY , THEN SUDDENLY
SOFTLY AND FADING.

RAPID, FORCED BREATHIN...
LOUD AND ENERGE...

U

S.

SAṄGAS TEṢŪ 'PAJĀYATE    SAṄGAS TEṢŪ 'PAJĀYATE

DHYĀYATO VIṢAYĀN PUMSAḤ    DHYĀYATO VIṢAYĀN PUMSAḤ

A.

SAṄGAS TEṢŪ 'PAJĀYATE    SAṄGAS TEṢŪ 'PAJĀYATE

DHYĀYATO VIṢAYĀN PUMSAḤ    DHYĀYATO VIṢAYĀN PUMSAḤ

T.

SAṄGAS TEṢŪ 'PAJĀYATE    SAṄGAS TEṢŪ 'PAJĀYATE    SOLO

T (trilled)
sf;

DHYĀYATO VIṢAYĀN PUMSAḤ    DHYĀYATO VIṢAYĀN PUMSAḤ

B.

SAṄGAS TEṢŪ 'PAJĀYATE    SAṄGAS TEṢŪ 'PAJĀYATE    SOLO
SH
sf;

SAṄGAS TEṢŪ 'PAJĀYATE    SAṄGAS TEṢŪ 'PAJĀYATE

DHYĀYATO VIṢAYĀN PUMSAḤ    DHYĀYATO VIṢAYĀN PUMSAḤ    SOLO

YA

CHOIR FADES OUT AS TAPE ENTERS

BASS SOLO

ca 2½"    ca 1½"

START
TAPE
CUE 20

(ORIENTAL PRIEST RECITING)

0"        5"        10"

ca 9'35"        9'45"

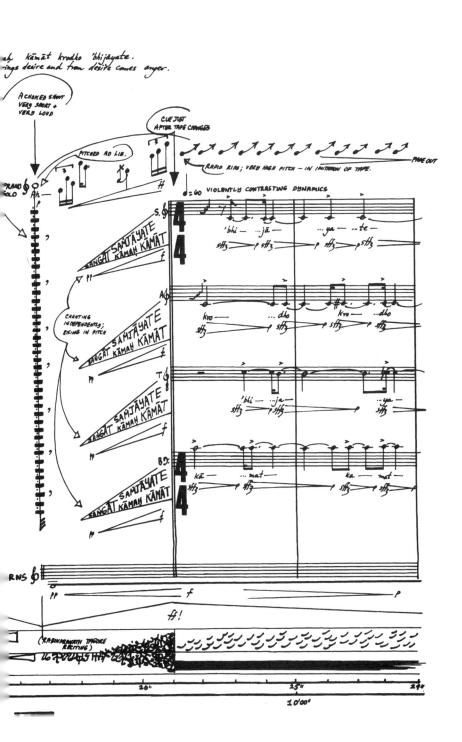

throughout the performance. Little by little the citizens arrive (for by now everyone is a citizen) and encircle the action. As police sharpshooters move into position on scaffolds and rooftops, reporters and television cameras dolly in on the floor. One of the first to arrive is the popular hero Eddie le Chasseur, who is instrumental in diverting D.P.'s attention in the final instant so that Ariadne may escape. As the audience sighs with relief, D.P. drives the knife into his own stomach, slipping to the ground with a single, broken, muffled sob.

Patria 1 was begun in 1966, the same year as Patria 2, but was not completed until 1974. The subject it deals with is familiar throughout the modern world as displaced persons everywhere attempt to make fresh starts in new countries. When I completed it I made the usual attempts to get it produced without any success whatever. I must have let fly a cry of despair one day when someone said: 'You'll never get it produced here, the subject is too hot.' It is true that the theme of immigration is a delicate one in Canada.[7] Canada is supposed to be a haven to the world, a 'free' country to which oppressed peoples of the world can turn for refuge and a new start. That is a very nice myth. The reality is that the country is the world's biggest refugee camp with all the problems attendant on helping to resettle enormous numbers of people quickly, find them jobs, teach them a new language, acculturate them. This creates strains on both sides; the new, living the disquieting experiment of learning new tricks for new masters; the established, watching the character of their towns and cities change and their culture and traditions erode.[8]

The successful immigrant adapts as quickly as possible, tolerates the rattrap of his first job, goes on to open up a business, make money, move uptown and contribute to the luxuriating of the economy. It is a happy if somewhat uninteresting story, and I am sure that Canada boasts more

---

7 According to the 1981 census, 16 percent of Canadians were not born in Canada. The figure climbs rapidly for urban centres: 38 percent of the population of Toronto are immigrants. The linguistic character of such centres is polyglot – a theme reflected in Patria 1 and 2. In Toronto, 30 percent of the population speaks English with greater or less proficiency as a second language. Source: Statistics Canada, Catalogues 92-913, 93-930, 95-901, 901, 98-906.

8 I have made my position on immigration in Canada clear: I am opposed to it, since I consider the country already overpopulated. Canada's most urgent problem is the discovery of an identity, an issue in no way served by the receipt of more strangers. If I put these remarks as a footnote it is only because they are *not* the issue in *Wolfman* since it does not deal with ideology but with a very concrete reality.

instances of it than most other countries. Assisting the newcomer on his way, the mythmakers have mounted a hefty public relations campaign at home and abroad to persuade the world that in this land of freedom and opportunity, all honest industry will be rewarded by a bountiful nest-egg; and the successful immigrant makes the same boast to his relatives back home in order to dilate his own achievement.

So much for success. What about the failures? What about those who don't get ahead? Those abandoned to loneliness and anomie? Those who after giving the country a try decide they hate it? Those who never wanted to come in the first place? Those who crack under the strain of irreversible displacement and murder their wives and children? This is why *Wolfman* had to be written.

The subject was a real displaced person. I found him in a Vancouver newspaper on May 28, 1966, a poor Yugoslav misfit who held a little girl at knifepoint while he emptied out an unprintable laundry bag of venom against Canada for deceiving him, then let the girl go and killed himself. I still have the picture that appeared on the first page of *The Vancouver Sun*. The terror in the eyes is unforgettable. Here was a man for whom the welcome mat must have been small and the two jobs he possibly held in order to make some advancement merely burned out his spirit so that in the end he just wanted to give up.

Of course I modified his story. In *Patria 1* we are really witnessing Wolf, chained as Odin chained Fenris, living the muzzled life of a dog, dodging cuffs and eating scraps – a not very successful reincarnation this first of several he will experience. And his Princess too has fallen to play out a pitiful role as a party girl and victim. We meet her only briefly in *Patria 1*; in *Patria 2* we will get to know her better. Had the two met they could have fortified one another against the snares of the pernicious world around them. The smallest but strongest social unit, we remember, is two persons. Even two weaklings can make a strength here. But the thread has snapped and the labyrinth is inescapable.

Unlike the model immigrant, D.P. shows little proclivity for adaptation. He seems to remain in a permanent state of shock and has protected himself by aphasia. He remains egregious – in the etymological sense, outside the flock – and by contrast to the swelling mob around him he raises the problem which confounds all civilization today, the problem of the one amid the many, the soloist in the crowd, the individual smothered by statistics. Bosch's painting 'Christ Bearing His Cross,' which is alluded to in editing unit 22, dramatizes the same issue of the individual with his soul alone in the mass of men. D.P. is also crucified by the masses, from whom he receives no love but only kicks and insults. As the crowd multiplies, so do alienation and fear. The little egoistic fire burning in him, like the little egoistic fire burning in you and me, is extinguished by simple Malthusian arithmetic. As Reverend Le Meul explains it: 'If a man has a soul, then two men have half a soul each,' and so on. Too many sacred fires are profane.

An editorial note in *Patria 1* calls (metaphorically) for a cast of thousands. Is it possible to love a multitude? Voltaire wrote: 'The greater a country becomes, the less we love it; for love is weakened by diffusion. It is impossible to love a family so numerous that we hardly know it.'[9] There is no love then in *Patria 1* and the only personal right remaining to the would-be lover is suicide.

What remains to be discussed is the method by which these themes can be brought out most effectively. *Wolfman* is conceived for the modern urban theatre, as distinct from *The Princess of the Stars* and some of the later *Patria* works which require more open environments. The present creation demands an enclosed space, a ghetto, walls, inside which the audience huddles and against which the music is hurled.

The moment you organize space you dictate the social actions permitted in that space. I have always been amazed at the tenacity with which the theatre building persists. Plays are produced year after year in conventional spaces which rarely vary and even then only by as much as a few rows of seats in order to give the playing area a different shape. Yet the world outside the theatre changes and has changed a great deal since these spaces set out the social division between the entertainers and the entertained, the structure of the text and the hierarchy of director, actor, technician, musician and customer. Even the most adventurous directors of the twentieth century respected that. All Meyerhold's, Piscator's, Brecht's and Artaud's productions were given in conventional theatres. Today one has three options with regard to the conventional theatre: to be sentimental about it, to exploit it, or to leave it behind. In *Patria 1* we exploit it.

I don't think it matters very much what shape the playing area takes, whether open or framed. I suggest that the technical crew running the show remain in full view, the technicians perhaps wearing white coats or uniforms of a quasi-military nature. The idea would be to let the 'seams' of the work show and to allow the technicians to pin it together openly in the manner in which all civic officials from janitors to policemen operate. At

---

9    *Philosophical Dictionary*: see under 'Country.'

one point D.P. may even attempt to secure a favour from one of these 'officials' who rebuffs him or kicks him, etc.

The relationship between the audience and the performers is a matter requiring special care. Although in one sense the audience and the immigrants are of the same mould – that is, the audience will easily be able to identify with the acquisitive instincts of the performers, or their appetite for a party or a blue movie – in another sense they are different, for there is a subtle line between the second-class citizens on the floor and the first-class citizens who are already in the theatre before them. This separation must be achieved by physical as well as psychological means in preparation for the final scene where the audience's hubris finally dissolves into sympathy.

The vertical dimension is extremely important in *Patria* 1. A sketch in the score shows a high modular scaffold on which the chorus is situated in order to maintain their *Entfremdung*, as mentioned previously. The precedent in my mind for this was probably Ernst Toller's *Hoppla, wir leben!*, where the author writes: 'All the play's scenes can be performed on a scaffolding of several stories which can be used unchanged,' a plan Piscator followed when staging the work.[10] The audience too, should be off the ground and to some extent, however slight, above the action.

In 'The Theatre of Confluence I' I stated that I did not wish to negate the individual personalities in the arts, but rather was seeking a means by which all levels of activity could be developed coevally and given equal status – a 'co-opera' rather than opera. It may be that at certain times a dramatic event may be best expressed by actions, unmolested by music, or at other times action should be suspended to allow the music to amplify a certain emotion.

I do not intend that one artist's *Fach* should become another's flop. It is not a matter of trying to do what one was never trained to do (actors

---

10   There are, of course, other precedents. In Metz in the fifteenth century there may have been a stage nine stories high, though the matter is disputed. Friedrich Kranich mentions it in volume 2 of his *Bühnentechnik der Gegenwart*, Oldenbourg, Munich, 1933, p. 294. But E.K. Chambers writes: 'These [scaffolds] were certainly known later, and the descriptions of some of them as no less than nine stories high have given rise to an erroneous theory that the plays were performed upon a many-storied stage.' *The Medieval Stage*, Oxford University Press, London, 1903, vol. 2, p. 86. Oskar Schlemmer also emphasized the neglected importance of the vertical dimension in his little book *The Theatre of the Bauhaus*, Middletown, Connecticut, 1961. In particular note the spherical theatre designed by Andreas Weininger in which the action takes place up and down a spiral ramp from floor to ceiling with the audience seated on all levels inside the sphere.

singing or a chorus acting) but rather of finding the means to pass, as if by sleight of hand, from one technique of presentation to another. The cast of *Wolfman* includes actors, singers, a mime artist and deaf mutes. What Eisenstein says about Kabuki Theatre is a useful instruction here:

> It is impossible to speak of 'accompaniments' in Kabuki – just as one would not say that, in walking or running, the right leg 'accompanies' the left leg, or that both of them accompany the diaphragm!
>
> In place of *accompaniment*, it is the naked method of *transfer* that flashes in the Kabuki theatre.[11]

Eisenstein continues:

> The Kabuki stage … gives each man or woman (courtesan, peasant, princess, samurai, merchant, demon) a different way of walking, a distinctive makeup (white face, brown face, red lines, black lines, purple lines, high eyebrows, no eyebrows, etc.) varying ways of using the voice (falsetto, broken falsetto, deep bass, musical intonations, guttural sputterings, etc.) and diverse colours and forms of costumes to suggest class, character and feelings.

This might be another useful instruction, particularly for indicating the ethnic diversity of the immigrants, stronger when indicated stylistically than literally.

In searching for precedents for the looping together of the various forms and activities of *Patria 1*, I came across a description of a banquet held in 1454 at Lille, France. Read it carefully and note the perfect counterpointing of diverse elements.

> The banquet took place in a great hall whose walls vanished under splendid tapestries depicting scenes in the life of Hercules. The chroniclers, besides describing the silken costumes, the elaborate table decorations, and the perfumes that scented the air, tell of the masques that were performed and of the part that music played in animating them, as well as in endowing the table decorations with the power of sound. In that hall there were three tables; on one there was a church, in which there were a

---

11    Sergei Eisenstein, *Film Form*, Harcourt Brace, New York, 1949, p. 21.

sounding bell and four singers who sang and played on organs when their turn came. On another table there was a huge pastry so formed that it could house twenty-eight living persons playing on diverse instruments. Later, on the main table, three little children and a tenor sang a very sweet chanson, and when they had finished a shepherd played on a bagpipe in most novel fashion.

We learn also of two trumpeters who sounded a fanfare while mounted on a horse that was led back and forth the length of the hall. Appropriately enough, considering the Order of the Knights, there were masques about the adventures of Jason. Before the first, those in the church sang, and in the pastry there was played a *douchaine* with another instrument and soon thereafter four *clarions* sounded very high and made a very joyous fanfare. These *clarions* were behind a green curtain, hung over a great scaffolding built at the end of the hall. When their fanfare was ended, the curtain was suddenly drawn, and there, on the scaffoldings was seen the personage of Jason. After this masque organs were played in the church for the length and extent of a motet, and shortly afterwards there was sung in the pastry, by three sweet voices, a chanson named *Sauvegarde de ma vie*.

Then, through the door, after those in the church and those in the pastry had each performed four times, there entered into the hall a wondrously great and beautiful stag; upon the stag was mounted a young lad, about twelve years old. The child held the two horns of the stag with his two hands. When he entered into the hall, he began the upper part of the chanson, very high and clear; and the stag sang the tenor, without there being any other person except the child and the artifice of the said stag; and the song was named *Je ne vis oncques la pareille*. While singing, as I have narrated to you, they made the rounds before the table, and then returned; and this interlude seemed to me good. After this interlude of the white stag and the child the singers sang a motet in the church, and in the pastry a lute was played with two good voices, and the church and the pastry always did something between the interludes.[12]

---

12    Gustave Reese, *Music in the Renaissance*, Norton, New York, 1959, pp. 57-8.

This example of delightful, unobstructive and carefully rehearsed interplay between activities is exactly what *Wolfman* should be on the stage – even though its tone is more sombre and brutal. A mosaic then, a galaxy. Let us never have competition for the spotlight. Rather let us simply have more spotlights.

The director can make *Patria 1* as political as desired, if that helps to bring the themes discussed in the above pages into focus. For instance, D.P. may be black and all the other characters white – though in the nature of things today it would perhaps be more appropriate if D.P. were white and all the others black.

The immigrants wear drab grey, one-piece uniforms with numbers on them at the beginning, but little by little they exchange those for gay, even gaudy costumes to emphasize their success in the new-found-land. Only D.P. retains his original uniform throughout, which in this case is powder blue (to suggest the sky into which his spirit will be released in the end) with the blood red numeral 1 on front and back.

In *Patria 1* I have tried to create a work as exciting as a football game. This mode of excitement and plurality of action should be the objective at all times. How it is to be achieved is, of course, up to the director.

Ah yes, the director....

*Patria 1* was first produced in November 1987 by the Canadian Opera Company. This is how it came about. The COC, which had not produced a Canadian opera in nearly twenty (20) years, was under increasing pressure from the arts councils to produce some native vibrations before the end of the century; so one day I was called into the COC office by John Leberg, director of operations, to be told that they intended to produce *Patria 1: The Characteristics Man*. It was to be co-directed by Guy Sprung and John Leberg. One is often approached about possible productions; it is wise not to let one's hopes soar too soon; I acknowledged their interest and left wondering whether it would really happen.

That was my mistake. I should have laid out my conditions for a production then and there. In all my theatrical works up to this point I had played an active role, functioning as artistic director in all cases and occasionally directing them myself (*Apocalypsis, Princess of the Stars*). This began out of necessity since at first there was no one else to take them on; later I felt it was desirable in each case to establish a historical precedent which later producers and directors would be forced to consider as they sought new methods of interpretation.

We know, for instance, that both Verdi and Wagner were very much involved with the casting and staging of their works, often dictating details down to the last lighting cue. Whether this improved the presentation is beside the point; students of these works have been provided with clear indications of the author's intentions as a record against which all future productions must be measured as improvements or deflections.

I knew that it was the success of such works as *Ra* and *Princess of the Stars* that had impelled the coc to consider one of my works in the first place and I naively anticipated they would respect me enough to allow me to assist in the shaping of this première also. In this I was totally mistaken.

When I was called back to the office a few weeks later it was to be told that the coc had been granted $310,000 by the Ontario Arts Council and the Canada Council to undertake *Patria 1*. Parenthetically I will remark that this was far in excess of any sum I or anyone else had ever been awarded before for one of my works, although by coc standards it was very slight – less than half of what they would spend on an average show. So far as I could tell, the money had been given to them on the basis of a few telephone conversations, for scarcely enough time had elapsed for written applications to be processed and juried – the procedure we artists are always forced to endure.

There was another surprise. Guy Sprung had disappeared and John Leberg was proposing to direct the work himself. Between meetings I had been doing a little telephoning myself and from conversations with performers had ascertained that Mr. Leberg was not exactly the Max Reinhardt of our time, so I tried to persuade him to consider at least a co-director and suggested several people, some of whom I had worked with before.[13] All my suggestions were rejected. I proposed that I direct the work and got a flat refusal. For some time the matter remained unresolved.

Next I heard that Chris Newton, director of the Shaw Festival, had been approached by the coc. I did not see why a director whose reputation was built on his skill at handling Shavian farces should be considered appropriate for the expressionistic complexities of *Wolfman*, but agreed to meet him in the hopes of finding a solution. I had a great deal of difficulty in deciding what to do. The coc was absolutely closed to all further discussion of the matter. When I delayed signing the contract which would release the work for production and force me to accept 'an advisory position,' I received a telegram as follows:

13    The names I suggested were Thom Sokoloski, Brian MacDonald and Leon Major.

HAVE NOT RECEIVED CONTRACT MAILED DECEMBER 1, 1986.
AMPLE TIME TO RETURN. DELAY SHOWS YOU ARE NOT INTERESTED
IN HAVING PATRIA PRODUCED. EFFECTIVE TODAY WE ARE
CANCELLING PROJECT.

JOHN LEBERG, CANADIAN OPERA COMPANY

It is difficult to explain to someone other than another creative artist how a work which took ten years to write and which lay on the shelf for another thirteen argues more and more restlessly with its author for the right to see the light of day. The score of *Patria 1* is very explicit and if the directions were followed it should be possible for a smooth machine like the COC to approach it with something like efficiency. I acquiesced, signed the contract and endeavoured to contact Newton, the designers, Jerrard and Diana Smith, and the music director, Bob Aitken, to begin production discussions. For this I received the following letter:

Dear Murray: We are disturbed by the confusion that has arisen surrounding the proposed production of *Patria 1*.

The decision to cancel the production was based on the apparent lack of interest in the contract mailed December 1, 1986. Since six weeks had elapsed from that date without receipt of a signed contract by the Canadian Opera Company.

We now understand you personally had convened a production meeting regarding the proposed COC production of *Patria* without informing or inviting a representative of the Company. It is unfortunate that you misunderstand the clauses embodied in the contract in your possession that we negotiated and sent to you December 1, 1986 and that this misunderstanding has led to a contravention of the clauses outlined therein on your part.

The contract outlines your involvement as Author in an advisory capacity and stipulates that the meetings were convened at the discretion of the Company to which you may be invited to attend. Clearly you have overstepped your authority as outlined in the contract by calling this production meeting. As a production of the Canadian Opera Company, the Company is financially and artistically responsible for the production and therefore any and all decisions concerning the production must be approved by the Company ...

Given this breach of contract we do not intend to create a

production of *Patria* without your agreement and adherence to the terms and conditions and understanding of the contract sent to you.

John Leberg, Director of Operations

And that was more or less the end of my involvement with the production. I attended two design meetings at my own instigation and managed to influence a few critical matters, or rather restore design elements described in the text (such as scaffolding for the choir) which were threatened with abandonment. I was invited to two production meetings. I had no further meetings with the director and was not asked to attend staging rehearsals. No one was interested in anyone else's part in the production. No one was interested in the whole. There were no meetings at which the artistic team shared ideas or sought to unify their concept of the work. Everyone went his own way, appeared when required and disappeared when not required. No one wanted to learn from anyone else. The director attended no musical rehearsals. The musical director was out of the country for the first week of staging rehearsals. The designers worked in a vacuum.

I have never felt that I suffer unduly from paranoia, but when at the dress rehearsal I watched D.P. receiving kicks from the grinning multitude I could not detach myself from the notion that we were one and the same person. 'D.P., *c'est moi!*'

A trashy poster advertised *Patria* 1 as a 'work about alienation and non-communication in the video age,' which is about as accurate as calling Faust a drama about a libertine who raped a spinning maid. The audience was provided with no introduction to the work in the flimsy program notes.

What the production amounted to is history.

The Canadian Opera Company charged me for tickets to attend the première. I did not attend any of the performances.

# Patria 2:
## *Requiems for the Party Girl*

*Composed*: 1966-72, Vancouver.

*Cast*: Ariadne (mezzo-soprano) and 12 actors (dancers).

*Orchestra*: Flute (piccolo, alto flute), clarinet (bass clarinet), French horn, violin, viola, cello, piano, percussion (1 player), electronic sounds on tape. Mixed chorus (live or pre-recorded).

*Duration*: 1 hour 20 minutes.

*First performance*: Stratford Festival, Ontario, August 23, 1972.

CANADA IS THE ONLY COUNTRY I know of in which new works of critical and public success are buried never to be revived. It is a country totally lacking curiosity about its own creations. It deserts them as a mother deserts an unwanted baby in a lavatory. The birth pains over, it kills its progeny and runs off to play prostitute with whatever foreigner is passing through.

So it is that I will now speak of *Patria 2*, a work premièred at the Stratford Festival in 1972, where it played for three nights to full houses, received excellent reviews in *Time* magazine and the national newspapers, is vividly remembered by its author and some of his acquaintances and has never been performed since. Not only has it not been remounted, there has not even been a tremor of curiosity about its existence from any of the national opera or theatre companies even though at the time of its publication copies of the score were sent to many of them. A whole generation of Canadians has died and another has grown up to replace them without knowing about this work. Several other *Patria* pieces have been performed successfully without stimulating interest in it, so that if it is raised again it will likely be through my own energy and money.

As the earliest work in the *Patria* cycle to be completed, *Requiems for the Party Girl* is the most conventional and also the most intimate. I don't recall exactly when I began to conceive it, but in 1966 I wrote a set of arias for Phyllis Mailing entitled 'Requiems for the Party Girl' and the drama inherent in that set is the sum and substance of the entire stage work. The arias were deliberately kept short (unlike those of *Loving*) so that dialogue and action could be interpolated. About 1970, John Roberts gave me the chance to produce an hour-long radio drama for the CBC; I used this opportunity to combine the arias with short scenes of dialogue and presented it under the title of 'Dream Passage.'

The final stage version differs only slightly from the radiophonic text. Michael Bawtree, then my colleague in the Communications Department at Simon Fraser University, persuaded the Stratford Festival (which had not yet become a mortuary) to undertake it on the Third Stage under his direction. The production adhered very closely to the text and therefore met with the author's enthusiastic approval if not with that of the lemon-faced administrators whose faith in the new Canadian work had risen to the exceptional height of offering the tickets for the ridiculously low price of three dollars (or something like that), so that I responded by ordering all the tickets for all three performances the first day they went on sale for a mere outlay of $3,000 (or whatever), intending to take ads in the Toronto newspapers offering them at double the price. But the lemon-suckers refused to cash my cheque, having abandoned themselves to the notion that the new work *must* fail.

All performances were sold out.

And they would have at double the price, too.

Three years later the Third Stage, the only experimental thing Stratford ever attempted, was snuffed out by the pommies.

I am not inventing the story about the tickets and I could tell you many other ridiculous episodes, so obtrusively colonial are the attitudes of almost every artistic director, administrator or cultural attaché I have ever met in the country I have often despaired of calling my own. Just recently, for instance, I read a report prepared by a team of cultural marketing experts who blocked a 1989 performance of *Princess of the Stars* by quoting a ream of inaccurate or exaggerated figures, to prove that Schafer productions always lost money. That these facts are turned against me and others like me, and are only infrequently levelled against Shakespeare, Verdi or Beethoven, who have lost more money in Canada than any of us will ever hope to see, is the cultural conspiracy of which I speak.

There was one major departure in the 1972 production from my original plan and this was in the construction of the set. I had originally imagined a central playing area with the audience ranked on two sides facing one another so that they could see themselves reflected across the stage and thus be encouraged to think that their own relationship to the insane asylum, in which the work takes place, is not altogether remote.

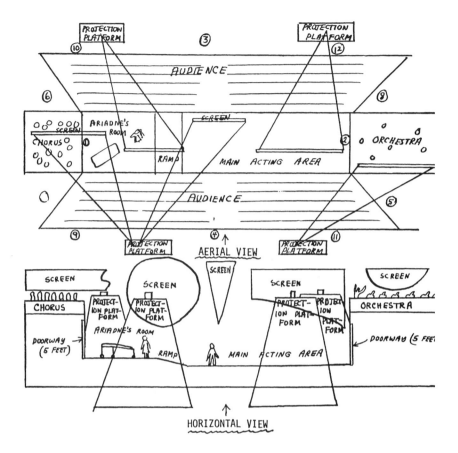

The stage Michael Bawtree and his designer came up with was a square pit about six feet deep with walls of translucent material on which lights and projections could be cast, with the audience ranged steeply upwards on all four sides so that they were looking down into it (from the superior position of the sane). Four corner platforms contained the orchestra, the choir, the stage manager and tape-playback operator, and the entrance stairs. A portable ramp, which could be raised and lowered, connected the rim of the audience area to the bottom of the pit and it was up and down this ramp that the doctors and nurses went in their visits to the inmates below.

I do not intend to give a running account of *Patria 2* here, first because it cannot be broken down linearly and second because the published score is available and can be followed easily even by non-musicians since it contains pictures, graphic images of some of the sounds, staging notes and a complete translation of the several foreign languages it employs. Although, like *Patria 1*, *Requiems* is divided into editing units, they flow together here more seamlessly. Where in *Patria 1* time jumped forward and backward on itself like a machine skipping keys, in *Patria 2* we encounter

the aberrational time of dreams or of the mental patient's mind; at times it stands still like dough in a bowl; at other times everything erupts and history is made in milliseconds. I wanted to create a work like a dream, no up or down, before or after, beginning or end, but only flow, musical flow, the flow of noises, of voices, near, distant, unintelligible.

Like *Patria 1*, *Patria 2* is a study on the theme of alienation, the consequence, as we know from the Prologue, of the Star Princess having been abandoned on earth by her father, the Sun, and being forced to wander here under the assumed name of Ariadne. As we encounter her she is a patient in a mental hospital, having presumably been brought there after her episode with the pistol in *Patria 1*. Her reign of terror is her own mind and, as we shall see, it can be reached by no medical telescope.

While writing *Requiems*, I imagined Ariadne as a prototype of one of those gay-tragic harlequinesque creatures I used to meet at Vancouver parties in the era of the LSD and magic mushroom craze, beneath whose furious demonstrations of gregariousness and *joie de vivre* one detected obscure signs of terror and alienation. As the gossiping voices around her whisper their absurd propositions into her ear, there is laughter in her eyes to disguise the anguish in her heart. She seems resolved to commit suicide and knows that no one will prevent her. 'Outstretched hands are rare,' she says.

By contrast to the absurd and often comical situations of *Wolfman*, the mood of *Requiems* is almost always sombre, malignant and shadowy. Most of the action unfolds in the darkened grottoes of the asylum rooms, which only dissolve to reveal nightmares or false apparitions of hope. The inmates grope about in semi-darkness; the doctors and nurses are uncomprehending and sometimes brutal; there are no exits. Ariadne is the only inmate who persists in hoping to find one.

I am not sure how the mental hospital evolved for *Patria 2*. Ever since Strindberg's *To Damascus*, German expressionist drama has had an obligatory asylum scene. I was familiar with a good many of these works.[1] A

---

1   I could point to several instances of 'borrowed' scenes or lines from German expressionism in *Patria 1, 2* and *3*. One instance, not acknowledged elsewhere, is the doctor in Walter Hasenclever's *Menschen* (1918) who 'demands sex from his female patients in return for performing abortions,' who is thus aligned with Dr. Ovid Klein as he appears in the Blue Theatre section of *Patria 3*.

stronger influence was several visits I paid to Riverview mental hospital in Essondale, B.C. Some of the less serious patients from Riverview used to attend noon-hour concerts I organized at the university, accompanied by a very enterprising nurse with whom I later became friendly. Miss Orno was her name. She had a thick Danish accent. I subsequently learned that *all* the doctors and nurses at Riverview were foreigners and that many of them scarcely spoke English at all. They were immigrants, trained in other countries and awaiting certification in Canada. They went to night school to learn the language and worked during the day in the lowest echelon of the public health service, the lunatic asylum. It was this that prompted me to have the doctors and nurses speak foreign languages in *Patria* 2 (there are ten of these) in order to distance them from the patients.

Some people have wondered why foreign or invented languages figure so prominently in the *Patria* works. The reason is that today more than ever before in history we live in a linguistic polyglot which has resulted in the polluting of all consistent linguistic paradigms. At times nothing seems to remain to us but a mass of jargon and gibberish through which, like Artaud's actor in the fire, we vainly try to signal in monosyllables, hoping that by shaving off all the nuances and refinements we were once taught, we will make our rudimentary and desperate messages comprehensible to someone.

This is why there has been such an infusion of recorded music into modern urban life, to bond people for whom advanced verbal communication is no longer possible. This is also the function of music in the *Patria* series; it is the keel-line sustaining the clear shape against the waves of verbal gibberish.

The situation at Riverview was pretty deplorable. I recall one ward, where the most hopeless female patients were kept, a row of spring beds without bedspreads placed no more than a metre apart with nothing in the way of private dressing rooms or tables. In the centre of the room, open to view from the barred door, was one toilet for about thirty women.

What I also recall is an incredible profusion of language, poetical language, lurid language, language veering off into silence or into grunting, bleating or screaming. These visits, together with the articles Miss Orno delivered up to me from the hospital library, provided almost all the textual material of *Patria* 2. It is in these articles that I made the acquaintance of J.L. Moreno, whose writings on psychodrama stimulated me. The brain of the schizophrenic is the repertoire for Moreno's psychodrama.

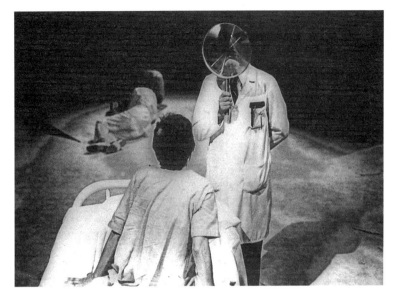

One of the doctors confronts Ariadne in *Patria 2: Requiems for the Party Girl.*
Stratford Festival production, 1972.

Sigmund Freud lectures the inmates in *Patria 2: Requiems for the Party Girl.*
Stratford Festival production, 1972.

The doctors operate on Ariadne's brain in *Patria 2: Requiems for the Party Girl.*
Stratford Festival production, 1972.

Ariadne asleep while her dead soul wanders. Phyllis Mailing and Suzette
Couture as Ariadne in *Patria 2: Requiems for the Party Girl.* Stratford Festival
production, 1972.

A production emerges, guided always by the doctor. It is fragmentary, checked by flashbacks, by the introduction of new characters drawn from the audience; halted by silence, tripped by irrelevance; and confused by the role reversals and various other techniques peculiar to the form. The production happens here and now although it may sometimes describe things that will happen in the future or have happened in the past. If the subject is 30 and refers to an event that happened when he was six, then he is six. And a moment later he is talking with God, and it is many years later and he is dead.[2]

I also find in my notes of the period this statement: 'Moreno-Ariadne-Berlin (1924). The theatre is a theatre of first nights only.'

Moreno and other psychiatrists have indicated that schizophrenics often speak a language intelligible to themselves or to other schizophrenics, though we cannot understand it. Thus while Ariadne speaks the *lingua materna* of the country in which the work is produced – I want her to engage our sympathy – the psychiatrists and nurses speak in their own (foreign) languages and the inmates speak gibberish or a branch of incoherent English, veiled in symbolism, or merely stuck together like Markoff chains from fragments of speech-patterns leading nowhere.[3] There are also a few statements from Dadaist or surrealist literature here (Tzara, Breton).

It was in the Riverview library articles that I first encountered the writings of Peter Ostwald, who has studied so intensively the ways in which mental patients communicate with their doctors not only by speech intonation but also non-verbally by means of coughs, grunts, stutters, etc. Ostwald's articles and his little book *Soundmaking* provided so many clues

---

2   J.L. Moreno, *Psychodrama and the Psychopathology of Inter-Personal Relations*,
    Psychodrama Monographs, No. 16, New York, 1945, p. 29.
3   The method I used for this was the party game in which the first person writes
    down three words then covers the first and gives it to the next to add a word, and
    so forth, so that each person extends the statement without knowing its origin,
    resulting in formations which may be grammatical but are absurd and often ridiculously funny. Another technique employed was that of copying out lines at random
    from other plays, say the top line on every tenth page, and using these as dialogue.
    I recall doing this on a train from Rapallo to Genoa one night after a visit to Ezra
    Pound's wife Dorothy. The note (p. 42 of the score) says that 'the director may
    construct an alternative aleatoric text of the same duration from a different play *ad
    libitum*, provided he does so on an Italian train.' He will, however, no longer have
    the good fortune of having just dined with the generous and intelligent Mrs.
    Pound.

Ariadne's dead soul reaching for the gem left by the alchemist in *Patria 2: Requiems for the Party Girl*. Stratford Festival production, 1972.

*Patria 2: Requiems for the Party Girl*. The empty stage showing raised catwalk down which the doctors and nurses travelled to visit the inmates in the pit. Stratford Festival production, 1972.

for the rhetoric and articulation-patterns of *Patria 2* that I later entered into correspondence with him, providing him with a copy of the completed score and soliciting comments. Some of these are woven into the text for the Blue Theatre psychiatrist, Ovid Klein, in *Patria 3*, though of course Ostwald is entirely guiltless of the malevolent streak in that individual.

If I have seen the doctors and psychiatrists who appear in the *Patria* series as corrupt and deceitful it is due probably to a personal experience I do not care to narrate. 'Beware of the doctor' reads one of the cards passed out to spectators at *The Greatest Show*.

From such remarks I explicitly exclude Ostwald, a very sensitive and intelligent man whose enthusiasms include the music of Schumann, about whom he has written a book. I seriously advise any prospective director of *Patria 2* to explore Ostwald's writings on bioacoustics. It is a field not much explored, and certainly not by Freud or Jung, who seem to have been utterly baffled whenever a patient offered them acoustic information.[4] On the other hand, Ostwald's remarks on the sound mannerisms of schizophrenics should furnish the director with a large repertoire of techniques for the actors playing the lunatics as well as for Ariadne.

Here are some of the sound mannerisms mentioned in Ostwald's articles:

| | | | |
|---|---|---|---|
| machine talk | stammering | retching | aphasia |
| staccato-articulation | stuttering | gurgling | glossolalia |
| flat vocality | stigmatisms | bleating | echolalia |
| lustreless monotony | coughing | grunting | fingernail-scratching |
| hyperinflection | gasping | growling | grinding objects |
| singsong voice | sneezing | panting | together |

speaking like dogs, cats, chickens, goats, monkeys.

We must now consider Ariadne. In *Requiems for the Party Girl* she is actually three persons: the party girl of, say, twenty to twenty-five, a little girl six to

ten years old (her innocent self) and a dead soul (her all-knowing self). The first two persons come directly out of *Patria 1*: Ariadne is both the girl D.P.

---

4  Jung's interpretation of the Miss Miller fantasies is a case in point (see his *Symbols of Transformation*, Volume 5 of the Collected Works). Many of Miss Miller's dreams were of an acoustic nature but Jung continually ignores this fertile theme or subverts it into myth-symbolism in which he, the psychiatrist, is more interested.

met briefly at the party in editing unit 32 of that work and she is also the child he holds at knifepoint at the end. We now realize the possibility that it was the memory of this traumatic experience that led to her ultimate break- down and institutionalization. Throughout the work she has glimpses of D.P. (Beast) as Nietzsche, Mozart or a handsome Greek youth (Theseus), but these glimpses are all so blurred and confused that they don't help her achieve the salvation she longs for and at the end of the work she describes her own suicide. Whether she actually commits suicide or only imagines it is intentionally left open. The scene she describes (with a revolver, an unusual instrument for a woman to employ to end her life) is the same as the *Patria 1* party scene, so that it could have been directly from there that she was rushed to the operating room which forms the first scene of *Patria 2*; but the recurrence of this scene at the end of the work also suggests an endless loop. Ariadne, like Uroboros, the self-devouring snake, is caught in an unsettled circularity where she will remain until Wolf, through redemptive love, can restore her to her native element in the heavens.

Originally, that is, in 1966, I had the intention of writing a triptych with the first two parts much as they are now, and a third in which the apotheosis would occur. The delusions of youth! Ariadne's thread has been broken many times; both she and the author have lived on to experience many more dreams and deceptions than first expected. Our goal has become more distant over the intervening years but the path more miraculous.

Is Ariadne mad in *Patria 2*? This is a question a director would want to consider carefully. Perhaps she is schizoid rather than schizophrenic, if the former can imply a less intense or durable condition. In my own mind I do not rule out the possibility that she is the victim of bioengineering by the dreaded doctors, for in the very first scene the stage directions tell us that the brain operation has proceeded to the third ventricle in the region concerned with the fluctuation of emotions. Certainly Ariadne passes through a great many widely contrasting moods in the course of the work. At times, like a hebephrenic, she reacts to her surroundings in ways that seem silly, shallow or bizarre. At other times she acquiesces to the will of others.[5] Her paranoia is extreme; she fears human contact and derives gratification and warmth only from the water of her bath, which she imag- ines as warm hands touching her, or from the music of Mozart played on a toy piano by one of the inmates (Nietzsche, Beast), who is the only character in the work to whom she speaks directly with any affection. Ariadne tells us

---

5   In the Blue Theatre of *Patria 3* the girl (Ariadne) indulges in echolalia, another token of her compliance with the doctor's wishes.

Things get out of hand, maximum frenzy.*  While the doctors and nurses strap
the patients one by one to the machine the lunatics scurry about shouting and
screaming.  Sometimes it is difficult to make out whether the patients are
giving shock treatment to the doctors and nurses or the other way round.  The
general noise continues - groans, screams, etc.  The voices of Nellie Frencheater
and Napoleon babble on simultaneously.

Nellie Frencheater:

A MAN IN NEW YORK INVENTED THE RADIO YEARS AGO, BUT ONLY GOD COULD TRAN
WAVES.  SINCE HE NEVER HAD TIME ENOUGH FOR THIS HE DECIDED TO CREATE A
WHO COULD DO THE TRANSMITTING FOR HIM.  HE CHOSE MY FATHER...AT THAT MC
STORM BROKE OUT.  THE LIGHTNING CAME IN AT FATHER'S MOUTH AND OUT AGAIN
HIS PENIS...I WAS IN MY MOTHER'S WOMB FOUR MONTHS PREGNANT AND WAS VERY
FRIGHTENED.  FROM THAT TIME ON I WAS MICROPHONIZED.

* Producer please take note:  the chaos here should not be sloppy, but carefully
choreographed.

ca 63' 48"

Napoleon:

SAY SI! SAY YES! I'D SAY OFFHAND GO RIGHT AHEAD AND CONTINUEZ S'IL VOUS PLAIT.
EXHUME THEM FROM BETWEEN HARD COVER TOMBS FILLED WITH UNEXAMINED PRINTING. THAT
SUNNY WINDY FRIDAY EARLY AFTERNOON CAME OFF IN MARVELLOUS BRILLIANCE,SAYS I
SITTING HERE IN QUERULOUS EXPECTATION WAITING...SECOND NIGHT OF THE ADVENT RETURN
OF SIX MONTHS GONE ABSENCE OF NIGHT SWEAT, HOPING AGAINST HOPE TO MADFUCK THE
AFFLICTION BEEN BROUGHT ON DELIBERATELY BY SOME SUBSTANCE INJECTED INTO ME...WHAT
BECOMES IN ROTATION DAMPISH THROUGH TO ICY COLD FEVERISH WILD TEMPERATURE SWITCHES
ERRATIC ENITIRELY BODY HEAT ALTERATION CHEST AREA SWEATS THERE.

au 6445"

nothing of her family, her parents, brothers and sisters, friends, lovers. How could she? As a castoff from another realm she scarcely knows these things; and yet she craves love as desperately as anyone on this earth, though she equally knows she will not find it in her present encapsulated world, where her keepers behave like android robots more interested in studying how the patients' brain cells are metabolizing oxygen than in helping them to rehabilitate themselves.

> I have never known a schizophrenic who could say he was loved, as a man, by God the Father or by the Mother of God or by another man. He either *is* God, or the Devil, or in hell, estranged from God. When someone says he is an unreal man or he is dead, in all seriousness, expressing in radical terms the stark truth of his existence as he experiences it, that is – insanity.[6]

Certainly, the asylum has its madmen. Napoleon, who keeps blowing himself up like a balloon and shouting, 'In slow increase my mood is improving,' is mad.[7] Perhaps all the inmates are carrying around a little of the heroic or divine buried under their skin like shrapnel as defence against the violations of their personages by the doctors and nurses.

But Ariadne really *is* divine, even though she is a divinity caught in the wrong element, a profane element peopled by creatures totally different from her true identity. For the time being her attempts to escape, either through the death ritual of the Tibetan *Bardo Thödol* (Book of the Dead) near the beginning or in the flying episode towards the close, prove futile. She must remain on earth with all its insecurities and perils until her final reconciliation with Wolf at the close of the cycle. But for the moment he too is a victim, a hunted animal, incapable of touching Ariadne in any way except painfully in the lesions of nightmares.

'They were afraid to kiss each other so they put on spectacles,' croaks one of the inmates after an abortive encounter between Beast (Nietzsche-Wolf) and Ariadne. Disguising the face to avoid detection is a well-documented form of self-defence. R.D. Laing (whom I have been reading

6  R.D. Laing, *The Divided Self*, New York, 1969, p. 39.
7  But even here there is irony for as Laing reports of another Napoleon in a real asylum who was given a lie-detector test in which he was asked if he was Napoleon and to which he replied 'No,' the lie-detector reported that he was lying.

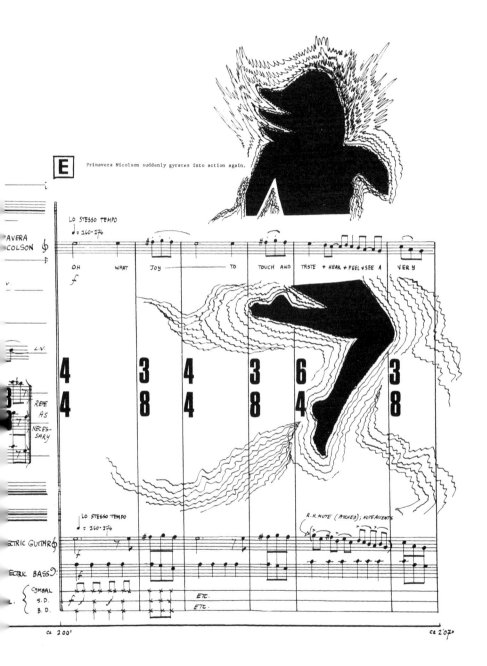

**E** Primavera Nicolson suddenly gyrates into action again.

LO STESSO TEMPO
♩ = 160-176

AVERA
NICOLSON

OH    WHAT    JOY ———————— TO    TOUCH AND    TASTE + HEAR + FEEL + SEE A    VERY

*f*

v.

L.V.

REPE
AS
NECES-
SARY

$\frac{4}{4}$    $\frac{3}{8}$    $\frac{4}{4}$    $\frac{3}{8}$    $\frac{6}{4}$    $\frac{3}{8}$

LO STESSO TEMPO
♩ = 160-176

R.H. MUTE (PITCHED); NOTE ACCENTS

ELECTRIC GUITAR

ELECTRIC BASS

CYMBAL
S.D.
B.D.

ETC.
ETC.

ca 2 00"                                                                ca 2'07" while writing these notes) has much to say about how the mentally disturbed often invent a false self to cover the real self. One of his patients caked her face with white make-up because it reminded her of her mother, whom she hated.

> She hated the face she saw in the mirror (her mother's). She saw, too, how full of hate for her was the face that looked back at her from the mirror; she, who was looking in the mirror, was identified with her mother. She was in this respect the mother seeing the hate in her daughter's face: that is, with her mother's eyes, she saw her hate for her mother in the face in the mirror, and looked, with hatred, at her mother's hatred of herself.[8]

Though she fears Wolf (Beast) Ariadne does not hate him. She would like to understand him by seeing him with his own eyes.

> And when you are near, I will tear out your eyes and will place them instead of mine, and you will tear out my eyes and place them instead of yours. Then I will look at you with your eyes and you will look at me with mine.[9]

Yet she is still not ready for the complete transposition of energies required for an affective relationship. Like Beauty in the fairy tale she is curious about Beast but regresses into the past rather than daring to advance the relationship. She says:

> O Beast, I begin to want to touch you ... but your face is all misshapen .. like a strange growth.

As I see it, the task for the director is to find a characterization for Ariadne as the victim she appears to be in *Requiems for the Party Girl* and the divinity we know her to be from the beginning and ending of the *Patria* cycle.

But why am I writing these notes for a prospective director? Do I really believe that *Patria* 2 will one day rise up out of the ashes like a neglected phoenix to play the major stages of Canada, or the world? I don't much care about that; but I do care that it should be restored as a vital link in the

---

8   *Ibid.*, p. 110.
9   This is a quotation from J.L. Moreno's *Einladung zu einer Begegnung*, Vienna, 1914, p. 3.

cycle as it has since unfolded, for some knowledge of this work would enrich the appreciation of both *Patria 1* and *Patria 3*, to both of which it is intimately linked.

# The Theatre of Confluence II

## 1. What Is the Purpose of Art?

FIRST, EXALTATION. Let us speak of that. The change that occurs when we are lifted out of the tight little cages of our daily realities. To be hurled beyond our limits into the cosmos of magnificent forces, to fly into the beams of these forces and if we blink, to have our eyes and ears and senses tripped open against the mind's will to the sensational and the miraculous. To feel these forces explode in our faces, against our bodies, breaking all encrustations and releasing us with a wild fluttering of freedom. Let us first speak of that. Of the newness that stuns the mind and sends it reeling. Let us speak of that. How everything becomes new. And if we return to our daily routines, they are no longer routines, but scintillate and have become magnificent by our sensing them with fresh eyes and noses and minds and bodies. Let us speak of this exaltation which has driven us out of ourselves to experience the life we have missed or only vaguely sensed, even resisted.

This must be the first purpose of art. To effect a change in our existential condition. This is the first purpose. To change us. It is a noble aim, a divine aim. And it existed long before the stale word 'art' was coined to describe the last tremor of this transformative power accessible to civilized man. Once it was drumming, prolonged drumming until its beats fused into a spell-binding hysteria. Once it was dancing, eternal dancing, until the dancer's feet left the ground and danced in the sky. Once it was singing, singing the turnings of the melody until they became the trail of life, following it back open-mouthed and breathless until the spirit became as light as a swan's feather and ascended out of this world. Once it was looking, intense looking and neither to the right nor to the left but directly at spectacles in which beating hearts were plucked from victims, in which dead men were brought back to life, in which gods boxed with thunderbolts, or the dead sun was kindled to life again and restored to the sky, or ghostly spirits were released from their wanderings – a world of miracles – that is what we were made to see. Once it was inhaling the thick fumes of incense as they ascended to the nostrils of the gods, making them laugh and dance on the mountains and in the stars. And the drumming, the singing, the looking and the motion carried us out of this world, hurled us into the spinning universe, making us aware of the unity of all things material, spiritual, natural and divine. Once art made divinities out

of humans, divinities out of animals, divinities out of trees, out of mountains, out of the sun and the sky, out of the sea and the moon and the stars.
Then there was no art. There were miracles. Then there was no music. There was tone magic. Then there were no artists. There were priests and magicians. Then the whole world of nature was a continuous, evolving hierophany. And man was dancing and singing and gawking at the heart of it.

Later, much later and gradually, as an ocean evaporates to become a tableland for a new kind of growth, civilization evolved. By the dawn of civilization humanity appears to have acquired a new habit: reflective consciousness. Perhaps it is the touchstone of civilization itself. When one sees oneself from outside the self, one's actions are made subject to review and preview; the critical dialectic of the mind comes into existence and begins to assert its prerogatives. The world of happenings begins to be replaced by the world of plans. That this represents a disinvolvement with the real world may not be immediately evident. It will take thousands of years to develop, but in essence this is what happened.

Little by little individuals began to draw out of the sacred circle, to watch in mute amazement the fervour of those who remained within. Perhaps they stood and tapped their feet in the distance, or merely hummed the songs, the words of which they no longer remembered. They began to be uneasy about the vividness of much of what they saw, and as their numbers increased, they insisted that no more living spirits be torn from victims, no more dead spirits be released, no more gods be set free. Then history was invented as a watershed to divide the mindless orgies of the past from the refinements of the civilized mind. Little by little, sensing was replaced by cognition, imagination by thoughtfulness. It was by intellect that humanity was going to pull itself out of its slobbering infancy. Science and machinery would raise it up; songs and dances belonged to the intemperate past. Then, when thoughtful bystanders became the majority, the magic circles began to disappear. The sacred bones and the drums and the harps were lost in the dust, the music stilled to a distant echo, perhaps even silence. And when men no longer put on the bird masks and the animal masks of the gods and no longer looked directly into their faces, the gods became bored and went away. The dancing fields in the mountains and in the clouds were deserted.

With the gods gone, humanity really began to angle in a different direction. Life ceased to be divine. It became a struggle to get ahead. Nature ceased to be divine. It became a resource to be consumed. With the desacralization of the world, man had only himself left to serve. Humanism was born. The Age of Enlightenment followed. Art as we have it today became a celebration of the human triumph over life in all its manifestations. It used the materials of nature in an increasingly refined manner to produce a mirror through which man saw the flattering reflection of his own countenance. Human loves, human joys, human griefs, human destiny – these became the subjects of art. What human would dispute their interest? And yet they represent a slumping away from something grander, a cooling, a contraction, a miniaturization of vision. The boiling fumes of the divine orgy had cooled. The volcanic eruption had been turned into a furious little glass of lemonade to be sipped between scene shifts in the drama of social interchange. This is the apotheosis of humanistic art, to study oneself, preferably while sitting down, preferably at a comfortable temperature, preferably on a full stomach – that is, when the juices of life are at their most stagnant.

Now the critics are released in order to ensure that the tone of all future undertakings should conform to civilized decorum. And the training schools oblige by teaching their students the art of restraint, so that when they put on their costumes and their wigs it is their technical agility that is to be admired, not their commitment. After all, don't they have to play a different character every night? And the more versatile they become, the more employable they are, offering by their graceful movements and their cultivated voices mere suggestions of something, yet never so intense as to lose the patronage of a public which has no intention of getting hurt by art. And so the final shift is to confiscate the word art and apply it to entertainment. Let the boulevard theatres have it and the pop concerts and the cinemas. Three-quarters of what today is called art and is subsidized as such is merely this. It is no longer exaltation, no longer a clearing of the path between ourselves and heaven. No longer does it teach us how to fly. It merely tickles what were once wings.

Have I gone too quickly? Have I bunched too much together? But that is how it happened, no matter how slowly. The roots I give are the true roots. And the evolution, for all the shading one might give it in a thousand paragraphs of intermediate explanation, is just as I have described it. Art and entertainment both evolve from the savage festival but their subject matter has shrunk to a tiny fragment of what it then was. Scope has been sacrificed to finesse. Intensity has dwindled to bemusement. Yes, the little orb of excitement which beats in your heart when you go to the theatre or hear an orchestra is the same as that bigger orb of vitality which animates the savage drummer or dancer, but his shakes him out of this world and yours merely bunts you back onto the same street.

## 2. The Recovery of the Sacred

Enough culture history. The art history books will tell you what has been gained in the evolution. I am concerned here with what has been lost. And what has been lost? The divine – the sensation of it and the ability to touch it. When I speak of the divine I am thinking of everything mysterious, everything beyond our ability to construe or temptation to dominate. But we can still feel it; we can still let it touch us. Grass is divine, clouds are divine, water is divine, sun and stars are divine. But that is not the end of it: electricity is divine, feathers are divine, mercury is divine, the proportions of the caterpillar are divine, the eye of the wolf is divine and the claw of the lion is divine. Man is also divine, not *more* divine, just divine along with all the rest.

Divinity is supposed to be the domain of religion and for us that has meant Christianity. Art has never been prevented from participating in this glorification of the divine, and even in these agnostic times many 'profane' artists have produced religious works, mostly borrowing from Christian liturgies or iconography, for instance Penderecki's *Passion* or Jean-Luc Godard's film *Je vous salue Marie*. But Christianity is a humanistic religion with an anthropomorphic godhead. Where is the place in Christianity for wolves and deer, flowers and trees, mountains and fish? Were they merely created for our aesthetic and culinary enjoyment during our life on this earth? Although some of the more unpleasant specimens of the animal kingdom may be found in the various hells envisioned by Christian artists, heaven has been reserved exclusively for the human herd; and if we are to believe John of Patmos even the sea is to be denied entry there.

Christianity has placed everything in the world on gradients below the human being and now overpopulation has obscured everything except human beings and their by-products from our view and apprehension. Everywhere the modern urban dweller looks he sees people. Everything his hands or feet touch has been made by people. Everything that goes wrong in the world can be fixed by people. He was born among people, he was educated by people in their ways, he will work among people, elbowing his way through a crowd all his life until he dies and is buried by people. It is scarcely any wonder that his imagination finds it difficult to contemplate anything beyond this environment.

Yet we need to go beyond it. Nature is not prepared to serve this foolish scheme any longer. It has been spoiled and polluted by our messy culture for too long already. Will it fight back? Somehow. If not with earthquakes and floods then with cancer and AIDS. But perhaps it will decide merely to desert us, to die on us, to leave us kicking for clean air, for water, for land on which to grow food. That could also be the final solution to the human problem.

One thing is for sure: the rampant destruction of nature did not get under way until the establishment of humanistic philosophies, of which in the West, Christianity has been the most influential. Another thing is for sure: pantheistic and totemic philosophies, such as those practised by the North American Indians enabled people to live more economically and ecologically. Nature is conserved when it is regarded as sacred. Strange algebra: religion and ecology. When a god inhabits a tree you think twice about knocking it down. When your ancestor inhabits an animal you pray for its soul before killing it and then only in necessity.

I am neither a Christian nor a humanist. I am concerned with environmental topics about which Christianity and humanism can teach me nothing. Whatever good they may have accomplished in the world, it seems now as if the law of enantiodromia has turned that good into evil. To be an *engaged* artist used to mean to be concerned with the restoration of certain social imbalances. Today, we could use the word 'engaged' with regard to the restoration of certain ecological imbalances. The artist assisting in the restoration of a holistic, natural philosophy, concerned with the preservation of forests and wildlife and clean water? At least it would be an enlargement of view over the beauties of the hosiery or toothpaste industry.

You can't go back, say the progressives, or rather the computerized clones who now speak for them. Of course not. To go back is always to go forward if you've never been there. Or would it not be better to say that once we are released from the notion of progress, the words *backwards* and *forwards* are no longer socially applicable? Lévi-Strauss, for instance, has shown that the savage mind is every bit as complex as the civilized mind though its areas of complexity lie along different tangents. By comparison, the pioneer expositor of primitive cultures, Sir James Frazer, saw civilization as an upwards streaking from jungle drums to the British empire.

Intellectual progress, which reveals itself in the growth of art and science and the spread of more liberal views, cannot be dissociated from industrial and economic progress, and that, in its turn, receives immense impulses from conquest and empire.[1]

For the word 'progress' we would now substitute the word 'appropriateness.' If it becomes *appropriate* to develop new techniques to deal with necessary issues then we must bend our energies to do so. For the development of a holistic philosophy we can scarcely turn towards humanistic art works for support and insight. Beautiful though they may be, they are no longer appropriate. It is in different sources, more ancient and strange, that we will find this ability to sense the divine in all things, this reverence for life and death, this acceptance of everything in the ordering and disordering of the cosmos, this ability to go with nature rather than against her. We do not know exactly how the ancient peoples or those living far from contemporary urban centres accomplished this. We have the anthropologists' records and we have certain artifacts and ceremonies used in their attempts to achieve these vital ontological insights. There are some hints then, and if the artist can understand them they can be put to good use again. Let us try to understand them.

## 3. Contexts and Environments

The sacred circle has been drawn but we cannot enter it directly. We are unprepared; our experience and our training has been in the profane theatre, and even if we decide to abandon it now, it will be a long time before we dare take full possession of the charmed new spaces which have been prepared for us. The profane theatre? What is that and why do we want to desert it?

Come with me then into the profane theatre where a new opera is being prepared. Outside the stage doors there are posters, many of them, large and small, announcing other productions here and elsewhere. The place is a veritable caravanserai of comings and goings in the world of entertainment. Many of the posters are torn, some of them bear dates long since past, of shows that have now moved on, or have closed early for lack of customers. The stage door foyer is littered with stagehands, loafing when not required to move scenery or adjust sets, bored men these who have seen a thousand stages prepared and struck. They slump in their chairs smoking cigars or playing cards.

We pass them and walk down a corridor filled with costumes from

---

1    Sir James Frazer, *The Golden Bough*, London, 1954, p. 48.

yesterday's shows, martial uniforms with bristling epaulets, a fool's patch-work tights, a countess's ballroom dress covered with sequins, furs, wigs, long flowing robes, dark villains' capes with high black collars, more dresses in red velvet, pink lace and yellow silk – and on top of the rack someone has carelessly thrown a T-shirt with the words 'Stick 'em up' tattooed on the breast.

We near the makeup room in which a radio is playing disco music. In the dressing rooms actors and actresses are bantering excitedly. 'How did *she* get that role? Must've slept with someone.' 'He *meant* to fall, to collect the compensation, and now he's suing the theatre.' '*Il teatro è la guerra.*' 'Better than singing this kitsch.' Now we hear the voice of the stage manager on the intercom: 'Five minutes to the orgy, ladies and gentle-men.' 'The orgy?' we enquire. We thought the setting was a monastery, but our companion merely smirks.

We make our way to the stage past a litter of coffee cups, some half full and cold with cigarette butts floating in them, left by the last troupe of performers, perhaps a jazz ballet or the Szechwan opera – for the theatre is multi-purpose and available to any organization that can pay the rent. From the director's table we hear raised voices; the conductor is arguing about a cut the director has just made in the music. The composer steps up to say something and is told to sit down. The friction between conductor and director has been communicated to the orchestra, who have begun to bang their chairs about and rattle their instruments. Somewhere a clarinet is tootling 'I love you Rosie O'Grady', while the first violinist is practising the cadenza of the concerto he will be performing next week; but both are soon drowned out by the percussionist who is gilding himself with his sizzle cymbal.

The rehearsal is about to get under way. The musicians light up a last cigarette and adjust the magazines they will be reading during the long gaps when they are not playing. We are waiting for the lights to be adjusted, but the conductor opts to attack the overture anyway. The singers stand akimbo on the stage while technicians put highlights on their faces and costumes. The leading tenor has a follow spot all to himself; it's in his contract. We were lucky to get him even though he can't act. The soubrette is from Bulgaria where they pronounce vowels darkly, but her shimmy compensates for her pronunciation. The bass is an egocentric American. The mezzo is German and looks like bratwurst. There are a few bit parts for local singers and of course a chorus for aspirants. This is instant opera and it is happening right here in our town.

The lights are finally adjusted and we are about to begin when the orchestra stand up and begin banging their chairs again. They are now on break. The steward is pointing at his watch and shaking a finger at the conductor. 'Half hour break!' hisses the conductor and everyone leaves the scene of the action. Only the composer remains in the darkened theatre, wondering whether it will all come together.

It does, but we do not remain to see it. We read about it in the paper a few days later. The critic had harsh words for the new work, a story of murder and intrigue set on Mount Athos. But he did think the part about the smuggled American Express cheques being hidden there by the heroine disguised in monk's garb an effectively contemporary touch. The music was described as 'near-wailing, jangling, giddy and bedraggled.' But the soloists came off better. The tenor, as the tempestuous, carousing abbot of the monastery was praised for his 'firm passionate instrument.' The soprano had a 'sheen the like of which has rarely been heard in this house.' There were complaints that the singers' words could rarely be distinguished, but this was attributed to the desultory vocal lines they were given to sing. The conductor was praised for his mastery of the fiendishly difficult score. The direction was lacklustre but the costumes and sets were considered superb. In conclusion, Mozart and Verdi were invoked as models and it was hoped that before any more young composers were given the 'rule of the house,' the works of these gentlemen would be more thoroughly inspected. The company and their sponsors were praised for their initiative. Next year's season, which was to include *Orpheus in the Underworld* and *La Bohème* was eagerly anticipated.

This scene, which occurs nightly all over the civilized world, includes one other vital ingredient: the customer. I could tell you how they spent their day at the office or the shopping mall, then hurried home to dress, dashed through a light supper (there will be a celebrity dinner after the show) and left for the theatre. After hunting for a place to park the car, they finally enter the grand foyer all aglitter with lights, champagne glasses, brilliant dresses and jewellery. We should never forget the foyer with its grand *escalier* and *piano nobile* lined with Greek columns, mirrors and chandeliers, for it is here that the public will play out their own small dramas. Indeed, it often receives more architectural attention than the house itself, certainly in grand theatres like the Opéra de Paris, designed by Garnier in 1875, who frankly admitted his flamboyant *escalier d'honneur* was more important than the theatre, which was designed on no acoustic principles whatever.[2]

Theatres for 'high art' are always designed to look expensive. Of course there are also flea pits for experimental productions where one can sit on boards and smell sweat, and there are places where one can stand and be deafened by the sonic shrapnel of popular entertainers, but all these venues have two things in common: performers and customers. Many studies have been directed towards this bifurcation, particularly by Marxist critics and sociologists. I don't want to go into that here except to point out that the purchase of admission tickets leads the audience to expect that they do not have to *earn* their way in; they are not required to work, learn, act, or extend initiatives suggested by the work or its interpreters, having already shown that they can afford the admission price. Thus art becomes a form of tipping – the demonstration of one's ability to pay out a little more than what is actually required by life's necessities to others, generally less fortunate, for the slight entertainment of their flamboyant personalities. The curtain call confirms this.

But let us look more closely at the physical environment of the theatre. Entertainers and customers face one another in spaces sealed off from the external world. These are man-fabricated spaces: there is not a bolt or a board in them that was not produced by human labour. They have roofs and walls without windows so that the outside world is prevented from intruding. They are kept at a constant comfortable temperature; their lighting is totally artificial and when empty they are acoustically antiseptic (though the rumbling of their heating and air-conditioning systems can often be heard). These buildings are generally situated in the centre of town and are run as a municipal service, usually by people who have no interest in the activities occurring within them.

Performances are usually given in the evening, sometimes in the after-noon, rarely in the morning. This plan interfaces with the work timetables of the majority of patrons and upholds the belief that work precedes pleas-ure or that art should not appear to resemble work. Moreover, one has at most three or four hours in the evening before the audience begins to fall asleep: this confers a consistent time-limitation on productions. Much clas-sical drama and most operas have been cut to meet this limitation and all contemporary works are expected to conform to it.

Within these confines of place, time and personalities, the action of the artistic enterprise can only fluctuate along the plane of style. And this is what we witness if we study the recent history of performance art. Just as

2   See: Michael Forsyth, *Buildings for Music*, Cambridge, Mass., 1985, p. 179.

diverse performance events can follow one another helterskelter on any stage, so performance theory becomes preoccupied with fashion fluctuation. Whole libraries are full of history books in which nothing is discussed but stylistic evolution. Whole university programs are modelled in the same manner. That is to say, the student is never given any accurate information or experience concerning art presented under different circumstances, say theatre in a cave, or on a consecrated mountain top, or music on a street corner or in a moving caravan. Such programs assume that high art does not belong in such environments, or, if it once did, it was inferior to that produced after the invention of the concert and theatrical stage; and subscribers to theatres have long since been conditioned to believe the same.

Modern theory teaches that revolutions in art occur when styles are challenged. But they ignore the bigger revolutions of context change. Styles vary constantly but it often takes centuries before an artistic tradition, locked into one environment, is released to find another. It is rarely something that is wished for by artists or their followers for it is very disruptive and in its early stages many more careers are lost than are advanced by it. It would seem that such changes generally come from outside, are forced on the profession by larger disturbances, social or environmental. When music moved into the Church in the Middle Ages, musicians who remained outside were quickly forgotten, to the extent that today it is difficult to reconstruct what actually happened there. Less dramatic was the shift from church to theatre, which occurred in the seventeenth and eighteenth centuries; for many generations the same musicians served both patrons. Walls, of one kind or another, have become the distinctive feature of Western performance art. Once these institutions were settled in their new homes, no amount of artistic agitation could drive them out again; thus when Gossec tried to move music back out into public squares after the French Revolution so that it could be repossessed by the masses ('*nos places publiques seront désormais nos salles de concerts*,'[3]) the attempt failed because the copyright owners feared their new enterprises would slip back into public domain. Something similar seems to have happened when agit-prop theatre retreated from the factories after the Russian Revolution. If, today, artists are again moving outdoors, it is partly from economic necessity, and partly in order to enjoy greater fluency with a larger public. Nothing within the artistic or educational world has

3   Jacques Attali, *Bruits*, Paris, p. 111.

encouraged them in this transfer or prepared them for the stylistic over-haul that will be necessary if they are to survive there.

Perhaps we are witnessing several contextual changes at once. The most obvious is that brought about by the electro-acoustic industries. I don't want to discuss that here because it doesn't concern me. For a long time I have sensed a limitation in the audio-visual media, for they are precisely that: aural and visual, and are therefore not comprehensive enough for the kind of change that now seems necessary.

To accomplish an art that engages all forms of perception, we need not only to strip down the walls of our theatres and recording studios, but also the walls of our senses. We need to breathe clean air again; we need to touch the mysteries of the world in the little places and the great wide places; in sunrises, forests, mountains and caves and if need be snowfields or tropical jungles. For too long the clement temperatures of our theatres have neutralized our thermic sensibilities. Why not a concert under a waterfall or a dramatic presentation in a blizzard? And why should we not feel the rain on our faces when we sing or a distant mountain throw back to us the voice we have just sent out to it? Why do we fail to notice the grass at our feet, the darkening of the sky or the sharp green eyes in the night air? Here are the divinities of our holy theatre, now so exceptional for having been ignored so long as to be overpoweringly real. These are the miraculous arenas of living drama inviting us to interaction; and the expe-rience is absolutely free. We will not try to change things here; we will let them change us. And if what we together produce is no longer art, it will be no great loss; for the urge for this new freedom did not come from the inner coil of art, but from the necessity to find a new relationship between ourselves and the wide cosmos.

## 4. Ritual

Ritual is older than art. Konrad Lorenz and others have shown that even animals practise it when they indulge in stylized gestures unconnected with any vital function. Every work of performance art is encased in a ritual. The ritual is axiomatic and performers rarely dare to challenge or break it. The repertoire varies, but the ritual appears to remain constant for it alters much more slowly. Thus one does not interpret rituals so much by their content as by their form: the special space and time they occupy, the ritual objects they employ, the roles of the participants, the decorum and ceremony. Yet when properly performed and experienced they can facilitate existential changes or become a palingenesis of spiritual renewal.

Among the oldest surviving rituals in the world is the Japanese tea ceremony, which has been practised with little variation for nearly a thousand years.

The tea-house is in a garden at the end of the *roji* (dewy path) which leads through the garden past pools of water, banks of shrubs and flowers to a gateway at the edge. The guests arrive at the gate which is closed, usually sealing the garden and the tea-house from view. They wait on a stone bench until the host has completed the preparation. When this is done a gong is sounded in the tea-house and the host comes and opens the gate to his guests. All bow. The host signals the guests to follow him down the *roji*. The particular path taken to the tea house has been selected from among several by the host in advance. It may be that he wishes his guests to pass by a particular pool of carp, or see a particular blossoming shrub or shadows across the grass in the afternoon sun; alternative paths not to be taken are marked by stones tied with twine.

Outside the tea-house the guests rinse their hands and mouth at a stone basin with a bamboo dipper. At this point I might mention that recent soundscape research has shown that many older gardens have resonating jars implanted in the soil beneath these washing basins so that runoff water would trickle into them creating a kind of waterharp.

The guests remove their shoes and enter the tea-house through a very low door. The act of bending to enter is said to be deliberately humbling and dates from a time when Zen monks acted as hosts of the tea ceremony. The tea-house, which may be four to six mats wide, is empty except for a scroll on the wall and a simple arrangement of one or two flowers in a vase, placed in a corner niche. The scroll contains a few words of poetry, chosen by the host to set the mood for that particular day, and the flowers have been arranged to echo that mood. The guests sit silently on cushions until the host enters through a sliding door on the opposite side of the tea-house. He bows and crosses the room in stocking feet, turning very ceremonially at right angles, bringing with him the special utensils that will be used in preparing the tea.

The preparation is executed with great formality as the guests nibble on sweet rice cakes. We hear the steam in the kettle. 'Wind in the pines,' is the way the Japanese describe the sound. The host pours fresh water into the kettle and then ladles it out for the ceremonial washing of the cups. From his waist he takes a cloth, turns it from side to side until all four edges have been held up, then folds it so that one corner points up, the other down before opening it again. The significance of this action has its roots in Zen philosophy. The four edges of the cloth are the four dimensions of the universe; the corner held upwards signifies heaven and the downward corner is the earth, while the opening of the cloth symbolizes the emptiness of the world.

We now hear the vigorous motion of the tea whisk as it mixes the finely powdered green tea with water poured from the kettle. Each bowl is prepared separately, the first being offered to the most honoured guest, either the oldest person present or the one celebrating some special day such as a birthday. This person always sits closest to the kettle. The cup is taken from the host, turned three times in the palm of the hand and drunk in one motion with a slurping noise. Sound, you will gather, is a very important ingredient of the tea ceremony.

After each guest has been served the host rises and leads the party to a second room in the tea-house which has been opened to a view of the garden. Here they all drink a second cup of tea which is salty to the taste and has an orange blossom floating in it. This is designed to clean the teeth of the sweet cake that was previously eaten. Here the atmosphere is more relaxed and the host converses with his guests, explaining the history of the bowls his guests have drunk from (they are all of great age though usually very plain) and the purpose of his having chosen the poem and the flowers for that particular day. He then accompanies his guests back to the gate where, with solemn bows and friendly farewells, the ceremony concludes.

Such was the ceremony as I experienced it in Kyoto in 1984. In this, as in its companion ceremony Ko-wo-kiku (*listen to the incense*) which is performed around the experience of inhaling various resinous incenses, we were led into a world that is exotic yet exceedingly simple. The earth has known countless blendings of the natural and the formal into sensory rituals with therapeutic and theological overtones, but what makes the tea ceremony and the incense ceremony special is that although they serve no sectarian interests they do attempt to transform us existentially by opening us to the profound mysteries of the simplest natural phenomena. They are about nothing yet they are by no means empty formalities. They show us that the fabricated world is always surrounded by the garden of the natural world and exists in symbiosis with it. In their slowness they allow the imagination to do its work in recognizing this relationship. In their simplicity they teach us how little we require to achieve a sense of fulfilment.

These are not old rituals. They are timeless and always new. Compared to them the rituals of modern life appear crude and self-serving: Christmas, New Year's Day, birthdays, wedding anniversaries, football and hockey playoffs. Suddenly we are plunged back into the world of technicians, stars and money. In the area of spiritual affairs our rituals are weak and emaciated. Death and dying is an existential crisis needing such attention. In some societies elaborate preparations assist the dying person to approach death by joining acts of compassion with the deepest human wisdom to create a bridge between the present world and the beyond. *The Tibetan Book of the Dead*, for instance, is devoted to this transformation and it is intoned constantly in the presence of the dying person who, even in this state of weakness, is always addressed by the dignified refrain, 'O Nobly Born.' In our civilized society we flounder towards death without counsel. If you think you are about to die, call the doctor or the crisis centre. Perhaps both lines will be busy.

The cycles of nature, which once received so much ritual attention, are almost totally neglected today. Only Thanksgiving remains to remind us of the harvest festival, but without the physical acts of growing and harvesting it becomes merely a prayer and a gobble.

Are these domains which modern art could begin to inhabit? Why not, since they have been deserted for so long? Imagine a ritual in which a garden is prepared and planted. Meeting at the garden plot, a group of participants together dig the soil, raking it and banking it up in preparation for the planting. The planters arrive with their seeds. They come in procession, singing and dancing, in costumes suggestive of the various plants whose seed they hold. There is special music as each type of seed is tucked into the soil. The water spirits arrive, sprinkling water over the plot. Bird dancers descend and peck at the newly planted seeds, but a ritual scarecrow is constructed to a rattling musical accompaniment and they are frightened off. The planting ceremony ends with an invocation to the sun to look kindly on the garden and ensure its productivity. Will this help the garden to grow better? It will help us to grow.

## 5. Celebration and Participation

Margaret Mead somewhere says that we need more celebrations in our lives, more experiences which unite us with others and with the treasury of the environment. Art is a means of accomplishing this, but societies which are celebration-rich are often art-poor. She cites the Balinese, who have no word for art. 'We do the best we can,' they say.

The other day in Switzerland I watched shepherds bringing cattle down from the alpine meadows to the lower pastures for winter. This simple event is an annual ceremony in the Alps and the shepherds dress for it in festive costumes of yellow and red. They wear long earrings and flowers decorate their hats. Arriving at the new pasture the cows are stripped of the bells, some of which are of enormous size and seem heavy when balanced, two on a yoke, by the shepherds, who now bear them off to a local *Gasthaus*, where they will have a glass of wine. On the way they sing folksongs in harmony to the rhythmic swinging of the bells. In a transformation, which Lévi-Strauss calls *bricolage*, the bells have become musical instruments and the shepherds have become musicians. Or have they?

The more we travel the world, the more we are made aware of how unusual our Western notions of art and music really are. The Eskimos have no word for music and the term is absent from many African languages as well. During the ten years I lived in Monteagle Valley among rural people of North-Central Ontario, I rarely if ever heard the word art. Art for them was something very distant, made by people who dressed strangely and behaved scandalously. They were assumed to be either very poor or very rich or perhaps both things at the same time since they were known to be living in the fast lane close to drugs and prostitution. For them the word 'artist' conjured a social problem for the tax department or the police.

We don't know how long art will last in the Western world. I have already described the tendency for it to erode before the broader appeals of entertainment. That is the word used by daily newspapers throughout North America to describe what both artists and entertainers do. The fact that the artist sees his mission as one transcending the production of various states of pleasure is of little consequence here. If he speaks of the height and depth of his work, he will be regarded as obscure. If he speaks of his work as prophetic, he will be dismissed as a quack.

> I was sent from the power,
> and I have come to those who reflect on me,
> and I have been found among those who seek after me.
> Look upon me, you who reflect on me,
> and you hearers, hear me.
> You who are waiting for me, take me to yourselves.
> And do not banish me from your sight.
> And do not make your voice hate me, nor your hearing.

Do not be ignorant of me anywhere or any time.
Be on your guard!
Do not be ignorant of me.

98    This is a gnostic text and its subject is divine epiphany; but we can almost imagine it being spoken by many artists from the Renaissance to the present, for their 'God' is also an alien and transmundane deity whose message, if recognized at all, can only be apprehended by those in possession of special (gnostic) powers.

The split that has occurred between the artist and the public is not the subject of this essay and it affects us only to the extent that artists have been disinclined or unable to assist in regaining the spirit lost in the long evolution of civilization. If this is the case, then we must cease to be artists. We must become something to which we cannot yet give a name, but which our works will reveal with increasing clarity. What they will reveal is man subdued by reverence for nature and the cosmos. What they will reveal is human dependence on an environment consisting of all things understood, misunderstood and mysterious.

A hierophany is an exposition of a sacred mystery. It need not be elitist, for nature, as Goethe said, is a great open secret. We must put aside the almighty importance of human society, its achievements and requirements. We must find ourselves fast-rooted in the soil and neighbours to the plants and animals. We must lie on the hill and turn our gaze to the mountains and the stars, our ancestors and the royalty of the universe. 'Who says the sun cannot speak to me!' says D.H. Lawrence.

> The sun has a great blazing consciousness and I have a little blazing consciousness. When I can strip myself of the trash of personal feelings and ideas, and get down to the naked sun-self, then the sun and I can commune by the hour, the blazing interchange, and he gives me life, sun-life, and I send him a little new brightness from the world of the bright blood.[4]

The African drummer can do this too, and the Swiss mountain herdsman, and so could the North American Indian before he was polluted by alcohol and Christianity. And so could we all if we would care to learn how.

---

4    D.H. Lawrence, *Apocalypse*, London, 1974, pp. 27-28.

To find performers in full control of a dozen musical or dramatic styles is today not difficult, but to find performers able to modulate their talents in order to perform around a lake at sunrise, or over a twelve- or twenty-four-hour period, or while hiking in a forest, is no easy task. The new techniques required for these tasks are missing even if the volition is present. We are all learners in this new environment, which as yet knows no distinctions between audience, performer and creator. This is the new Theatre of Confluence which is now opening its doors to all participants who would accept the challenge of admission.

# Editing Unit 5: WOLF'S ARIA

WOLF'S ARIA BEGINS AS THE DRUMMING FADES DOWN. AS HE CHANTS
WOLF SLOWLY CIRCES IN THE CENTRE OF THE LAKE.

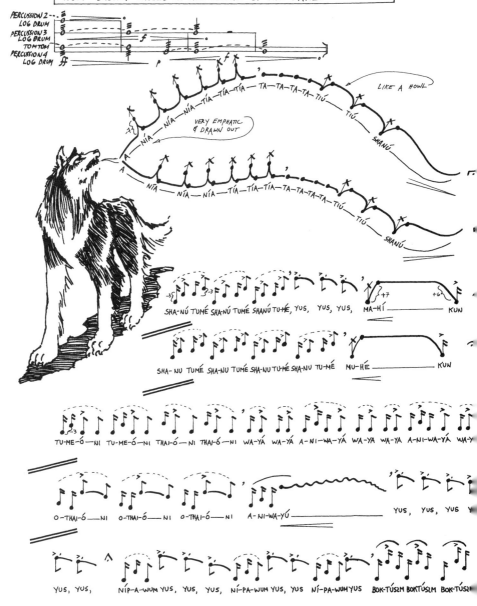

# Patria: Prologue
## *The Princess of the Stars*

*Composed*: 1981, Monteagle Valley, Ontario.

*Cast*: Solo soprano, two mixed quartets or choruses, 4 actors, 6 dancers, and about 20 canoeists.

*Orchestra*: Flute, clarinet, trumpet, horn, trombone, tuba, percussion (4 players).

*Duration*: 1 hour 20 minutes.

*First performance*: Heart Lake, Ontario, September 26, 1981.

## 1. The Legend

*'Without man the world was born and without him it will end'*

This is the story of the Princess of the Stars,
daughter of the Sun-God and herself a Goddess.
Her name is in the stars and you have seen it there.
Each night she looked down on earth,
blessing it with kisses of light.

One night she heard a mournful cry coming up from the forest.
It was Wolf, howling at the moon, his double.
The Princess leaned over the forest to see who was singing,
but in leaning down so far she fell from heaven.
Suddenly she appeared before Wolf in a great flash of light.
But Wolf, frightened to see the stars so close,
lashed out at the Princess,
wounding her.

She ran bleeding into the forest, leaving dew wherever she went,
which was nearly everywhere, since she had no idea where to run.
By morning she found herself at the edge of a lake
and slipped into the water to bathe her wounds.

But there something caught her, dragging her down.
In vain she struggled:
in the end the waters closed over her.
You may see the stars of her crown at the tip of your paddle,
but the Princess you will not see.
The Three-Horned Enemy
holds her captive at the bottom of the lake,
and the dawn mist is the sign of her struggling.

## 2. The Action

All this has happened during the night. The story continues as the audience arrives at the lake in the darkness before dawn. In the distance we see a pinpoint of light moving slowly towards us from the opposite shore. At the same time the voice of the Princess is heard, singing an unaccompanied aria across the water. (The singer is a kilometre away.) Her haunting aria has something of the quality of a loon. Soon other voices from far and near begin to echo it as the light-point continues to move towards us. When it reaches the shore, dawn has broken enough for us to see an old man in a canoe, the Presenter. He tells us of the happenings during the night, then turns and calls across the water.

Wolf arrives to look for the Princess. He enlists the help of the Dawn Birds (dancers in canoes) who arrive to comb the water with their wings; but they are prevented from rescuing her by the Three-Horned Enemy, who is keeping her captive beneath the lake. A battle develops but is interrupted by the arrival of the Sun Disc (sunrise) who comes to demand what has happened to the stars. The Sun Disc drives the Three-Horned Enemy away, sets tasks for Wolf before he can release the Princess, and exhorts the Dawn Birds to cover the lake with ice and sing there no longer, until Wolf succeeds.

The Princess of the Stars is to be performed as a ritual in canoes at the centre of the lake, some distance from the audience, who are seated on the shore. The principal characters are either costumed and masked (e.g., the Dawn Birds) or are enclosed in large moveable structures fastened to the gunwales of voyageur canoes (Wolf, the Three-Horned Enemy, and the Sun Disc). Since the characters in the canoes chant an unknown language, the audience is informed of the action by the Presenter, a kind of earth spirit or medicine-man, who acts as an interpreter between the observers and those performing the ritual.

The work is designed for performance at dawn on an autumn morning. It forms the Prologue to the entire *Patria* cycle and introduces the central theme of the works to follow. From this lake, Wolf will go out in search of the Princess, seeking her forgiveness and compassion. If he can find her, he will also find himself. Then she will at last return to the heavens, and he, redeemed, will also rise to inherit the moon. Wolf's wanderings will take him to many distant lands and he will visit many historical periods before he will return to find the Princess in the same natural environment he deserted at the close of the Prologue.

The unifying motif of the *Patria* works is Wolf's journeys through the many labyrinths of life in search of the spiritual power which can both release and transfigure him. He will travel under many names and assume many guises, impersonating a human as the displaced immigrant D.P., as the Greek hero Theseus, as the dead pharaoh seeking to be raised to heaven by the sun, or as antimony in the 'chymical marriage' or hieros-gamos of the alchemists. At times, he may assume great pre-eminence; at other times he may be chased away as a fool, a criminal or a 'beast.' As the labyrinthine nature of his wanderings intensifies, the Princess becomes personified for him in the figure of Ariadne, who helped Theseus escape the Cretan labyrinth in the well-known Greek myth. The thread-gift provided by Ariadne in the *Patria* cycle is the thread of music. Ariadne's gift is her haunting voice; this is what sustains and transforms Theseus-Wolf during his life journeying.

Each of the *Patria* pieces is designed to exist on its own and many explore different theatrical settings and techniques, but all follow the theme of Wolf's search for his spirit in the guise of the Princess as it was introduced in *The Princess of the Stars*.

## 3. The Environment

The environment of *The Princess of the Stars* is extremely important, not only for the effect it has on the audience, but also for the ways it is intended to affect the performers. It relies entirely on what the Japanese call *shakei*, borrowed scenery; that is its entire décor. While the principal characters are on the surface of the water, the musicians and singers are positioned around the perimeter of the lake, which should be rural, showing as few signs of civilization as possible. The lake should be about half a kilometre wide and a kilometre long, with an irregular shoreline to allow the principal characters to enter in their canoes from 'off stage.'

The Sun Disc flanked by Wolf, the Three-Horned Enemy and the Dawn Birds in the prologue to the *Patria* cycle, *The Princess of the Stars*. Designer: Jerrard Smith. Banff Festival production, 1985.

What distinguishes this from the traditional theatrical setting is that it is a living environment and therefore utterly changeable at any moment. The lighting alone is in a constant state of change, and atmospheric disturbances can descend or retreat to affect a good deal more than the audience's state of mind or comfort. Having witnessed a good number of performances of *Princess* I can say that it is a different theatre every time. Will there be a sunrise? Will there be dew on the ground or mist on the water? What if it is raining or windy? Wind in particular is the enemy of the production, for not only can it make the canoes difficult or dangerous to navigate, but it can totally destroy the music, carrying the sounds off in unintended directions, so that not only will the audience miss much, but also there is a risk that performers will miss vital cues; for the work is structured to function largely without the direction of a conductor, the musicians listening and reacting to one another by ear rather than eye.

Hence, the living environment enters and shapes the success or failure of *The Princess of the Stars* as much as or more than any human effort; and knowledge of this must touch the performers, filling them with a kind of humility before the grander forces they encounter in the work's setting. But as we participate with these forces, allowing them to influence us in every way, is it not possible to believe that we as performers and audience are influencing them as well? We disclaim belief that we can make the wind rest or the sun shine, though this latter is the principal motive of *Ra*, one of the later works in the *Patria* cycle, and it is certainly not remote from the ancient peoples, whose rituals were often conducted in the open environment. Then one danced to make the rains come or cease or to make the corn grow or the caribou appear. Yes, there must be something of that kind of faith in the minds of the participants as they approach a performance of *Princess*. I have seen beautiful performances in the Rocky Mountains when the sun stroked snow-capped mountains just at the moment of the Sun Disc's entry and I have seen haunting performances when the lake was enshrouded in thick mist. The production of this work will always be tinged with the excitement of a première. It will always be a theatre of 'first nights only.'

Though the text of *The Princess of the Stars* is original, the work is clearly related to Indian legends, for like them it employs a story to account for various natural phenomena. There is dew on the grass because the Princess ran through the forest; and the mist on the water is the sign of her struggling to be free of the Three-Horned Enemy. The Dawn Birds appear at precisely the time the real dawn birds are waking up, and singers and

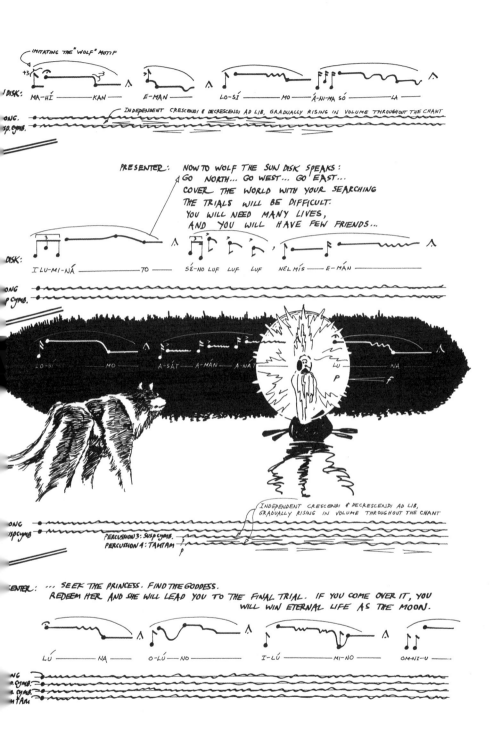

instrumentalists around the lake coax them into song by imitating their calls. To know that one is affecting the environment in this way can fill one with awe. On more than one occasion loons or Canada geese flew across the lake in front of the bird-dancers mixing the real and the imitative to beautiful effect. The entire work is timed according to the sunrise; for the real sun should sychronize with the arrival of the Sun Disc, who has received messages of the distress on earth from the birds who have awakened just before him. When, at the conclusion, the Presenter tells the Dawn Birds to leave the lake as it will be covered over with ice and snow, we know that this is precisely what will soon happen.

What is the effect of treating nature in this way? By mythologizing the fluctuations of nature we have intensified our own experience of it. We begin to flow with it rather than against it. We no longer spite it or shut it out as we do in covered theatres. This is our stage set, and we have become one with it, breathing it, feeling it in all its mystery and majesty. Of course, there will be problems, for nature is fickle, though as Jung reminds us, she is never like man, deceitful.

*The Princess of the Stars* is conceived for a situation. It should only be presented when the conditions are right. But since no producer can predict this and no union can enforce it, this is both its birthright and its stigma. Like the art of ancient times, it is wedded to its time and place by indissoluble links which guarantee that no counterfeit experience could ever be a replacement for it.

## 4. The Tempo

The tempo of a production of *The Princess of the Stars* is never fast. Even when Wolf and the Three-Horned Enemy engage in battle, they move at the pace of an armada rather than that of modern warfare. It will take the Presenter fifteen minutes to come down the lake to the audience area at the beginning of the show, an act which prepares us for the tempo of the entire work. But something strange happens when nothing happens. The senses are sharpened with alertness, ready to print the decisive action when it occurs. There can be little doubt that primitive rituals are deliberately structured in this way. Long informationless interludes are punctuated by sudden events, which cause an adrenalin rush to the brain, making the experience memorable.

And so in the slowness of the breaking dawn we are alert to the smallest change. Perhaps the eyes wander to the hills and notice they have become lighter. Or we notice a ripple on the water as a breeze skims across it. Or we hear an animal scurrying for cover in the underbrush. (On one occasion an instrumentalist had an animal run between his feet while playing in the darkness.) In the slowness tiny events become magnified; large events are haunting. I have seen small children transfixed as Wolf comes on the lake with head lowered and swinging from side to side in the long hunt before he arches his neck and lets forth a blood-freezing howl.

The music of *Princess* also participates in this slowness. Since sound travels at slightly more than 330 metres a second, it will take the music of a performer at the far end of the lake three seconds to reach the audience area and another three seconds for the echo to return, if there is one. When we performed *Princess* at Two-Jack Lake in the Rocky Mountains, we gave the singers megaphones with which to focus the sound, bouncing it now off one mountain, now off another. The idea of employing megaphones in outdoor performances is certainly not new. There are diagrams of such instruments in the writings of Athanasius Kircher (*Phonurgia Nova*, Campidonae, 1673, pp. 117-143). And Sir Samuel Moreland published a brochure in 1672 describing a twenty-one-foot horn he made by which the human voice could be projected up to a mile (*Tuba Stentoro-Phonica*, London, 1672).

If the lake is surrounded by mountains and forests, echoes become a special feature of the performance. The feedback in the echo will soon begin to modify the production which lengthens and lingers in breadth and resonance as performers learn how to turn this into advantageous cybernation. At Two-Jack Lake we were able to position the musicians so that their sound was funnelled indirectly to the audience area, the auditor sometimes receiving the echo more prominently than the original sound. Indirect reception removes much high frequency sound, giving the tone a mysterious, remote quality – an effect, by the way, which was aimed at by Wagner, though in quite different circumstances.

## 5. The Ritual

In one sense the comparison with Wagner is not inconsequential. Wagner wanted to hide his musicians in a pit, their appearance distracting from the drama. The result was the creation of a *mystischer Abgrund* (mystical abyss) which separated the audience from the action on stage, thus taking on many of the aspects of a ritual. In *The Princess of the Stars* the musicians are hidden from view by the trees; we do not know from where the sound will issue next; and the action is distanced from the audience by the lake, for only the Presenter comes close to shore.

But there are other features which draw *Princess* closer to ritual. When he speaks to us for the first time, the Presenter tells us that before we may observe the 'sacred actions' performed on the lake by 'gods and animals,' he must first prepare us. In a short thaumaturgical incantation, he turns us into trees, in order that we may observe the events without interference. In one sense, this distances us from the action, and, in another, it implicates us as part of the natural décor of the production. We are reminded of the motto of the work: 'Without man the world was born, and without him it will end.'

Language also contributes to the ritual effect of *The Princess of the Stars*. The gods and animals speak an unknown language, or to be more precise a series of unknown languages, which the Presenter alone can interpret for us. Wolf chants an invented language incorporating some morphemic and phonetic elements of North American Indian dialects. This lends it an ancestral dignity, but has a practical significance as well, since Indian languages not only have an abundance of long vowels but also contain few labials (such as 'm') or compact vowels (such as 'i' [bit] or 'ê' [bet]) which do not carry well in the open air. Similar considerations also affected the choice of instruments: for instance, tests proved that log drums, so dull and muted when played indoors, took on an exciting resonance in their natural environment, particularly if they were placed over pits or gulleys, which acted as sound boxes. And so log drums and tom-toms became Wolf's accompaniment, four sets of them, played by drummers at the four corners of the lake.

The singers' texts contain actual Indian words: 'star, lake, princess, wolf.' These are not employed syntactically; they are colour words, chosen from a cross-section of languages, those of the eastern woodlands predominating. Another series of colour words is that forming the Sun Disc's welcoming music. Beginning with the ancient Japanese word for sun, *ohisama*, sun words follow in a geographic curve around the world through the languages of Asia, Africa and Europe. The Sun Disc himself speaks an invented tongue with a strong suggestion of Latin cognates. The Three-Horned Enemy's speech contrasts sharply with that of Wolf and the Sun Disc; neologisms, notable for their monosyllabic abruptness of compact vowels and waspish consonants, are given additional bite and distortion by means of a loud hailer implanted in the Enemy's costume. A further independent vocabulary is that of the Dawn Birds' chorus, this deriving partly from ornithologists' notebooks and partly from personal listening experience plus imagination.

Enough about the polyglot nature of the work; it is an affair that will recur repeatedly throughout the *Patria* cycle, though not always with the same intention. The important thing to stress here is that when we come to witness a performance of *The Princess of the Stars* we are already at some remove from the action as suggested by the real and implied antiquity of the languages its characters speak.

All rituals are rooted in antiquity or must appear to be. If they have not been repeated uninterruptedly throughout the ages, archaic dress, conduct and speech can assist in creating this impression. When we performed *The Princess of the Stars* on Two-Jack Lake, gaunt black-robed ushers conducted the audience from the road to their places at the edge of the lake. In a more complex handling of ritual, more elaborate preparation ceremonies, including the consecration of the site may be desirable, but here 'holy nature' and the strange timing of the event seemed sufficient.

When the site is legendary its attraction is intensified. In his review of *Princess*, the Banff poet Jon Whyte related a legend from Lake Minniwanka, which immediately adjoins the site of the production. In 1909, an Indian family was crossing the lake carelessly singing.

> Suddenly out of the water appeared the huge back of a fish many yards broad, only to disappear, when out shot a beautifully shaped arm and hand, which clutched not in vain at one of the singers. Immediately a companion seized a knife and stabbed the arm through and through. The hand only clung the tighter to its victim and the surrounding waters were churned and lashed about as if the winds of heaven were let loose all at once.[1]

So there was a monster in the lake. And there was a woman possessed. Who can say she was not a princess? Of all the things said at performances of *The Princess of the Stars*, to me the most beautiful was that of a four-year-old child who murmured to her mother after all the characters had departed, 'The animals were just pretend, weren't they, but the Princess was real.'

We depart from the lake, as the sun rises majestically above the mountain peaks, bathing them in crimson and gold. Is this the same sun that left

---

1   *Crag and Canyon*, Banff, Alberta, August 14-20, 1985.

The Presenter, bpNichol in *The Princess of the Stars*. Banff Festival Production, 1985.

us yesterday, or is it not the Lord of the cosmos who has 'set his commands for all to hear?' Perhaps for just a moment we feel what D.H. Lawrence intended in *Apocalypse* when he wrote:

> Don't let us imagine we see the sun as the old civilizations saw it. All we see is a scientific little luminary, dwindling to a ball of blazing gas. In the centuries before Ezekiel and John, the sun was still a magnificent reality, men drew forth from him strength and splendour, and gave him back homage and lustre and thanks. But in us, the connection is broken, the responsive centres are dead. Our sun is a quite different thing from the cosmic sun of the ancients, so much more trivial. We may see what we call the sun, but we have lost Helios forever, and the great orb of the Chaldeans still more. We have lost the cosmos, by coming out of responsive connection with it, and this is our chief tragedy. What is our petty little love of nature – Nature!! – compared to the ancient magnificent living with the cosmos, and being honoured by the cosmos![2]

## 6. The Pilgrimage

For centuries our art has been produced for indoor environments. I will not dwell on the ways this has altered music, how it has conditioned the search for purity of expression and the suppression of all distractions, bringing about an intensification of acoustic image, hi-fidelity, amplification, and sound presence. Everything has been arranged to enhance these values. Musicians sit in a group on the opposite side of the building from the listeners, often disciplined by a conductor. They have set up unions to ensure that their working conditions are appropriate. Times of work and rest are dictated by contract. Light intensity must be sufficient; adequate warmth and controlled humidity for instruments must be guaranteed; proper sound amplification must be maintained. For this a whole battery of non-musical specialists is engaged: stagehands, caretakers, lighting engineers, acousticians, recording engineers. Now the public needs to be informed of the undertaking, and to do this another fleet of experts is required: publicists, box office attendants, managers,

---

2   D. H. Lawrence, *Apocalypse*, Penguin, 1974, p. 27.

promoters, printers, critics. All this apparatus is very costly to maintain. It will have to be paid for one way or another, and if the public cannot or will not do so, foundations and government agencies will be expected to come to the rescue, bringing new confederates onto the scene: boards of directors, accountants, planners, arts administrators, more managers, heiresses, royalty, etc.

The model I have given of the current musical or musical-theatrical undertaking was once very efficient, in fact such a paragon of efficiency that by the eighteenth century it actually served as the model for all future capitalistic enterprises. Here labouring professionals were harnessed and yoked under the leash of a foreman, promoted by expectant owners and backers before the first paying public in history. The commodification of art dates from this time and it extends today to all the auxiliary agencies who expect to make greater profits from it: publishers, broadcasters, recording companies and performing rights societies. I do not allege that this model works efficiently all the time. In fact, as time goes on, it works less and less effectively or, at least, only works effectively when the cash flowing in from the public exceeds the cash flowing out for the services.

*The Princess of the Stars* is a work which, simply by moving outdoors, challenges us to breathe again. But disguised beneath its simple plot and musical textures are timely questions – big ones. When musicians play across a lake at a distance of half a kilometre or more, how are they conducted or supervised? Of what value then are conductors and managers? When everything is muted at long range (like the tinting of colours at a distance) how is presence to be obtained in the sound, or is this ideal to be abandoned? How do performers cope with unpredictable weather conditions, cold, dampness or the difficulties of transporting themselves and their instruments over uneven terrain? Can we arrange a contract to remove the hazard of rain? And what about the managerial staff? We need boatmen, not caretakers; trailblazers, not electricians; naturalists, not publicists.

And the audience? Instead of a somnolent evening in upholstery, digesting dinner or contemplating the one to follow, this work takes place before breakfast. No intermission to crash out to the bar and guzzle or slump back after a smoke. No pearls or slit skirts. It will be an effort to get up in the dark, drive thirty miles or more to arrive on a damp and chilly embankment, sit and wait for the ceremony to begin. And what ceremony? Dawn itself, the most neglected masterpiece in the modern world. To this we add a little adornment, trying all the time to move with the elements, aware that what can be done will be little enough in the face of it all. Here is a ceremony then, rather than a work of art. And like all true ceremonies, it cannot be adequately transported elsewhere. You can't poke it into a television screen and spin it around the world with anything like a quarter of a hope that something valuable might be achieved. You must feel it, let it take hold of you by all its means, only some of which have been humanly arranged. You must go there, go to the site, for it will not come to you. You must go there like a pilgrim on a deliberate journey in search of a unique experience which cannot be obtained by money or all the conveniences of modern civilization. Pilgrimage; it is an old idea; but when more than five thousand people travelled to a remote lake in the Rocky Mountains to see a performance of *The Princess of the Stars*, it was evident that this old idea is one for which there is a contemporary longing.

Ellen and Michael Waterman as the phantom musician and Tycho Brahe in the game Dodecachordon from *Patria 3: The Greatest Show*. Peterborough Festival production, 1988.

# Patria 3:
## The Greatest Show

*Composed*: 1977-87, Monteagle Valley, Ontario, St. Gallen, Switzerland.

*Cast*: About 150 actors, singers, dancers, musicians and carnival people.

*Duration*: 3 hours

*First Performance*: Peterborough Festival of the Arts, August 6, 1987.

## Parabasis

IN PREPARATION FOR their later reconstruction, *Patria 1* and *2* are broken in
*Patria 3*. They are taken apart, dismantled, pulverized, shaken down scene
by scene and action by action until only the siftings remain, then mixed
with alien and catalytic elements that will lead to the myth-apotheosis to
follow in future works. According to the alchemists, the base metals
cannot be transmuted into silver or gold without being first reduced to
their *prima materia*. This reduction to prime material is the action which
takes place in *Patria 3* and their reconstruction will be the subject of *Patria
4: The Black Theatre of Hermes Trismegistos*. The destructiveness of *Patria 3* takes
many forms and is immediately apparent at the beginning with the disappearance of the hero and the dismemberment of the heroine. This is in
keeping with ancient practices, for the destruction and dismemberment of
the hero is frequently encountered in religious and psychic processes.
Often it is the enemies who do the destroying and quartering, but sometimes it is also the faithful followers, even priests, and while the intention
may sometimes be that of limiting power, it is often consciously
performed to ensure the divine status of the hero.[1]

Failing protagonists, the plot of *Patria 3* crumbles, or at least is reduced
to small-scale counterplotting and frog-croaking. If there is a major story
here, it has been forgotten, even by the participants, and survives only in
sword dances, mummery plays and freak shows. All events are minor,
though they may have the seeds of deeper intention in them, as when
masks are put on as sport and only inadvertently reveal deeper mysteries.

---

1   For the hero to live the hero must die. The fate of Osiris, paralleled in many religions, is also the fate of the artist, who is plundered and torn to pieces by his critics
and his epigone alike – a necessary prelude, it seems, to his final apotheosis.

All speaking is superficial as if before a thousand invisible microphones. But this need not be unpleasant for the audience. On the contrary, it is very relaxing not to have to stand at attention and endure 'another major contribution to culture.' Sometimes it is useful to be able to lift one's legs and escape.

Searching for a medium in which such a fissiparous work could be contained, I thought of the model of the village fair. In one form or another this type of entertainment is known throughout the world, but the fair I have endeavoured to depict is the North American fair of my childhood. In those days (unlike today when the fair, like everything else, suffers from too much electricity) spielers and talkers mounted bally platforms and, by their fast talking, persuaded cynical but inquisitive customers to enter their tents to witness their shoddy and sometimes shady acts. Here was a very special ritual – completely without a sense of striving, and promising no rewards. You wandered about amused and amazed, never sure whether you were there to be entertained or entertaining – for the moment you won a balloon or lost your money while upside down on a sky ride, you became an actor, watched by others and excited by their watching. The fair conformed perfectly to the rules of capitalism and democracy: it tossed everyone into the limelight for two minutes and charged for the thrill.

What was the theme of the fair? Where was its message? Its utility? Who were its organizers and heroes? No one knew or cared. It arrived by stealth one night and would depart furtively the next morning. A bare tract of ground aglitter for a few days, then bare again.[2]

Visibly the fair functioned without any of the necessary characteristics of a work of art, for it neither educated nor enlightened. So it wasn't a work of art then? But what a challenge that question offers! Let us return and stir its embers and see what we can produce. So what if the protagonists never appear and the main themes are all splodged like a bad paint job. So what if instead of a five-act *fauteuil* monstrosity we produce a confection of a hundred atrocities; amusing, ironical, linked only in the head of the wandering visitor.

So *Patria* 3 has no heroes or heroic pretensions. But such a state of insouciance cannot exist for long, especially when there is a suspicion that it has been devised out of mischief and staged perhaps over the very graves of

---

2  I am aware that by locating the fair historically I have set it at a certain distance, even from those who remember it. Perhaps this introduces more irony than is desirable. The extent to which it may have to be modernized, for its illusions to work effortlessly over an audience, will be a director's decision.

Rabindranath LeMeul (centre) delivers a monologue on the lost gods and heroes, accompanying himself with a razzle-dazzle of instrumental effects, in *Patria 3: The Greatest Show*. Peterborough Festival production, 1988.

The semaphore flasher, Hvar Mullin, signals to the god Baal to enter near the conclusion of *Patria 3: The Greatest Show*. Designers: Jerrard and Diana Smith, Peterborough Festival production, 1988.

those whose destruction it celebrates. And so in the very midst of this giddy carnival we begin to long for something which, as in a dream, we are given clues, hints, hopes and even promises of. And what is it that only towards the end begins to take hold of the action? It is nothing less than the resurrection of hero and heroine and their transformation into the androgyne of the alchemical wedding. But such a forging of unity out of disparate elements takes great skill. There is a right and a wrong way, a true *solve et coagula* and a paste-up concoction. *Patria 3* goes about it one way, *Patria 4* another. Whether individual visitors experience the right or wrong solution (or no solution at all) is not in itself important. *Patria* pursues its inexorable course towards its conclusion regardless of those who bear witness to it.

## *The Setting*

The setting is outdoors at night. A network of booths, towers, tents and kiosks is grouped about like those at small-town fairs of days gone by. There is one large stage, the Odditorium, on which the show opens and closes, and three large appropriately-coloured tents to house the Rose Theatre, the Blue Theatre, and the Purple Theatre – the 'restricted shows,' so-called because one cannot obtain entry with normal coupons but has to win entry by playing the game shows or participating in other activities offering tickets as prizes. But there are many other nodal points in the setting as well, such as the tents of the Gallery of Heroes and Heroines and the Palace of Mythical Beings, the Minotauromachy Maze or the continuous cabaret performances on the converted stage of the Odditorium. There is even a University Theatre where various professors pontificate and wrangle about the significance of the *Patria* works before a single bench seating, at most, four people. I myself give a lecture in this tiny theatre, dressed as Wagner. The loops of the work are the small sideshows, the open booths and alleys between them, where solo performers and small groups play close to the public and interact with one another in competitive synergy.

    *The Greatest Show* is simultaneously a setting of traditional theatre spaces where the audience and performers confront one another at a distance (the audience seated passively in the darkness, the performers active and lit), and of elastic spaces in which the performers can move right in on the audience, often jostling them or engaging them in conversation. These are lively and intimate environments but they can easily be dissolved when the spectator strolls off to another attraction. This conjunction of contained and open spaces allows for a great variety of performance tech-

niques in *The Greatest Show*; in fact I can think of no other work for the
theatre which approaches it in this respect. Having twice participated in
productions of the work, I can attest to the invigorating environment of
this spatial variety which is never geometrical or finished off but is broken
unpredictably by wing flats, soffits and coulisses, suggestive of the
labyrinth which is the subtext of the entire work.

Standing at any point on the grounds you might see groups of people
lined up waiting to enter a tent, others exiting from somewhere else, knots
of spectators around roving performers, a distant group being led off into
the darkness, only to be taken unawares by an actor as close as your nose,
through whose gesticulating arms and raspy voice you catch the shrieks of
an opera singer or of an Indian war dance behind your back. One feels at
the epicentre of a great and uneven disturbance of colours, noise and
music erupting everywhere throughout the grounds.

Yes, all this is similar to walking down a busy street in one of the more
cockeyed towns of the modern world. Both are colourful, simultaneous
and haptic. But the fair is not contoured for quick passage. It leads you out
in all directions and holds you back at the same time. It demands participation; the hooks, yanks, lunges, and thrusts of the hawkers and hucksters
make *you the centre of attention.*

Few works of traditional theatre produce this sensation. Ben Jonson's
*Bartholomew Fair* may be an exception.

*Enter Costard-monger, followed by Nightingale*

COST.      Buy any pears, pears, fine, very fine pears!

TRASH.     Buy any gingerbread, gilt gingerbread!

NIGHT.     Hey, now the Fair's a filling! (sings)
           O, for a tune to startle
           The birds o' the booths here billing,
           Yearly with old Saint Bartle!
           Buy any ballads, new ballads?

'The marvel of the play,' said T.S. Eliot, 'is the bewildering rapid chaotic
action of the fair, it is the fair itself, not anything that happens to take place
in the fair.'[3]

---

3   The quotations of Jonson and of Eliot are from Marshall McLuhan and Harley
    Parker, *Through the Vanishing Point*, New York, 1960, pp. 82–83.

Ideally this activity should extend vertically as well as horizontally, which is why I added a tight-rope walker and Mr. Daedalus on stilts. I wanted spectators to gawk upwards at times and at others to search the ground for shadow-clues or unsuspected tricks and traps. I found it useful to make a close inspection of Hogarth's painting, *Southwark Fair*, which shows how the vertical dimension can be amplified; and Jerrard Smith's design for the Odditorium stage, although it inclines more to Russian constructivism, emphasizes this dimension as well.

## *The Text*

To open the show, the Showman, Sam Galuppi, calls for two volunteers to become hero and heroine for the night. A man and a woman are found. Their names? Ariadne and 'Wolfie.' 'What a spectacular pair of ordinary mortals,' proclaims Galuppi, and he calls on the Black and White Magicians to turn them into hero and heroine. The Magicians appear in a puff of smoke and go to work: they saw the woman to pieces and put the man in a cage, then make him disappear. 'What a spectacular beginning,' shouts Galuppi, and he declares *The Greatest Show* open. Immediately all the sideshows go into action.

The text is printed and available[4] so I don't need to go on discussing it here. Anyone reading it will discover that it encompasses an enormous variety of playing styles.

*The Greatest Show* aims to seduce its public by ruthlessly plundering the past, conjoining belly dancers with tragedians, slapstick with expressionism, vaudeville with opera, voodooism with pulpit and lectern demagogy. In fact this stylistic impurity is the source of its attractiveness to a modern audience. Of course there is irony here, the irony that living in an era which claims to be able to access every theatrical style, even the anthropological rituals familiar from *National Geographic* specials on TV, we have slipped into the trap of being acquainted with everything and knowing nothing. Superficiality is the badge of our time, so that when we observe actors doing *lazzi* from *commedia dell'arte* or a mock vegetation ritual from medieval England, we know that they are mumbling lines and enacting ceremonies only partially understood. Like the clapboard surfaces and eccentric spaces of *The Greatest Show*, the conflation of texts mocks any claim to true mastery of the proceedings. The degeneration of the Mighty

---

4   Arcana Editions, Indian River, Ontario KOL 2BO.

Finale is a reminder that dangerous subjects played with ignorantly can erupt into monstrosities.

Some of the texts are borrowed; others lean on a known style; some are complete and detailed; others are suggestive only and indicate a general character to be developed and maintained in a variety of ad lib situations. This is particularly true for the strolling performers, who interact closely with spectators and encourage banter and repartee from them. In some cases only a scenario is given, the fulfilment of which is left entirely to the performers. In sum, there is something to every taste and skill.

In discussing the transition from folk tale to printed tale performed by the Grimm Brothers in their famous collection of *German Nursery and Household Tales*, Maria Tatar comments:

> Every storyteller has a unique repertoire of tales, one developed in collaboration with an audience. Much as the tellers of the tales may appear to exercise unilateral control over their material, their powers of invention are to some extent held in check by their audiences. The successful retelling of a tale requires the narrator to take the measure of his listeners, anticipate their wishes, and veer away from what might offend their ears. Even in the heat of narration the teller may allow his story to take new twists and turns as he trains his powers of observation on the audience, watches their reactions, and becomes attuned to their likes and dislikes. Thus the teller of tales works in concert with his audience to create popular tales. Or, to put matters differently, the folkloric community operates as a kind of censor, endlessly revising the content of a tale until it meets with full approval.[5]

It has been interesting to observe how the texts, and sometimes the music of *The Greatest Show* have been modified by the performers after engagement in a sufficient number of audience situations, so that ungainly material is reshaped and new lines are improvised in the hope of drawing an additional laugh or a tear. Already many performers have performed the same roles in productions in two successive years in Peterborough and I can only imagine what a lifetime of performances could accomplish as the players internalize their roles and unite them with their own personalities.

---

5  *The Hard Facts of the Grimms' Fairy Tales*. Maria Tatar, Princeton University Press, 1987, p. 25.

The Black and White Magicians, about to transform Wolf and Ariadne, in
*Patria 3: The Greatest Show.* Peterborough Festival production, 1988.

Ideally what has to be created is the impression that the performers are a
troupe who have been together for years, who know one another's secrets,
phobias and diseases and can play off this material as easily as they can play
off the script. We are at a new flashpoint as the script dissolves back into
the teller's art.

I once had a dream in which I was explaining to the actors in *The Greatest
Show*, especially those who play in the alleys and game shows, that they
should avoid level eye contact with the audience and seek to position
themselves to look up or down at them, crouched like an animal or peer-
ing like a hawk, either cowering or commanding, all reflected in the height
of shoulder and the angle of vision. The actor is always indifferent to the
audience, but at close quarters this indifference, even contempt, can be
effectively conveyed by a few inches up or down.

In one of his notes to the performers in the Peterborough production
Thom Sokoloski wrote:

> The performer should understand that it is the spectator who
> becomes the surrogate hero or heroine [or victim] once the
> volunteer hero and heroine have disappeared and been chopped
> up respectively during the opening unit.

In this way the audience is encouraged to wander still deeper into the maze of intrigues which make up *The Greatest Show* until it becomes impossible to distinguish the actor from the acted upon, the author from the listener – or the hero from the victim.

## The Music

If I were beginning to write the music for *Patria 3* now (1988) rather than eleven years ago when it was actually begun, I am sure it would be different. *La Testa d'Ariadne* (1977) was the first piece composed. The remaining pieces were added at various times over the years as opportunities arose. The all-interval *Patria* tone row is present in a few of them and it makes its appearance in the Mighty Finale, but most of the musical items adhere to lighter styles. It is as if the Great Bass of *Patria* were crumbling, being ground up for easier consumption or perhaps in preparation for its coagulation into some new form.

One thing I know would be different. I would be less inclined to indulge in dynamic nuancing, realizing, as I now do, that in outdoor performance the dynamic of the music is a function of the distance between performer and listener, rather than an expression of emotion or sentiment. Music is loud when present, and soft when it goes away. It is quite as simple as that. When von Békésy was conducting his *Experiments in Hearing* and asked a gypsy violinist to play more quietly, he simply stopped playing. Either the music was present, or it was not. It didn't move about in the metaphorical space to which the modern concertgoer has grown accustomed and which dates back to the influence of perspective painting, with its illusions of distances, on the musical tableaux of the seventeenth and eighteenth centuries. It is part of the inherited tradition of the Western composer and it was only after the experience of some of my other environmental works that I was able to unlearn it. It may be, therefore, that a work like *Beauty and the Beast* (1980) is too refined for presentation in a tent where the cascade of noises from without too frequently covers its delicate dynamic tremblings.

The real musical interest of *The Greatest Show*, its final excitement and satisfaction, is not to be found in the individual attractions, but in the interaction between them, the interstices, the sound spill, the cross-talk – what one hears peripherally as much as directly. This is why amplification needs to be kept out of *The Greatest Show*, since amplification merely substitutes uniformity for diversity, by inflating one sound image at the expense of all the others. Still it had to be resisted stubbornly and if in production meetings I said 'no microphones' once, I said it a thousand times over the pleas of actors and the general insistence of the electric clones that the show would be improved by a wattage boost.

The question of how to shape and scale the soundscape back to human proportions has concerned me for a long time and so while writing *The Greatest Show* I found myself again studying Brueghel's painting *The Battle Between Carnival and Lent* (1559) to determine how this proportion was maintained in the Age of Humanism. The painting contains well over a hundred people of all ages, some happy, some miserable, some producing sounds, some silent, almost all in motion. The spirit of Carnival, to the left of the painting, is followed by a group playing an assortment of bizarre instruments, while the spirit of Lent, to the right, is pursued by a caravan of children, beggars and nuns producing a competitive disturbance in which the children are playing wooden ratchets. But these are by no means the only soundmakers in the picture. There are two street theatre performances in progress and several other groups of children and musicians are in evidence, each producing sounds with musical instruments or objects quite different from any other group. Yet no group is dominating any other. The essential vitality is the dialectic of the sounds and the excitement and satisfaction for the listener is in overhearing as much as in hearing. There are also quiet zones in the picture, quiet enough for a baby to sleep in its mother's arms or for penitents to kneel in prayer under the arches of the town church. We are witnessing a busy soundscape, but it is not a noisy one, or at least no one seems to be protesting the noise. On the contrary, the doors and windows of the buildings are all open, as if to suck up the soundmaking in the square.

This is the soundscape after which I have sought to model *The Greatest Show*. If technology intrudes, and it does, it is to remind us of that other scale, the sublime one, in which human beings are quite incidental.

## Technology

The Three-Horned Enemy, who slithered to the bottom of the lake at the end of *The Princess of the Stars*, returns at the end of *Patria 3*. He has been alluded to throughout the evening, both directly and indirectly (there is even a Dunk the Three-Horned Enemy game) but his once dreaded power is assumed to be long since exhausted, just as that of all ancient gods has withered or gone into hiding. They are here, together with their prophets

(Baal, Mithra, Buddha, Apollonius, Mohammed, Hermes Trismegistos), often mocked or trivialized in the same way that Hallowe'en is a travesty of All Saints' Eve or Christmas has become a vulgarization of Christ's birthday.

So when the Three-Horned Enemy appears at the end of *The Greatest Show* to tear it to pieces, it is like the revenge of all the gods against the forces which have torn the modern world away from their veneration. The Three-Horned Enemy makes his appearance in the apparatus of technology (his voice is hideously amplified and is accompanied by electronic noises), but the violence of his appearance blows out the entire system, lights, amplifiers, the works, so that the show closes in darkness with a pair of lonely trumpets playing the last post over the deserted grounds.

We are now in a position to identify at least one of the horns of the Three-Horned Enemy: it is blind faith in any system that would replace the power of the gods. Today it is electricity that has seduced the age, substituting glare for beauty and convenience for enterprise. I remember, in the days when I taught in the Communications Centre at Simon Fraser University, reminding students after they had spent four years in intensive media studies in our department that everything they had learned depended on one fact. They looked up brightly, perhaps for the first time. 'The plug,' I said. 'Pull it and you're all out of business.'

As an individual with sympathies towards the philosophy of the anarchists, I have never subscribed to mega-technology, believing that for each job there is an appropriate form, the high-powered sort for high-powered jobs and a diversity of other forms for jobs that can just as easily be done in other ways. But we are purblind today, believing that no human undertaking can occur without the assistance of an electrical support system, whether it is light, sound or the typing of this article. Yet there are and have been many other solutions to these issues throughout history and some of these solutions may still be appropriate to any undertaking in which one seeks to provide people with more independence from the power barons, and with humility before the true forces that rule the universe.

When I look back on the first production of *The Greatest Show*, I realize how much of our time, energy and budget were surrendered to finding solutions to the power problems, to the detriment of other things which might have been achieved. The inadequate power of the park had to be strengthened to light the show. But when rain and wet grounds occurred, none of the lights could be turned on for fear of electrocuting the audience. We lost several performances this way and $30,000 in anticipated box office revenue.

Are there other ways to light a fair? Of course, and we could have researched them. Here's an account of a travelling fair in Ontario in 1850. 'The whole space is lighted by... tin holders, filled with very bad, greasy, tallow candles.' Can you imagine how the sinister side of a show could be brought out by that? 'Imagine a tall, thin, bearded American, exhibiting himself at a small wooden desk between two dingy tallow candles and holding forth... on mesmerism, phrenology, biology, phonography, spiritual communications, etc.'[6] That's the kind of lighting *The Greatest Show* needs. That's the atmosphere for its menagerie of freaks and hucksters.

## Variety Theatre

I append some remarks, without comment, by T.F. Marinetti, leader of the Italian Futurists, from an article entitled 'Variety Theatre,' written in 1913. I hope that future performers of *The Greatest Show* will find them appropriate, for although Marinetti's world and ours are widely separated, some of the ghosts he wished to expel remain the same.

> The Variety Theatre ... is lucky in having no tradition, no masters, no dogma, and it is fed by swift actuality.

> The Variety Theatre is absolutely practical, because it proposes to distract and amuse the public with comic effects, erotic stimulation, or imaginative astonishment...

> Today the Variety Theatre is the crucible in which the elements of an emergent new sensibility are seething. Here you find an ironic decomposition of all the worn-out prototypes of the Beautiful, the Grand, the Solemn, the Religious, the Ferocious, the Seductive, and the Terrifying, and also the abstract elaboration of the new prototypes that will succeed these...

> The Variety Theatre offers the healthiest of all spectacles in its dynamism of form and colour (simultaneous movement of jugglers, ballerinas, gymnasts, colourful riding masters, spiral cyclones of dancers, spinning on the points of their feet). In its

---

6   Susanna Moodie, *Life in the Clearings versus the Bush.* Toronto, 1989, pp. 95-97.

swift overpowering rhythms the Variety Theatre forcibly drags the slowest souls out of their torpor and forces them to run and jump.

The Variety Theatre is alone in seeking the audience's collaboration. It doesn't remain static like a stupid voyeur, but joins noisily in the action, in the singing, accompanying the orchestra, communicating with the actors in surprising actions and bizarre dialogues. And the actors bicker clownishly with the musicians...

The Variety Theatre destroys the Solemn, the Sacred, the Serious, and the Sublime in Art with a capital A.

The conventional theatre exalts the inner life, professorial meditation, libraries, museums, monotonous crises of conscience, stupid analyses of feelings ... *psychology*, whereas, on the other hand, the Variety Theatre exalts action, heroism, life in the open air, dexterity, the authority of instinct and intuition. To psychology it opposes what I call 'body-madness' (*fisicofollia*).[7]

7    'The Variety Theatre,' in Marinetti: *Selected Writings*, London, 1972, pp. 116-120.

The Three-Horned Enemy destroys the fairground in *Patria 3: The Greatest Show*. Peterborough Festival production, 1988.

Theodore Gentry as Hermes Trismegistos in *Patria 4: The Black Theatre of Hermes Trismegistos*. Festival de Liège production, 1989.

# Patria 4:
## The Black Theatre of Hermes Trismegistos

*Composed*: 1982, Monteagle Valley, Ontario; revised 1988, Montreal–Indian River, Ontario.

*Cast*: Countertenor, 2 sopranos, boy soprano, mezzo-soprano, tenor, bass, mixed chorus, 11 actors, dancers (optional).

*Orchestra*: Piano (celesta, electric organ), harp, violin, cello, flute (piccolo), clarinet (bass clarinet), alto saxophone, horn, trombone, percussion (3 players).

*Duration*: 2 hours.

*First Performance*: Festival de Liège, Belgium, March 9, 1989.

FEBRUARY 25, 1989.Sabena Airline flight to Belgium, where we are to give the première of *Le Théâtre Noir* for ten nights in Liège. Thom, Jerrard and Diana have preceded me by several weeks to begin work with the Belgians.

A dark night, a black ocean, and a third alien rushes forward in the frictionless air of the streaking jet to join the other two, the aspirant earthling and the fallen angel, set adrift so long ago in this cosmological drama of arrivals and departures, of ascents and descents, this time into the furnaces of medieval alchemy. There is no moon. The flames of the sea could devour us in an instant or a terrorist bomb could blow us into ashes in the booming stratosphere just beneath heaven; still the pretty stewardess clears away the tray of food just consumed in the hopes of tomorrow's continued existence on the mortal shores of Europe, and now the movie flicks on proclaiming enlightenment to the darkened cabin. I lay out my notes and read again the introduction to the score I worked on all last spring and summer.

The subject dealt with in *The Black Theatre of Hermes Trismegistos* is the Chymical Marriage as described in the writings of the medieval alchemists. Alchemy consisted of subjecting the base minerals to various processes of dissolution and coagulation (*solve et coagula*) by means of smeltings and burnings in the hope of

8.

producing precious metals such as gold and silver, but as Jung
and others have been able to show, the minerals were also viewed
symbolically as aspects of the human personality so that the goal
of alchemy, regarded philosophically, was nothing less than the
attainment of spiritual purification and excellence. But this
harmony was not produced without great difficulty.

> Just as the outward work of the metallurgist with ore
> and fire has something violent about it, so also the
> influences which bear back on the spirit and the soul –
> and are inescapable in this calling – must be of a danger-
> ous and two-sided nature. In particular, the extraction
> of the noble metals from impure ores by means of
> solvent and purifying agents such as mercury and anti-
> mony and in conjunction with fire, is inevitably carried
> out against the resistance of the darksome and chaotic
> forces of nature, just as the achievement of 'inward
> silver' or 'inward gold' – in their immutable purity and
> luminosity – demands the conquest of all the dark and
> irrational impulses of the soul.[1]

Psychologically considered, the alchemical operation consisted of
separating and distilling the basic elements (sometimes called
the *prima materia*) then reuniting them in purified form in the
*coniunctio* or chymical marriage. This conjunction was personified
as a ritual cohabitation of gold and silver or sol and luna (sun and
moon). From this sprang the *filius sapientiae*, the transformed
Mercurius, who was thought of as hermaphroditic because of his
rounded perfection. This in essence was the shape of events; but
the subject was never stated so simply. The doctrine of *al-Kimika*
hides in riddles because it is not intended for everyone. As the
alchemist Artephius wrote: 'Is it not recognized that ours is a
cabbalistic art? By this I mean that it is passed on orally and is full
of secrets.... I assure you in good faith that whoever would take
literally what the alchemists have written will lose himself in the
recesses of a labyrinth from which he will never escape.

---

1   Titus Burkhardt, *Alchemy*, London, 1967, p. 13.

February 26, 9 a.m. Claude Micheroux meets me at the airport and we drive directly to Liège where we lunch and then go to the orchestral rehearsal, already in progress in the Vertbois, an antique chapel with large murals of biblical scenes glowering down from all sides. From the pulpit above the orchestra Theodore Gentry has just begun to sing the opening lines of Hermes' aria in his fluty countertenor. As the only black person in the assembly he really does look like the prophet of an alien culture.

> I come from far to speak the truth.
> That which is above is like that which is below,
> and that which is below is like that which is above,
> to accomplish the same miracle.
> The moon is the mother.
> The sun is the father.
> The wind carries it in its belly.
> Its nurse is the earth.
> It is the father of perfection throughout all the earth.
> Separate the earth from the fire and the subtle from the gross,
> carefully and with great prudence.
> It rises from earth to heaven and comes down again to earth,
> and thus acquires the power of the realities above
> and the realities below.
> In this way you will acquire the glory of the whole world,
> and all darkness will depart.
> The microcosmos is formed according to the laws of the macro-
> cosmos.
> For this reason I am called Hermes Trismegistos,
> for I possess the wisdom of the whole world.[2]

This is the text which served as the inspiration for *The Black Theatre*, the so-called Emerald Tablet or *Tabula Smaragdina* of Hermes Trismegistos, a text which must be read as a philosophical explanation of the alchemical process, and was understood as such by all the medieval alchemists, who accepted Hermes as one of the founders of their art. Hermes: Greek for the Egyptian god Thoth; Trismegistos: 'thrice great.' Hermes Trismegistos was believed to have lived in ancient Egypt. His grave was supposed to have

---

2   I have adapted the text somewhat, following the translation of Titus Burkhardt in *Alchemy* (Penguin Books, 1971, pp. 196-97) with some reference to the translation by John Read in *Prelude to Chemistry* (London, 1936, p. 54).

been discovered by Alexander the Great; his writings are known first from Arab sources in the eighth century and were later translated into Latin under the title *Corpus Hermeticum*.

Hermetic: obscure, dark, magical. In alternatively commanding and beseeching tones the hierophant promises secret knowledge (gnosis), to those who listen carefully. The tone is confident, arrogant, arcane. The entreaty is addressed to everyone, but the revelation will only come to a few. 'I am the hearing which is attainable to everyone,' runs a gnostic text from Alexandria, 'I am the speech which cannot be grasped.'[3]

Such texts do not originate in low civilizations. They occur in the highest. A few individuals – at first a very few – sidestep society to regard it in a totally different manner, from a transmundane perspective, accessible perhaps only to the physically inactive. Such were the gnostic philosophers; such were the alchemists to whom they are related. And by a comparative gradient so far unexplored, we see resemblances between these individuals, hermetically sealed off from the masses, and certain modern artists: Joyce, Kafka, Beckett. We see it also in the arrogance of d'Annunzio, the spinsterish voice of Eliot, the fustian politics of Pound, wherever figures of maximal intelligence have been isolated or have sought isolation from the public arenas of social life.

Truth is only true when it becomes so. What serves as the mightiest expression of it in one society will become a lie for the next. It is the law of enantiodromia, the tendency of everything to move to its opposite, which Hermes announced and the alchemists practised. Gold becomes vulgar and decays; the King dies. Lead is raised up and transformed into gold; the King is reborn. To rise up we descend. To reach the light we move into darkness, and out of this pit the fire will throw up personalities from our own unconscious, archetypes from the various stages of rotation and ascent: Melusina, Mercurius, Ariadne, Wolf, the Green Lion, Sol, Luna and finally the Divine Child, all presided over by Hermes, floating above the action, initiated by his singing of 'The Emerald Tablet'.

I was hearing the music for the first time, but it didn't surprise me as much as first rehearsals sometimes do. The orchestra consists of very young players, technically adroit and well managed by a quite young conductor, Patrick Davin, who reads the music from a scattering of single sheets spread out on a table before him. He promises to have memorized the passages to be conducted in darkness by the time we move to the Cirque d'Hiver.

136

---

3   'The Thunder, Perfect Mind,' in *The Nag Hammadi Library*, New York, 1981, p. 277.

*Cirque d'Hiver*: the venue I have chosen for the work, in conformation with my belief that *The Black Theatre* should not be performed in a traditional theatre. One should never underestimate the value of an alien location for a work of this kind. The producer should also realize the effectiveness of disorienting the audience before their arrival. For instance, they might be asked to meet at an assembly place some distance from the actual venue and be led there in darkness.

I wanted to do *The Black Theatre* in a deserted mine, in order to stimulate the sensation of being at the source of the telluric kingdom. There are many coal mines near Liège, but they proved unsuitable. Finally, Micheroux discovered this nineteenth-century circus building where, among other attractions, Buffalo Bill's Wild West show had once appeared while on a European tour. Sometime in the early twentieth century, this perfectly circular structure had been turned into a parking garage; the space was divided by three levels of cement flooring and an elevator was installed for raising the cars to the desired level. When this proved too time-consuming, the parking lot was abandoned, leaving several old cars stranded on various levels. The top level is surmounted by a high cupola with a star-like grid beneath, from which trapeze ropes once hung and from which we intend to 'fly' Theodore. The whole structure is now locked up and is completely unknown to the contemporary public. Windows are broken, rain drips in, birds flap under the dark ledges. As soon as I saw it, I knew it would work for us.

Jerrard is at work on the décor. In the centre sits the athanor in a large puddle of water. The work is at a standstill until the roof can be repaired. I can't imagine anything further from the athanor as the fiery centre of the whole production than the black ribs of this skeleton in the wet, grey light. Actually I am still wondering whether my own design of an egg-shaped athanor wouldn't have been symbolically more potent than the open-arched construction conceived by Jerrard. It would have been more compact, warmer, a filled space rather than an implied one. Then I learn that we are having problems with lights and that the circuits installed in the structure before it was shipped from Toronto cannot be used, so that the athanor will have to be lit from outside or beneath rather than internally.

Athanor: *at-tannor*, Arabic for oven, a glass vessel which lies in a sand-bath immediately above the fire. A *fire*, not a puddle!

We discuss ways of feeding the tubes of the heating fans into the base so that the audience, who will be seated in a circle about the edges, will feel the athanor as a source of heat. Secretly I regret that I didn't research the use of real chemical transformations, the flash of magnesium or other pyrotechnics, rather than accepting the impotent alternative of electric lights.

Those colours the alchemists so vividly attached to the various processes of the work, *nigredo* (blackening), *albedo* (whitening), *citrinitas* (yellowing), *rubedo* (reddening), and *cauda pavonis* (peacock's tail), they are thermic, hot and cold, with the ability to sting, freeze or burn the observer; that is how they differ from the pale emulsions of movie colours, theatre colours. I wanted the colours of the athanor to explode out of the darkness into the viewer's face and body. Now I realize that a little spilled light is all I can expect, and even less of that than Jerrard had planned. I am disappointed but remain silent, knowing the difficulties of working in the inhospitable space I have insisted on having for the production.

Evening. Dinner with Thom in a sawdust-floored restaurant specializing in twenty-five recipes for *moules*. He tells me of the problems in getting the Belgians to realize the magnitude of the project. We discuss our idea of using pieces of stone inscribed with alchemical signs as tickets. There is a blue-grey slate-like rock around Liège that is often used in buildings. Micheroux liked the idea of using it for this purpose and promised to try to obtain some. In this way the known takes on a mysterious quality. The different signs on the stones could accord with one's birthday, underlining the astrological influence in the alchemical processes. The stones could be offered up by the audience at a certain point or points to become ingredients in the transformation.

Lights again come up for discussion. Sylvain has not brought enough instruments. It is a good thing that Beate has come from Germany to help us. I am apprehensive, but am too tired on this first day in Belgium to fathom the problem. Certainly Sylvain, who works with Micheroux as chief factotum, has done some creative publicity: I've seen my face, or to be more precise the left half of my face, staring back at me from half the kiosks and shop windows of Liège; black saturation with white lettering: *Le Théâtre Noir commence à minuit.*

It took a lot of persuasion but I finally convinced Micheroux to have the show start at this hour. 'Liège is dead at nine o'clock,' he said. 'All the more reason,' I replied. 'Then they won't know what we're up to.'

Thom and I leave the restaurant to the sound of clocks striking eleven. The taverns are all still full of baggy Brueghel-like youths, seated around beer bottles, in an array of sizes and shapes, laughing and swaying in the foggy yellow light. Walking down the wide tree-lined avenue, I hear a mellifluous bird which I am later told is a nightingale.

February 27. We are staying on a *péniche*, I in the captain's cabin aft, the others in the forward compartments. Several of these barges lie tied up along the banks of the Meuse, many, like ours, made over into floating hotels. The common room is well equipped with easy chairs and television and at one end there is a sunken kitchen with a large refrigerator and a washer and dryer.

To get into my cabin I pass through the wheelhouse, then step down four steep stairs, assisted by a brass railing, into a little cabin with two bunk beds on one side and two square portholes on the other. All the woodwork is heavily shellacked, and there are numerous built-in cabinets around the room, suitable for any number of small containers and bottles, but scarcely suitable for clothes or papers. An adjoining bathroom with a shower (chronically plugged) completes the *ménage*.

Throughout the day and night barges flying Belgian, Dutch and German flags pass, motors throbbing; then the *péniche* rocks, squeaks and gurgles gently in its moorings. Various generators and sump pumps go on and off unpredictably in this unfamiliar soundscape, but I sleep well with my earplugs in and only rise at noon.

February 28. I walk to the Vertbois. The Melusina and Mercurius arias are to be rehearsed today. Melusina belongs to the watery realm of nymphs. She is not strictly speaking an alchemical personage, but comes out of French folklore. I added her in the rewrite, partly in order to strengthen the music by incorporating the song cycle *Arcana*, but also to add drama to the work. Jung says Melusina belongs to 'the lower, denser region' of the blood. She has the magic love potion which seems a necessary ingredient in the revivification of the dead king. Twice she emerges from the athanor as a presage of disorder, arising from her 'Nymphidida' like a lamia or succubus to seduce the unwary. Thom is having her infatuate Magister with her siren's voice, so that at one point the Brotherhood have to pull him back to prevent his leaping into the athanor after her.

Half drew she him
Half sank he down
And never more was seen.

Trans. "Questions for midnight..."

8

VERY DRAMATIC
♩=ca.76

MELUSINA

PICCOLO

CLARINET

SAXOPHONE

HORN

TROMBONE

VIOLIN

CELLO

ELECTRIC
ORGAN

HARP

4 BONGOS
(HARD STICKS)

JAPANESE
BELL TREE

BASS DRUM

TIMPANI

Jung says that Melusina 'must return to the watery realm if the work is to reach its goal. She should no longer dance before the adept with alluring gestures, but must become what she was from the beginning: a part of his wholeness.'[4]

Melusina is traditionally pictured as having a fish's tail or the tail of a snake. Diana has encircled her blood-red costume with snakes and a wig suggestive of Medusa.

As the symbol of transformation, Mercurius is central to everything in the work. His material is quicksilver, hence his slippery changes of character and appearance: he is both water and fire, vaporous and combustible, soul and stone; and when he takes a human form, he is quite amoral. He is simultaneously father of the metals, the *prima materia*, and also the *ultima materia*, the tincture, Adam, the lapis. He is the shape-shifter, an event rather than a substance, which is why one of his favourite forms is Uroboros, the self-slaying, self-begetting dragon.

> I am the poison-dripping dragon, who is everywhere and can be had cheaply. My water and my fire separate and coagulate. Therefore I am called Mercurius, for I am light and dark, changeable and deceitful, equally in the company of saints and sinners. I am known yet do not exist. All colours shine in me and all metals. I beget myself as Uroboros the dragon. I impregnate myself, bare, devour and slay myself and raise myself on high. I am the beginning, the middle and the end. Understand me and you may pass through, but if you do not have exact knowledge of me, you will drown in the flames of my fire.

I like this aria, composed of tritones and minor seconds and accompanied by saxophone, trombone and bass drum. At one time Thom thought of having the instrumentalists move about the athanor as if taunting the spirit, but whether this will be possible remains to be seen.

The French bass needs to loosen up in his singing. He has power enough but he doesn't beguile as yet. It is hard for me to know how to pronounce the French words in a beguiling manner to help him, and we have a little session on this subject together with Patrick Davin after the rehearsal.

I have now heard all the music except for that of Sol, Luna and the Divine Child at the end and I must confess I am pleased with it.

---

4   See: C.G. Jung, 'Paracelsus as a Spiritual Phenomenon,' *Collected Works*, New York, 1959 etc., vol. 13, p. 180.

Back in my little cabin, further thoughts on the relationship between Mercurius and Hermes. Both come from the Egyptian god Thoth. I have split them into two characters, Hermes above as the prophet of wisdom, descending from heaven, and Mercurius below as his agile and dangerous counterpart, rising from hell. The colours I have given them, green for Hermes, red for Mercurius, are complementary (when mixed they produce black) to draw attention to their polarity.

That which is above is like that which is below ... to accomplish the same miracle.

March 1. At the *Cirque*, where things are still stalled on account of the rain, I go down to the Preparation Hall, below the Alchemical Theatre where the Brotherhood will give the audience a crash course in alchemy. Jerrard is building a nice environment here out of old boxes, rusty metal sheets, crumbling bricks and a few benches. Various alchemical signs have been painted on the walls and the whole is gloomily lit by work lights. I trace the two signs for Mercury on the dusty windshields of old cars:

 and

Above, again in the Alchemical Theatre, we discuss ways of giving the cranking mechanism of the athanor door a concatenated sound. There are times when I want us to hear sounds from the mundane world, for unlike music, they are never abstract, but are always referential, and are therefore loaded with a different kind of symbolism. I've mentioned in the notes on the score how I wanted the sounds of dripping water and the flapping of birds or bats to suggest the subterranean world. Here we have both.[5] There are others: the tapping cane of the old King, the wheezing of the athanor bellows, the turning of keys in metal escutcheons and the bolting of heavy doors. As much energy needs to be expended in getting these effects to sound right as on any passage in the music.

---

5 Actually, by the time of the performance we lost them. The weather was dry and the birds departed or were still. Another time I would make sure we had water, preferably dripping from a great height into two or three cisterns. The sound of flapping wings is uncounterfeitable and failing real birds or bats should be left alone.

Eleanor James and Christian Crahay as Melusina and the Magister in *Patria 4: The Black Theatre of Hermes Trismegistos*. Festival de Liège production, 1989.

Ariadne and the Magister in *Patria 4: The Black Theatre of Hermes Trismegistos*. Festival de Liège production, 1989.

March 2. Thom is rehearsing the actors at the Conservatoire. Everything seems too loud. I wish I could rehearse them in darkness and teach them how to see with their ears. The presence of women's voices among the Brotherhood is an appalling anachronism which could be neutralized if they were whispering instead of declaiming. This is what I originally wanted. The whisper draws us in; the declamation drives us back. I speak to Thom about it once again, but he is worried about audibility in the great space of the Alchemical Theatre.

Darkness would also be useful in training actors in the precise measurement of pauses. Maeterlinck once spoke of the 'overwhelming influence of the thing that is not spoken,' believing that 'the profounder vibrations of the soul are more easily communicated by silence than by speech.'

I am, however, much impressed by the voice of Christian Crahay as Magister: deep, rich but with an urgent edge, suggestive of the ferocity of Paracelsus, who served as a model in the creation of this character. It is said that Paracelsus slept with his clothes on and his dagger strapped at his side, such a fugitive he was or considered himself to be; also that he appeared perpetually intoxicated, but at the same time sagaciously sober.

Diana yesterday showed me some rusty old keys and chains she picked up for a hundred francs to sew onto his coat, another example of what I said about sounds above. I am a little less enthusiastic about the boots she wants the Brotherhood to wear, fearing they may be too difficult to keep quiet in the dark sections, but we will find out.

Still on the subject of voices, I wish the Brotherhood were not so young (they are students); ideally we want a cross-section of adepts from sixteen to sixty, suggesting various stages of apprenticeship. This is a problem I have faced before in both *Patria 1* and *Patria 3*, where there were too many young actors and too few older ones.

As if the bright lights of the rehearsal hall did not countervail enough against achieving a subdued tonality, we are also being treated to the sounds of Henri Pousseur's latest orchestration from across the hall.

Last May, together with Claude Micheroux, I had lunch with Pousseur (whose daughter, Marianne, is our Ariadne). He looked young for a man of sixty. As an *enfant terrible* who has been somewhat abandoned by fashion, he seemed simultaneously proud and frightened, smiling rarely and seemingly with difficulty. Among other things we discussed Kafka's *Castle* and the description of the telephone system there, the perpetual humming and singing in the lines. Pousseur's eyes lit up suddenly: 'Just like Stockhausen's *Gesang der Jünglinge*.' When I indicated I would be returning in the spring he said: 'Good, you'll be able to hear my new piece in honour of the French Revolution!' His body grew visibly stiffer over the plate of rather Germanic stew we had been eating. Micheroux smiled broadly, confident that I had not yet been designated as an enemy.

I go across the hall to hear part of the rehearsal. Henri is at the knobs of the elaborate sound system, confronted by banks of knobs and faders and aided by two assistants. On stage is one of the biggest orchestras I have ever seen. The music sounds apostrophic, in total contrast to what we are trying to achieve in the other room.

March 3. At last we are working on the music for Sol and Luna. At first it sounds terrible; the orchestra plays too continuously and has not learned how to fold their lines under the voices of the singers to produce a heterophonic extension of the vocal lines. The section can't be conducted, but must be felt by the musicians themselves. We are hampered by a weak tenor who curls his upper lip when he sings. The duet never reaches a climax. Thom urges me to consider adding the choir for power; I agree it might help, but can't find a way to fit them in since the fabric here is so free. Patrick Davin is opposed and says he'll try to get the tenor to uncurl his lip and sing louder.

I am also worried that we have not yet found the music to illustrate the seven signs of the metals; but Patrick promises we will begin this tomorrow.

March 4. Again I would like to be working in darkness. When I worked through the music for the signs with the group in California,[6] we did so in the presence of a single candle, holding up the image of the sign before it and then trying to find the sound. We have no candle and so I begin by explaining how the alchemists gave the names of the metals additional resonance by associating them with the heavens.

Lead – Saturn
Iron – Mars
Copper – Venus
Quicksilver – Mercury
Silver – Moon
Gold – Sun

6   A workshop of *The Black Theatre* in an earlier version was given at the California Institute of the Arts in 1984.

I describe how the alchemists thought the heavens worked cooperatively with the elements and quote a line from Hermes' opening aria explaining this relationship:

> The microcosmos is formed according to the laws of the macro-
> cosmos.

The orchestra is puzzled and I rush through everything so we can begin experimenting with sounds. I want sounds that don't seem to be produced on traditional instruments; I don't want that kind of association; and I want them so soft as to be scarcely audible. At the end of two hours we have found only three. For Lead (Saturn) very slow glissandi on a muted trombone and *scordatura* cello.

For Silver (Moon) a sequence of artificial harmonies on the violin, some of which are extended by bowed *crotales*. The cello also sustains the odd harmonic from time to time.

For Gold (Sun) the clarinet, saxophone and flute sustain a very long cluster together with a bowed cymbal.

We will have to return to these another day.

March 5. I am dissatisfied with the movements of the dancer playing Wolf (editing unit 7). He twitches too much and the pair of red eyes he has been given to move in the dark are too bright and the wrong shape – round rather than oval, tapering upwards. They look like the tail light of an erratic automobile.

I mention to Thom how two weeks previously I had watched a wolf-dance at an Indian powwow in Calgary, the way the dancers scarcely moved at all, darting their heads furtively from side to side. I really wish I could rehearse this unit myself....

Although his appearances are brief, Wolf is a major character in *The Black Theatre*. He brings the *prima materia* and returns to battle the Green Lion as a prelude to the final production of gold (Sol). In alchemy the Grey Wolf is antimony, a corrosive or 'biting' agent used in purifying molten gold – the impurities being removed in the form of a scum. This is how the alchemist Basil Valentinus describes the process in *Viridarium Chymicum:*

> From the yellow metal let a crown be made; let the modest bride [Luna] be united to her bridegroom. Then hand over the King to be eaten by the ravening Wolf, and that three times; and stoutly burn the Wolf in fire. Hence the King will come out cleansed from every spot, who can renew thee with his own blood.[7]

Wolf and Ariadne both contribute to the conjunction of Sol and Luna but they are not conjoined here. It is rather as if the Chymical Marriage is a simulacrum to which they bear witness, a pointer towards their own eventual union. In this sense perhaps *Patria 4* marks a certain halfway point in the entire cycle – or at least I tend to think of it in this way at the moment.

Over beer after the rehearsal, Thom discusses with me how he had Magister enter the athanor after the slaying of the Grey Wolf and the Green Lion, turning back momentarily to glance at the Brotherhood and his successor, Iliaster. A nice touch, I thought, as if his death was a sacrifice to the gods, necessary if the purified forms of gold and silver are to unite in the Chymical Marriage.

---

7   *Musaeum Hermeticum*, vol. IX, Frankfurt, 1678, p. 394. In Michael Maier's *Scrutinum Chymicum* of 1687 there is an illustration of a wolf devouring the King in the foreground while in the background the wolf is burnt (calcinated) as the King steps out of the fire. This picture is reproduced in the score.

One of the actors, Septhura, asks me what his name means. I consult my notes and find entries for Ion, Iliaster and Aquaster, although I have none for the other members of the Brotherhood. Ion is 'the priest of the inner sanctuaries' in the first of the *Visions of Zosimos*. Iliaster is the name Paracelsus used to describe the 'life principle,' and Aquaster is also Paracelsian, meaning 'water star' from *aqua* and *astrum*.[8]

March 6. The original idea of giving the audience pieces of stone or metal inscribed with the alchemical signs as tickets could not be effected. Now we learn that little metal discs, acquired too late for this purpose, cannot be inscribed at all. Damn!

This was to be a way of having the audience participate in a tactile manner in the work. I had hoped that they could be collected or exchanged during editing unit 6, where Magister is calling forth the various elements. It would have been nice to have had them placed in the athanor. I am afraid that after the interesting interaction with the audience planned for the Salle de préparation, they will mount up to the Alchemical Theatre and be treated as mere spectators for the remainder of the evening. Thom says it would be nice if they all stood up for the Chymical Marriage, but I think we would need previous interaction with them for that to work. Now our most effortless chance of achieving this has been lost.

March 7. Perhaps the most daring gesture in the whole of *The Black Theatre* is the long pause at the end of the Scarlet Mass, after Wolf and the Green Lion have killed one another, and before the Chymical Marriage – daring because nothing really happens. The question is: how long can we sustain the darkness and silence with only the sounds of the elements occasionally heard in *pianissimo*? The score leaves some latitude: between two and ten minutes. Tonight in rehearsal we achieved about five minutes but the musicians were fidgety (I must speak to them). One giggle from the audience and the whole effect will be ruined. But we must try it, we must!

I was thinking of the alchemists' regard for astral time when I conceived it. If the metals are related to the stars, they, like us, must wait for the proper conjunctions to take place in the heavens before the corre-

---

8   All these references will be found in Jung, *The Collected Works*, vol. 13, p. 60, 135, and 138. Zosimos's 'Visions' also furnished me with some material for Ariadne's description of her torture at the hands of Mercurius. See Jung's 'The Visions of Zosimos' in the same volume, pp. 59-108.

sponding events can occur in the womb of the earth or the artificial womb of the athanor. But of course medieval humans could wait much more unselfconsciously than we can and that is what makes me worried.

150 March 8. Dress rehearsal before a few friends of the cast. Some people comment that the show is too dark and gloomy. A few people giggled at Wolf's eyes, but during the long pause before the arrival of Sol and Luna they were very quiet. The rain was beating heavily on the roof and the sound, intermingling with that of the orchestra softly playing the elements, was magnificent.

I thank all those performers I can find in the dark after the show and walk back to the *péniche*. Soon Thom joins me, and later Jerrard and Diana. Theodore (who has to wait until they get him down from the catwalk) and Beate are the last to arrive. As stage manager and lighting designer, Beate has been working non-stop for days and is exhausted. She goes right to bed. The rest of us have a late-night dinner and chat over a couple of bottles of wine. Diana's beautiful costumes are suffering because of the lighting problems. We all know it, but no one has an easy solution at this point. The pacing of the performers is off in a few places, but that is easier to fix when Thom gives them his notes. The sun is rising over the still city when we go to bed.

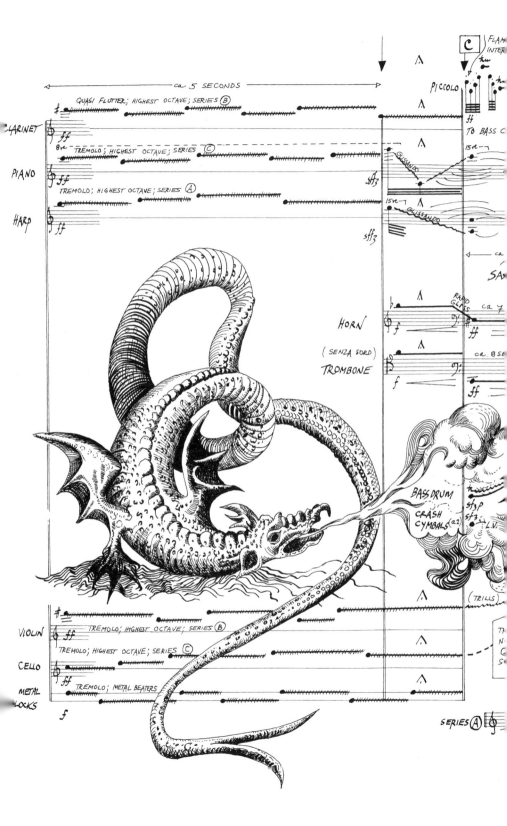

Sketch by Jerrard Smith of the Minoan court from *Patria 5: The Crown of Ariadne.*

# Patria 5:
## The Crown of Ariadne

*Characters*: Pasiphae, Minos, Ariadne, Theseus, Minotaur-Asterion, Daedalus, 4 Soothsayers, Satyr, 6 Beautiful Boys, Courtiers, Soldiers, Priestesses, Workmen, Handmaidens.

*Musicians*: Mixed chorus (16-32 voices), solo harp and orchestra.

*Duration*: 2 hours 20 minutes.

*Composed*: 1982, Monteagle Valley, Ontario; completely revised 1990, Indian River, Ontario.

*First Performance*: Concert version, Toronto 1991.

THERE COMES A TIME when everything must be told simply, or as simply as it can be told. The classical myth of Theseus, Ariadne, the Minotaur and the Labyrinth has been encountered many times throughout the *Patria* works; now in *Patria 5* it is told in the form of a dance drama. *The Greatest Show* contained numerous allusions to a myth apotheosis which would restore the world to the gods. *The Black Theatre of Hermes Trismegistos* showed that process beginning by leading us into the world of alchemy where, by means of a simulacrum, the legendary and the divine are blended. *Patria 5: The Crown of Ariadne*[1] extends this work further. What we see here are heroes conjoined with the gods; the apotheosis has begun.

The story is well known: the Cretan court at Knossos is ruled by Minos and Pasiphae. They have two daughters: Ariadne and Phaedra (though I have left Phaedra out of my treatment). The sea god Poseidon has sent a white bull to the court for ritual slaughter, but Minos has declined to kill the animal. Poseidon, in revenge, makes Pasiphae conceive a lust for the bull and the result of their coupling is the Minotaur, a creature half man and half bull. Minos has the architect Daedalus construct a labyrinth for the Minotaur and feeds it victims taken from tributary states such as Athens. This continues until the young Athenian prince, Theseus, arrives as a prisoner, destined, like the rest, to be sent into the labyrinth as food for the Minotaur. But Ariadne falls in love with Theseus and gives him a

---

1  The Cretan Poet Epimenides, who lived in the sixth century B.C., says that Theseus was aided in his escape from the labyrinth by means of light radiating from a crown of blazing gems which Bacchus gave to Ariadne.

thread by which he may retrace his steps and escape the labyrinth. Theseus kills the Minotaur and sets fire to the palace, escaping with Ariadne. In the original myth Theseus deserts Ariadne on the island of Naxos, where Dionysus finds her and marries her, though I am not concerned with this development here.

The story is a mix of history and legend. The palace of Knossos existed, and still does in Sir Arthur Evans's reconstruction. The fire which destroyed the palace can be dated to about 1250 B.C. Theseus is acknowledged as the founder of Athens and there are enough references to Minos among Greek poets and historians to establish him as a tyrant in the Aegean, though the name may have applied to a series of kings forming a tyrannical dynasty when Crete was the centre of Mycenaean civilization, circa 1600-1400 B.C. The rest is legend, unverified by history or archaeology.

I chose dance as the primary medium in which to tell this story, because I want it to be sensed physically, proprioceptively, as if foaming out from inside the body rather than trickling down from the mind as a textbook memory. Actually I would have liked it very much if the whole drama had unfolded during a lull in a Dionysian marathon of dancing, indulged in by the whole audience. I wanted everyone to dance, to lift their feet and dance with rose-wreaths on their heads, to dance all day to cymbals and tambourines, to sistra and krotala, until they sank exhausted on the seashore as quinqueremes arrived bringing gods and heroes to enact the ancient ritual before the sinking sun and into the torch-lit darkness of the summer night. The labyrinth would be spread out across the sand, the Minotaur at the heart of its darkness, and when it was destroyed, the whole beach would be set on fire while Theseus and Ariadne would depart across the clear water of the ocean by torchlight.

I searched both oceans touched by Canada for a beach on which to perform this dance ritual, but found nothing suitable. Either they were too populated, or too noisy with incessant surf. Somewhere the perfect beach does exist, I know that, but I have limited time to look for it. I had already composed some rather delicate music for harp and strings, intended for incorporation into the work, and anxiety about whether it would be heard – and some rough tests suggested that it would not – forced me to consider another setting.

I have spoken before of my dissatisfaction with modern theatre build-ings as impediments to the existential changes we would like to achieve in those who attend our productions. Perhaps the problem is not the build-ings but the uses to which they have been put by a contemporary entertainment industry that mimics art and specializes in nothing but forgetfulness. The fabrication of a drama from an ancient myth, involving cult practices as well as historical events in symbolic form, is hard enough to achieve without its effect being devastated by the expectations of customers who slump in from the box office, simply because they have enough money to purchase tickets. If only they would take off their shoes!

Perhaps there is a setting somewhere that would allow a large surface of water to be used creatively while still providing an enclosure to protect the music for Ariadne's delicate dances. For the moment, an interior space seems obligatory, though I hope it is not a theatre. The work will remain a dance drama, wherever it is performed; above all I want to preserve the terra cotta earthiness of an event centred in pagan Crete, the visceral uneasiness and sensual excitement of being under the sun and stars. The clash of Dionysian and Apollonian themes is everywhere evident in the story I have to tell, for although it is replete with lust and cruelty, we should never forget that the Minoan story is also civilized: its main prop is a palace.

Daedalus epitomizes the civilized aspect of the myth. He is the reasoner to whom others turn for advice. The palace is his creation, as is the labyrinth. The conjunction of aloofness and guile that animates him is the hinge over which terrible events grate into a new historical ordering. He is the shape-shifter who, like his successor the modern technocrat, blithely produces what everyone wants without concern for the consequences. Beside the other characters, he is cold-blooded, almost lifeless – a computer among soothsayers and satyrs. He neither speaks nor dances but moves slowly with the precisioned throb of the motor inside him. Ariadne, in total contrast, is all life, moving with the delicate grace of *appoggiaturas*. Theseus is raw masculinity and it is difficult to appreciate him, even in the long account of his life left by Plutarch, as anything more than an ignorant hero, a sort of classical Siegfried. One day I would like to shape him into a more elevated character but for the present he must be left as the Greeks presented him. It was his biceps not his brains that attracted Ariadne. Like her, he will be a dancer. Minos and Pasiphae are actors. Minos's voice, normally pinched and squealing, drops at times from head-tone to bowel-tone, into a ferocious growling below speech, terrifying in its sudden release from nowhere. Pasiphae's voice is also coarse and brutish and may actually be that of a man chanting falsetto. Certainly she must not be presented as temptable flesh. She is very fat but her corpulence does not weaken her; in fact, during the first part of the drama she dominates the scene.

The historical evidence for all this is sketchy, and I have embellished what is known for purposes of the drama. Let us suppose that Crete is a matriocentric civilization in decline. Then Theseus arrives and kills the Minotaur, sacred offspring of the bull and the moon goddess, sets fire to the palace and escapes with Pasiphae's daughter, the future Moon Queen, Ariadne, thus breaking the royal line. Theseus returns to Athens to become its King. Crete disappears from history and the Golden Age of the Hellenes follows, of Homer, Aeschylus, Socrates and Aristotle; the age of the patriarchs, setting the tone for the whole later development of Europe. An inversion of sexual-social power is encoded in the myth of Theseus, Ariadne, the Minotaur and the labyrinth, approximately the opposite of what seems to be happening in North American society at present.

I was unconcerned by all this when I first planned to write a work based on the myth, nor was it as topical as it might be considered today. My intention was to treat Theseus and Ariadne as equal partners, the animus and anima symbols they have consistently been throughout the *Patria* cycle, ultimately destined to blend together in perfect wholeness. The first complete draft of the work dates from 1982 (the same year *Ra* was written) but I was not entirely satisfied with it and it was never offered for production. I am completely rewriting it now (1990) at the same time as I write this essay, and the intervening years have stimulated me to rethink a number of issues both technical and psychological. Contemporary public attitudes may have provoked me to fire up the sexist theme by making Pasiphae the focus of power and corruption rather than Minos, as was the case in the first draft, but it has done nothing to alter the relationship of Theseus and Ariadne, which is archetypal and timeless. Sexual abrasiveness is stimulated in the rewrite by the incorporation of four speaking parts for soothsayers, who comment freely on the actions both as guardians of the matriarchal traditions and prophets of its downfall.

The soothsayers speak the 'demotic' language of English in contrast to the 'sacred' language spoken by the divine and heroic characters of the drama.[2] Originally this was Ectocretan, a language I invented myself and used in the novel *Dicamus et Labyrinthos*. But Ectocretan has a very Celtic-sounding phonology and as a private creation it would, I fear, strike most people as more perverse or ironical than sacred. To have been able to tell the story in Mycenaean would have been the most appropriate and I spent a lot of time between 1975 and 1980 studying Michael Ventris's decipher-

---

2   Afternote (1999): In the final version of *The Crown of Ariadne*, the four soothsayers were compressed into a single role to achieve greater clarity and precision.

ment of Minoan Linear B, the only Cretan language yet deciphered.[3] But its vocabulary, consisting mostly of palace records and inventories, is too impoverished to handle the nuances of a complex myth. Since the Cretan language is now indisputably regarded as a cognate of Greek, the next best thing seemed to be to put the text into ancient Greek, and to do this I went to Professor Michael Silverthorn of the Classics Department at McGill University. Michael has put the texts spoken by Minos, Pasiphae and the Chorus into the most ancient Greek known. It still means that the declamation and chanting is anachronistic by eight hundred years or so, but for the eternal gods this is no doubt pardonable.

Returning to the soothsayers: they are the articulate spectators of the ancient Greek drama. Since my chorus will be unintelligble to the audience, they become nothing more than a human wall, the fleshly side of the palace set. The soothsayers provide comprehensible if contradictory points of view on a story, running the risk of seeming too remote to attract contemporary attention. They force us to take sides by their auguries and questions, but like the oracle of Delphi, they always speak the truth and never give a straight answer. They agitate but they also narrate those portions of the drama needing explanation. This is why I want them placed in the midst of the audience where they can comment to those around them liberally and vociferously. Missing in the first draft, their interventions have become a vital ingredient of the rewrite, though the drama itself swings inexorably forward, regardless of their commentaries.

Pasiphae personifies the decline of Crete. Pampered as the Moon Queen, she has grown fat and has become sexually depraved to a point where Minos, or whatever succession of consorts she has enjoyed, can no longer satisfy her. When Poseidon sends the white bull, her open expression of desire for it is a humiliating insult against Minos, who, in failing to sacrifice it according to Poseidon's requirement, has already demonstrated his psycho-sexual impotence. The bull cult of ancient Crete is quite well known and there are many illustrations of women turning somersaults over the backs of bulls as if to arouse their passion in preparation for their ultimate sacrifice, perhaps by the two-edged axe that was so conspicuous among the decorations of the Knossos palace. In the original myth Pasiphae has Daedalus construct a cow in which she may hide to court the bull since, as Jan Kott reminds us, 'in order to unite with a god, one has first

---

3   Michael Ventris and John Chadwick, *Documents in Mycenaean Greek*, Cambridge, 1973. This book, which still glowers down from my library shelf, was also the inspiration for my novel *Dicamus et Labyrinthos*.

to be an animal.'[4] But Pasiphae's coupling with the bull could also be a distortion or pollution by the Greeks of an earlier story in order to discredit the bull rituals so prominent throughout the Middle East. In any event, the incident gave rise to one of the most disturbing and unforgettable characters of any mythology: the Minotaur.

Then who or what does the Minotaur symbolize? Traditionally he was a chthonic figure, dark, blood-thirsty and evil. With his cloven hoof or horns (for he is sometimes depicted as a bull with a human head and sometimes as a man with a bull's head) he is a prototype of the devil, ruling his underworld labyrinth with a ferocity that chilled the hearts of the entire Aegean. No one entered his abode and came out alive. But just as there is ambiguity about his appearance, we cannot forget that this dark prince was the half-brother of Ariadne and the son of the Moon Queen of Crete. I see him as one of the ambiguous figures of the unconscious, that is, everything we do not or cannot know; and by having the Soothsayers refer to him alternatively as Asterion (Star Creature), I mean to imply that like Ariadne, to whom he is related, he retains the divine spark of some nebula we cannot fathom. As with her, there is a fascination about him that draws us on, urging us to confront something hidden, perhaps something lying deep within ourselves. In order to rise up, the hero must first descend into darkness, into the ocean or the labyrinth, there to confront the deadly antagonist face to face. It is a task we must all face at some point in this miraculous passage called life. To accept the challenge gives us the chance to become true men and women, heroic and divine; if we avoid it, we remain victims of the labyrinth, aimlessly wandering its dark passages until sooner or later we are devoured by the beast of oblivion.

*Asterion* is the title of one of the later works in the *Patria* cycle in which I want to develop this theme of individuation through a series of personal trials. For the present, Minotaur-Asterion is maintained in his simple mythic splendour as a bull-man, dangerous to his adversaries, but not so menacing that he does not attract the affection of Ariadne, who, with the purity of her girlish heart, seems to understand her own strange affinity with him. This is why, aside from giving Theseus the thread to escape the labyrinth, she enters it herself to be present at the fateful encounter. And when, at the moment of that encounter, a bird escapes and flies upwards while two shadowy figures make their exit, we are left in suspense as to precisely what has happened. I can do no more for the present. The rest remains to be dealt with in the sequel.

4   Jan Kott, *The Eating of the Gods*, Evanston, Illinois, 1987, p. 34.

*Some property matters.* The palace dominates the scene. It may also simultaneously be the labyrinth or may be transformed into the labyrinth, for at least one researcher has suggested that the Minoan palace was not at all the abode of kings and queens, but rather a vast necropolis where the mummification of the dead was practised.[5] At any rate the palace should not appear as the elegant and almost cheerful structure Sir Arthur Evans reconstructed. It must bristle and I suggest it might be constructed almost entirely out of shining metal. In fact, it is a huge sound sculpture or instrumentarium, consisting of many parts, each of which gives off its characteristic sound when set in motion by men pulling cranks and ropes. Like the *deus ex machina* of the ancient Greek theatre, it is a divine engine or series of engines providing a turbulent commentary on the entanglements of the plot. What I have in mind would be in the tradition of the *bronteion*, the instrument used in Greek drama for imitating thunder. Here I am also reminded of Pliny's description of the Egyptian labyrinth which had huge stone or metal doors that opened with 'a terrifying sound as of thunder.'[6] I have given the various instruments names to suggest their functions: 'Machine of Eternal Splendour,' 'Numina of the Sacred Bull,' 'Wheels of Ominous Destiny,' 'Gateway to the Sun,' 'Gems of Asterion.' They are large, these sound machines, and they are frequently heard choking the merely mortal music of the choir and orchestra.

My stage notes say that the palace is to be lit so that one side is light and the other dark. The light side faces the sea and the dark side faces inland towards what might be the labyrinth, though a second thought is to make the labyrinth the forecourt of the palace, hinged so that it could be drawn up vertically to reveal the maze of passages through which Theseus and the Minotaur will climb.

One advantage of the dancing floor serving to cover the labyrinth is that all the actions performed above it would be inextricably united with it, a notion preserved in the extensive meander-pattern floor tiles of Knossos itself, and also in the legends connecting Ariadne's dances with the labyrinth, of which they form a kind of decipherment. The dancing floor could be raked up to the palace so that the open spaces of various depths and configurations beneath would also serve as resonators for the dancers' footsteps, or at any rate for objects forcefully struck on the surface, each

---

5   Hans Georg Wunderlich, *The Secret of Crete*, New York, 1974.
6   Pliny, *Natural History, xxxvi*, 19, quoted in W. M. Matthews, *Mazes and Labyrinths*, New York, 1970, p. 10.

area resonating differently according to the depth and size of the cavity beneath it. The technique of resonators is used on the Kabuki stage even today where large jars are placed in different positions beneath the floorboards to echo the actors' footsteps. I have given the male chorus poles to strike on the floor with the intention of utilizing this feature, and various dancers could also have poles, for instance in the Dance of the Double Axe. For this idea to be truly effective the labyrinth would have to be constructed along 'musical' lines. Each chamber or tunnel would have its distinct *Eigenton* and the various zones of the stage above could be played almost like a giant marimba.

*Masks*: 'Everything profound loves the mask,' said Nietzsche. It is our way of touching the supernatural, of manipulating our identity to align ourselves with deeper worlds, intensifying our existence by contact with spirits and essences – what the Greeks called *enthousiasmos*, 'having the god within one.' The mask tells a single truth where the face tells many truths in the creases of its fluctuating deceptions and doubts, and in the multitude of signals brought to the surface by nervous discharges and inadvertent muscle spasms. To bring these fluctuations under control is part of the actor's training and the actor succeeding best at it is said to be good at 'psychological' drama. But *Patria* is not concerned with psychological drama; its characters are unflinching and timeless. If you catch Wolf (Theseus) or Ariadne today they will be the same tomorrow; though the circumstances around them may alter their deportment, their destiny does not change and their character reveals no departure from it.

Among the Greeks both the mask and the actor were called *persona* – the term Jung borrowed to suggest the image we all try to wear when confronting the outside world. A mask is a face that lives without living. Its immobility provides its fascination and its limitation. Its unchangeableness suggests one of its original connotations: its affinity with death. It also suggests that the wearer is an eternal being, an archetype in a timeless pantheon of entities whose reality is undeflected by history.

The first masks were those of the gods: Ra, Anubis, Horus.... The earliest mention of masks in Greece is in connection with the mystery cult of Dionysus. The Greek dramatists employed them to enlarge the actor's presence, especially when playing the parts of gods or heroes. I want masks in *The Crown of Ariadne*, particularly for the characters of this sort: Minos, Pasiphae and, of course, the Minotaur. Perhaps the whole cast is masked, though dancers have traditionally practised the art of facial immobility in their marionettish manoeuvres to the extent that masks may not be necessary for them.

One interesting feature of the mask, which cannot be ignored, is the way it alters vocal resonance. *Persona* is derived from *personare*, meaning to sound through. Greek masks were equipped with a bronze mouthpiece to amplify the voice, but with or without the mouthpiece a clever designer could experiment with resonance chambers within the mask structure to disguise the voice just as the mask disguises the face. As Gordon Craig warned long ago (1910): 'it is not the Greek mask which has to be resuscitated: rather it is the world's mask which is going to be created.'[7] And so I leave the matter to the designer to do just that. For Minos, two masks, a pleasure mask at the beginning and a tragic mask after the death of Pasiphae – also a rather ridiculous bull mask for his pursuit of Pasiphae in the 'Dance of the Cows.' Pasiphae, herself, needs only one mask, to an extent bovine, but by no means weak, rather glowing with the splendour of ripe fruit or the full moon. There is nobility as well as ferocity in the Minotaur mask and, in keeping with his appearance in other *Patria* works, I would ask that he have not two but three horns.

The designs for *The Crown of Ariadne* should incline towards visual symbolism. In particular, the curves of the moon, and its echo the *labrys* axe, should be replicated throughout the set so that everything has a convex-concave feel, corresponding to the domination-submission theme that lies at the core of the myth. The bull is related to the sun as the moon is related to femininity and the phasing of the sun and moon throughout the drama is a kind of 'pathetic fallacy' in which the elements reflect the events of the narrative. When the full moon slowly sinks into the sea on the final night, the civilization of Crete comes to a close.

*Colours.* Graves tells us that red, white and black are the colours of Minos's heifer and also of the moon-cow. Certainly they are among the predominant colours in Cretan frescoes. Others are yellow, often with a lemon tinge, ochre, ivory, a range of blues from powder to aquamarine and a few greens. Terra cotta is the predominant colour, serving alternatively as skin tone or background. Although there seems to be no preference of colours accorded to the sexes, this might be a distinction the designers could develop in whatever ways their taste inclines them.

*A final note on the music.* It is as Greek as I have dared to make it. I have borrowed numerous melodies from Greek and Cretan folk music, gathered at the time of my visit to Knossos in 1956. I am ignorant of the provenance of this material, or to what extent we might assume that it corresponds to ancient Cretan music of which nothing is known. That the tunes

---

7    *Craig on Theatre*, ed. J. Michael Walton, London, 1983, p. 21.

should provide good rhythms for dancing was my chief concern. Layered over this is my own music and also the 'infernal machine' of the palace-labyrinth instrumentarium. There is a good deal of drumming, particularly in the earlier sections of the work to accompany Minos. The harp is Ariadne's instrument and her solo dances are all accompanied on it. The building of the labyrinth is accompanied by specially-constructed xylophones made from two-by-four-inch planks of cedar or maple, graded in lengths of about two to four feet. These instruments might be mounted as part of the palace. The sound of four of these instruments, played in a resonant room by sixteen performers or more, is unforgettable; and when Minos orders Theseus to be thrown into the labyrinth it would be wonderful to have the entire chorus join the percussionists to produce an overpoweringly oppressive polyrhythm of sound, suggesting the complexity of the structure Theseus is about to face.

The chorus's role in *The Crown of Ariadne* is as large as that of the orchestra, and includes some choral pieces previously written ('Epitaph for Moonlight,' 'Fire'). Whether or not the vocal quality of their singing inclines toward the Near Eastern, I suggest that at times they may hint at singing techniques known from that part of the world, for instance the habit of pinching the larynx with the fingers to gain tension in the high notes, or beating the breast in rhythm with the music. The Greek word *commos*, which came to be the name applied to a lamentation in classical drama, originally meant stroke or beat and referred to the beating of the breast. The custom is known throughout the Middle East even today. Elias Canetti reports that Shiite Muslims 'form their right hand into a kind of shell and violently and rhythmically beat themselves with it beneath the left shoulder.'[8] The sound of a chorus striking hollow metal breast plates with metal gloves could be electrifying, and one might look at the large figure-eight shields conspicuous in Minoan illustration with regard to designing them as percussive instruments for the chorus.

I cannot say where the musicians and chorus should be arranged; certainly they should not be stuck in a pit. At times they are central to the action and should expect to participate in it to whatever extent the director desires.

Failing the sea, a tape recording of ocean waves may connect everything in the drama in the manner of what Ezra Pound used to call the Great Bass.

---

8   Elias Canetti, *Crowds and Power*, New York, 1981, p. 176.

# The Theatre of Confluence III

Note (2001): Although this essay was written in 1997, several years after some of the Patria works that carry its philosophy into practice, I am placing it here, as an introduction to those works that endorse it. Its tone is strident. My impatience with consumerism in the arts increases as I get older.

Let's start with what's wrong. Here's my list.

THEATRE:            Anthropocentric. A human universe of lusts and fears.

OPERA:              Hypertrophy of the voice. A glorious bandy-legged tenor loves a fat cow with flowing appendages. The story of real life.

MUSIC:              Electrified sex industry, best mixed with drugs. Guitar slung at the crotch. Microphone as phallus. Lollipop-sucking in the bar, the restaurant and the dentist's office...

DANCE:              Twitter-boned exercise on boards. The body as marionette.

LITERATURE:         What commuters read on their way to work.

FILM:               Gorgeously coloured roll of plastic.

ART:                A commodity exported from centre to margin with the intention of displacing the local by merchandise that is not ideologically neutral.

ENVIRONMENT:        Urban; synthetic (now called 'virtual'); electroacoustic mooze from a nozzle in the wall; moving pictures on a screen; fake flowers in a vase, etc.

CRAFTS:             Gone.

MATERIALS: Imported. Not found in your own backyard.

SITES: Rented. Polyfunctional. Desacralized.

CULTURE: Profitable if possible. Cream off the profits and leave town.

AUDIENCES: Larger and lazier. Mob art.

OBJECTIVE: To entertain while sliding in the controls. Our culture is the best in the world. Ram up the price for it.

VERSUS:
Contemporary Requirements:

THEATRE: Hierophany. The return of sacred drama: gods and nature.

OPERA: Gone.

MUSIC: Made by everyone. Songs to enchant, songs to heal, songs of birth and death. Music for any and every occasion. Mysterious music. Music that mixes with nature and the stars.

DANCE: The ripple of flank, the pleasure of movement... maybe just learning to walk beautifully.

LITERATURE: 'News that remains news.' E. P. 'The book should be a ball of light in one's hand.' Pound again.

FILM: Unnecessary in the ideal state.

ART: One of a kind. No copies. No photographs. No reproductions.

ENVIRONMENT:   Natural if possible. At any rate with enough non-urban
               flora and fauna to divert one's attention from cement,
               plastic and electricity.

CRAFTS:        Reintroduction of the homemade object.

MATERIALS:     Local whenever possible.

SITES:         Sacred energy points.

CULTURE:       A satisfaction like learning how to swim. Nothing to
               shout about perhaps, but a distinctive and useful
               accomplishment that may help one to save oneself and
               perhaps others.

AUDIENCES:     The big challenge will be to wed audience, performers
               and the work in a single unity.

OBJECTIVE:     Existential change, transformation, rebirth,
               palingenesis.

Now for a few crosshatchings on these themes.

June 30, 1995. I'm reading Canada's national newspaper, which I never do,
but I'm in an airport and the paper is free. First page of the 'Arts' section
contains a promo for a new TV series on ghost stories, a report on the first
week's sales of Michael Jackson's new album (400,000 copies), an article
about the police seizure of a sadomasochistic sex manual, and a review of a
new jazz CD. Second page: two film reviews, an obituary on a film writer
and a review of a book on Ingmar Bergman. Third page: three film reviews;
five video reviews. Fourth and fifth pages: ads for films. Sixth and seventh
pages: promo for a 'Controversial twenty-four-hour look at Teens, Sex and
Drugs' made by Disney (!), a jazz column, review of a theatre adaptation of
Chaucer, more promos for movies; and on the last page more movie ads,
an article on an American TV news network, and an article on strawberries!
    What is here described, and is every day described in every newspaper
in the nation, is not Art but Entertainment. It's another case of the pollu-

tion of vocabulary indulged in by the media world-wide. It is the elevation of slime and the bullying of the public into accepting it as elixir.

The task of the writer, Ezra Pound said in 1927 or '28, is to maintain

the clarity and vigour of 'any and every' thought and opinion. It has to do with maintaining the cleanliness of the tools, the health of the very matter of thought itself ... When their work goes rotten – by that I do not mean when they express indecorous thoughts – but when their very medium, the very essence of their work, the application of word to thing goes rotten, i.e., becomes slushy and inexact, or excessive and bloated, the whole machinery of social and of individual thought and order goes to pot ... One 'moves' the reader only by clarity.[1]

The degeneration of the word Art is now so massive, and its theft by every entrepreneur attempting to enchant us so overwhelming, that we may have to find another word with which to anoint the few modest activities still conforming to the accurate dictionary definition of art as 'the quality, production or expression, according to aesthetic principles of what is beautiful, appealing or of more than ordinary significance.' The five last words could be underlined.

What the media consider as the 'constituency' for Art is enormous. It includes everyone. Well, not exactly. They mean consumers. Not a single item in the reportage presented above is free. Not a single item involves people actively. Everything there is to be bought and passively digested. Then where do we, who would speak of art in the active sense, find our voice? Do we have to invent a whole new vehicle of publicity for ourselves to secure a hearing?

I am in France, in a hotel room, bored, thumbing through tourist brochures. I come across a glossy colour production for the Disney park 'Le Tour d'Europe en huit heures,' showing people of all ages, all wearing big smiles as they visit shows and entertainments (rides, spectacles, restaurants, etc.). With nothing else to do, I tabulate the people in the pictures. Only 36 customers are standing or moving about; 139 are seated while the entertainments spin about them. That's the kind of rigor mortis that has gripped the modern entertainment factory. Can life be renewed here, or are the perpetrators of this opiate so self-satisfied and the public so doped that only an explosion could clear the ground for any alternative type of aesthetic (or athletic) activity?

1  Ezra Pound, *Literary Essays*, London, 1954, pp. 21-22.
2  *Wer sichert den Olymp? Vereinet Götter? Des Menschen Kraft, im Dichter offenbart.* (lines 155-56).

Am I saying that a fundamental revolution is necessary if we are to restore dignity to art as a force capable of transforming society and setting it on a higher course with intensified spiritual, intellectual and moral values? Who keeps the Gods intact if it isn't the poet? asks Goethe in the prelude to Faust.[2] Are there still Gods then? Of course there are, and I've just named them: spirit, intelligence and morality. No, they don't congregate at your local golf course, or at the Cannes Film Festival either.

## Why Not Film?

I need to explain its deficiencies. It merits attention by the sheer volume of its production and the captivity it holds over modern audiences. In fact in the late twentieth century it became very much what opera was in the nineteenth century, an escape for the masses; and in this guise it has been promoted as the art form of its time. I am not going to say that it did not produce its masterpieces. I am simply going to say it became a bad habit, and habit, as Montaigne said, 'stupefies the senses.' The original promise of film has been undermined by its success. We know why it succeeded: because as a cheaply produced commodity it could be born everywhere at once, thus becoming an icon of glorious merchandising. What about the original promise?

Film could have introduced us to alternative realities. It could have achieved the syntax of dreams, by which I do not mean carrying us over into dream moods, but by montaging structures analogous to dream life. It could have gone abstract like symphonic music or post-Kandinsky painting, revealing essential realities in light, colour and sound beyond the figurative or narrative. But the box office quickly put an insurmountable obstacle in the way of the few courageous filmmakers who wanted to move in these directions.

Sergei Eisenstein was one of them. Eisenstein not only theorized brilliantly about this new medium but made significant contributions to its initial years of greatness. To read *The Film Sense* or *Film Form* is to enter the mind of a great intellectual, weaving together threads of all the arts, both East and West, and of all periods, placing them at the disposal of the incipient film maker. To achieve 'the synchronization of the senses,' which he sought, the thoroughness of his investigation led him not only to study the great painters from Dürer to Kandinsky, but poets such as Rimbaud and the Japanese haiku poets and took him deeply into areas of music and colour theory.

Even today his self-critical analysis of the montage is worth restudy, and his 'chromophonic,' sound-colour montage as well as his albeit disputable theory of the function of music in counterpointing the visual image could have been of benefit to those who followed him, had they possessed anything like his inquisitiveness into how the film might have developed before Hollywood bleached all intelligence out of the medium.

I have never known a movie audience to refrain from feeding itself while watching a film. This single fact exposes the weakness of the film: something is missing here, and the film audience is evidently more aware of this than theatre or concert audiences who, for the most part, seem to forget their stomachs while engaged with the presentation. Yes, I am suggesting, in spite of the vigorous denials I hear all about me, that an audio-visual event in a plastic medium is somehow unsatisfying, leaves a gnawing in the sensorium or a frowziness in the mind requiring compensation; either a sweetheart or a bag of popcorn, and that this spreading of focus, regardless of whatever pleasures it may provide, does not produce the concentrated aesthetic experience that the best art can provoke.

Beyond the undeniable power to persuade us that we are inhabiting the world of the screen characters, there is at the end the acknowledgement that it was all just a sham of coloured lights. If only we were given time to study the situation before the next bedazzlement, but the industry will never permit that. The consumption of movies by modern human beings is breathtakingly unstoppable. It belongs to the world of the electric information flow and will only cease when the whole system is short-circuited. But I am not predicting the future; I am only describing the reason films seldom achieve the experience of art, no matter what the media tell us. Pulp novels were an earlier opiate of the same order, whose exclusive function was to alleviate boredom. Today everything possible is electrified. We call that progress. Progress – the faith of the lazy that it even continues while they sleep.

## Commodity Art

Is all artistic duplication bad? No, merely suspect. If I excoriate it, it is simply because it pretends that life's peak experiences can be repeated, and for as many people as submit themselves repeatedly to the experience. The poet e.e.cummings once said that a person is a poet maybe half a dozen times in a lifetime. And probably we all achieve transformational aesthetic experiences no more than that. If these occur so rarely why do they require such massive expenditures of money and enterprise to persuade them to occur? If a song sung across a lake at dawn or twilight can change my life, why do I need the Metropolitan Opera Company? And I can't get that where I live either except on the radio.

Commodity art flows from centre to margin. At the centre are the stars, managers, dealers, promoters, producers, administrators, manufacturers, and the copyright lawyers. This is a one-way street. Consequences: erosion of the local, the homemade, the unique community, in favour of bought merchandise that (I repeat) is not ideologically neutral.

One of the most appalling achievements of capitalism in the twentieth century was to have turned virtually every aesthetic undertaking into an economic exercise. Of course the spectacles of the past also cost money, but never before were the profits or losses rendered so visible or used, as they have been during recent decades, to applaud some achievements and extinguish others. Virtually all activities have been forced to adopt their method and charge for admission, which increasingly has become the dividing line between success and failure. Artists have evaded many masters over the centuries, many of them equally nefarious. Often they have had to fight openly to achieve more ideal states for the pursuit of their work.

## Back into the Future

Art is not a mirror; it is a hammer. Today it might be civil defence against media fallout. It is also a means of transforming that which is no longer into that which was before its corruption, and that which is not into that which ought to be.

Art is a cry of protest against anything that is being threatened. This means that the task of the artist is to maximize anything that is being minimized. Bad artists maximize what is being maximized. Nietzsche: 'The artist who knows his public has nothing to say.' 'My aspiration,' said the painter Hundertwasser, 'is to free myself from the universal bluff of civilization.' Largely this has to do with escaping the egosystem of techniculture. 'The straight line is a man-made danger. There are so many lines, millions of lines, but only one of them is deadly and that is the straight line, drawn with the ruler ... The straight line is completely alien to mankind, to life, to all creation.' (Hundertwasser)

Nor is the straight line the only crime against art. So is electricity – or at least when used to extend the outreach of the work imperialistically, to multiply it, to speed up its discharge, or to amplify it to the occlusion of other art forms. In the rage to electrify everything for better distribution, and by this I refer to the cornucopia of CDs and movies that spill down on us from everywhere, we have all but obliterated simple forms that are homebred, homemade, derived from the commons and free: for instance choral singing and storytelling. They are still around but are downgraded, deranked or dismissed as poor persons' culture. Yet they are as close as your fingertips, ready to be reclaimed, and will be when the rage for over-consumption passes.

'Is there too much music in the world?' is a question I still ask students, and they look at me stupefied. You could ask the same question about food in the fat-assed society where obesity is an obvious health problem, and you might also get an amazed look. Would a diet be a good thing? Is self-denial valid? Might the voluntary renunciation of all art stimuli, at least for a certain period of time, be useful as a preparation for a meaningful aesthetic experience? Could this be arranged by placing art in a situation where it is not immediately accessible? Could certain forms of art be celebrated in secrecy? Certainly all these things were abundantly practised in the past.

For a long time I have been maintaining the originality of the wilderness – originality in the sense of "origins" – against the claims that our history is "European" and has now become cosmopolitan, or universalist. I have insisted that context is more important than style, especially slick styles imported from anywhere, and to counteract this I have avoided all-purpose theatres and sought out unusual settings (sacred energy points) or situated productions at special times (sunsets, dawns, commemorative days, equinoxes, etc.). I am arguing that art might answer the questions where? why? and when? rather than who? and what? Where or when a song is sung or a story told could be more important than who sang it. We need to shift the emphasis away from superstars and their droppings. We need to get back to celebrating special times and places; and where they have been forgotten, we need to reinvent them. The rule ought to be: foreign materials only when necessary and neither those that have been exploited from others nor those that enslave us to others.

You can't go back, say the critics. I answer: It's not going back if you've never been there. It is only the ideology of an age that keeps art works secure; when it changes, the art is abandoned, crumbles and turns to dust. There is no universal art and there is no timeless art. Everything has to be continually reinvented.

That is always our mission. To reinvent art within a changing society. In this struggle, institutions, even the most benign, are the artist's greatest enemies. Yesterday it was the state. Before that it was the church, and today it may be the university. But the biggest threat is everything that the media call Art.

The initiates gather to accompany the dead King into the underworld. Holland Festival production of *Ra*, 1985. Director, Thom Sokoloski; designers, Jerrard and Diana Smith.

The birth of Ra in his ram-headed nocturnal guise in the 1985 Holland Festival production of *Ra*.

# Patria 6:
# *Ra*

*Composed*: 1982, Monteagle Valley, Ontario.

*Cast*: Approximately 25 solo singers, actors and dancers; male voice chorus.

*Orchestra*: Qanun, ud, darabukkah, violin, harp, percussion, tape and electronic sounds.

*Duration*: 10-11 hours.

*First Performance*: Ontario Science Centre, Toronto, May 1983.

> *You are not permitted to look directly at Ra,*
> *but you may touch the sun with your face.*

MOST SIMPLY, RA is the story of the Egyptian sun god, particularly during the hours between sunset and sunrise. The myth tells how Ra (or Re) passes the night, travelling from west to east through the Netherworld, a dangerous time for him and filled with encounters with his vilest enemies, in particular the serpent Apophis. It is easy to see how the myth satisfies the cosmological problem of how the dying sun can rise up newborn the next morning in the opposite sky.

Ra is what might be called a hierophany, a religious drama. While in broad outlines it is easily comprehensible, I have sought in many ways to retain an aura of mystery in certain details. Much of the text has been retained in Pharaonic Egyptian. This is the language of the gods, which appropriately distances them. But it is interpreted, as the drama proceeds, by a high priest or Hierophant, together with his assistants (I call them Hierodules) and, in explaining, they embellish the myth, adding details suitable to a contemporary audience.

The audience is limited to seventy-five – necessary because of the location changes throughout the work, and fitting because this corresponds to the seventy-five magic names of Ra, one of which each individual will carry throughout the night as a seal of divine protection.

But audience is the wrong word here, for those in attendance are more like initiates being conducted through a mystery ritual, and must consider themselves as such if Ra is to have meaning for them. They are clothed in white robes, and are given amulets as a sign of their acceptance as initiates in the 'Mystery of Ra.' During the early part of the work, they undergo numerous preparation exercises designed to assist them when they eventually descend into the Netherworld. They learn breathing exercises; they learn to distinguish the gods by their appearance as well as the sounds and perfumes associated with them; they learn to chant in ancient Egyptian and to perform a little dance in honour of their patron divinity. The Hierodules then accompany them to the Netherworld, where Anubis will guide them, showing them the manner in which Ra's miraculous rebirth is carried out. There are many spectacles in the Netherworld, but the work is experiential in other senses than the visual, with particular emphasis on the senses which function best in darkness: touch, hearing and smell.

Ra is certainly not intended for everyone. In a sense the initiates must be cast, and play their roles, as carefully as the actors, dancers and musicians who present the work. Perhaps a few lines from Serge Saurenon's book on The Priests of Ancient Egypt are not out of place here:

> The Egyptian temple does not admit the crowd: from the entrance of the sanctuary, a series of doors more and more effectively protects the holy place from the dangers of the open air. The darkness deepens as, room by room, one penetrates to the heart of the edifice; the floors go lower, the earth approaches, and, with an apprehension which increases from moment to moment, the visitor finds himself before the entrance, carefully closed, of the chapel where [the divinity] consents to embody itself. It is this sacred effigy that the priest contracts to maintain religiously, to clothe, to nourish, and above all to protect from the attacks of evil spirits....'(p. 35)

Symbols loom large in Ra, as they do in all Egyptian religious writings. In fact, as Henri Frankfort explains in Ancient Egyptian Religion, 'they constitute in the case of many a god all – or almost all – we know about him' (p. 7) producing an 'irreducible unity of image and thought' (p. 28). Then what does Ra symbolize? Ra, who in late Egyptian religion had become the chief or universal deity, moves in a perpetual cycle of ascent and descent, up to the heavens as the sun and down to the Netherworld, to the realm of the dead. Yet, in death, Ra gathers new strength for his resurrection, and in life he perpetually moves towards death. Life means slow dying and death means resurrection and new life.

The 'Weighing of the Heart Against the Feather of truth' ceremony in *Ra*. Ibis-headed Toth (centre) inspects the scales, presided over by Osiris (below) and Maat (above). Holland Festival production, 1985.

Eleanor James as Hasroet, goddess of the necropolis in *Patria 6: Ra*. Toronto premiére, 1983.

Other religions, exhibiting cosmic dualism (Zoroastrianism, for instance), are not fluid in this way. Light and darkness remain in fixed positions, good and evil in changeless combat, and death is irreversible. Judaism and Christianity have inherited these ideas directly from Persia. For me the appeal of the Ra myth is its circularity, its recognition that everything changes into its opposite, that one moment after midday midnight begins, all of which accords very well with Jung's law of enantiodromia where, in psychological terms, an excess of light (intelligence) bends back towards the mysterious, just as conversely the forces of darkness must be travelled through to reach the light.

Light and darkness, high and low, good and evil – they are recurrent themes in the Patria series right from the outset of *The Princess of the Stars* where the savage unconscious (Wolf) is drawn out of the dark forest by the spark of starlight (Ariadne) into the presence of the omniscient sun. The theme can be traced repeatedly in the ensuing works.

One of the problems of modern life is the avoidance of darkness as the nadir of 'enlightenment' in the great swing of cosmic evolution. Just as today we deny the dark side of our nature, we have also choked off physical darkness in our lives – a matter, incidentally, which makes it increasingly difficult to find suitable playing spaces for the *Patria* series. It is precisely at night that humanity's arrogant conquest of the world is most evident. Everywhere there are puddles of electric lights, even when there are no humans about, like urine traces to which their owners will eventually return to establish their territorial sovereignty. From the air at night one views the earth in ripples of electric lights like strings of pearls or the starry sky turned upside down. Even in cloud or fog one sees the blush of civilization reflected thickly in the air. How far must one travel to find darkness? No city knows it any longer, nor even most rural areas as the electric glare worms its way into every crevice of existence.

The text which forms the basis of *Ra* is a work entitled *The Litany of Re*, or to give it its proper ancient title, 'The Book of the Adoration of Re in the West and the Adoration of the One-joined-together in the West (i.e., Osiris).' It is one of several mortuary texts popular during the New Kingdom (c. 1550-1070 B.C.), all dealing with the theme of Ra's nightly passage through the Underworld (the Duat) in the course of which he unites with Osiris. In the process of describing this union of the creative solar principle with the passive hypostasis of fertility, these texts, with such names as the 'Book of Gates,' 'Book of Caverns,' 'Book of What-is-in-Hell,' etc., provide ample details of the twelve sections of the Underworld and their divine denizens. The *Litany* is built up around the invocation of the sun-god by his seventy-five names and the role played by the deceased in assisting and participating in the descent and reemergence of the solar deity at dawn. The text appears on the walls and shrouds of many tombs, the earliest being that of Thutmosis III (c. 1504-1450 B.C.). Originally the deceased was the Pharaoh but it is clear that the text was used to assist other members of the nobility and finally the entire upper-class citizenry in their passage to life after death. The written directions accompanying the book indicate that the entire text was to be recited at night over the seventy-five representations of the sun-god, drawn in colour on the ground.

So far as we know, the *Litany* was never performed dramatically, although sacred dramas were certainly known to the Egyptians and one work, *The Triumph of Horus*, has been restaged in modern times. Myths of importance were commemorated in simple 'mystery' plays in which priests and laity took part, playing the parts of divine protagonists and their supporters. The action was symbolic and the dialogue brief; occasionally mock combat was staged and processions were especially popular. However, no text was ever recited or dramatized for pure enjoyment, rather in the firm belief that re-enacting the myth in some form on earth would be magically effective in the realm of the gods and prove beneficial to the well-being and salvation of the individual as well.

I am paraphrasing the words of Donald Redford, the Egyptologist who helped me to comprehend the mysteries of ancient Egyptian social and religious life and, more important, provided me with the original hieroglyphs of *The Litany of Re* together with a phonetic gloss. In order to round off the drama, and also to give some definition to the character of the King, I also incorporated some passages from the *Am Duat* and the Egyptian *Book of the Dead*, notably the ceremonies known as 'The Opening of the Eyes and Mouth' and 'The Weighing of the Heart Against the Feather of Truth.' These texts were also prepared by Redford, together with one or two lines we concocted ourselves for continuity. All the English texts are my own, some borrowed from Egyptian material and others leaning on the psychological ideas of Jung.

A large team of people assisted in preparing *Ra* for production, in particular Thom Sokoloski, who directed the work, Jerrard and Diana Smith, who designed it, Sally Lyons, who choreographed it, Bentley Jarvis, who created the electronic music, George Sawa, who supervised the Middle-Eastern music and Billie Bridgeman, director of Comus Music Theatre, the producer. Finding venues for *Patria* works is never easy and finding a site for *Ra* was especially difficult, since the action was to be itinerant and called for twenty-five to thirty locales, both indoors and outdoors. Of all the sites I saw in Toronto (not the heliotropic centre some people believe it to be) the Ontario Science Centre seemed the best, mainly owing to some monolithic exteriors and the park surrounding it. Aside from a few corridors, the interiors were useless and the Smiths spent a good deal of time trying to cover up display cases so they wouldn't intrude. For permission to use the space the director had to be convinced. He was a sclerotic old man whose speciality in younger life had been rocks. 'Young man,' he said, 'the kind of thing you are proposing is precisely what delayed science for two thousand years.' But when the proposal came up at a board meeting, Rocky was napping in his chair and the board approved it.

The next thing to do was to spend a night in the Science Centre, walking the route in real time, reading the texts, imagining the action and, above all, testing our boredom and arousal curves over a twelve-hour period. We did this twice, the second time bringing a few actors and some tape-recorded sounds to enliven the experience, also a hamper of sandwiches and coffee to serve as the feast after we had danced around killing an imaginary dragon at 2 a.m.

The attraction of undertaking a work that will last all night is the challenge of comprehending how the rhythms of boredom and arousal work over a long period and then adapting the material in such a way that it will support or counterpoint them. The arsenal of quick thrills depended on by the normal opera and theatre industry has no place here. *Ra* begins to approach the time interval known to anthropology students in folk rituals the world over, particularly those celebrating or concluding with some form of palingenesis or rebirth. Approaches it, I say, though it still falls short by many hours or days. Nevertheless, to take a group of modern metropolitan adults on a trip lasting longer than a subway ride to a movie and back seemed quite enough of a challenge. When they arrived they would be excited and giddy. The problem here would be to settle them down quickly to the seriousness of a ritual for which they had very little knowledge or preparation. By midnight they would be growing tired. Would they want to continue through until the dawn and should they be allowed to leave if they wished?

The itinerary of active and passive episodes, of participating, observing, walking, sitting, standing and lying down was as vital in the structure as any pacing of music and dialogue – more vital. Sometimes natural inclina-

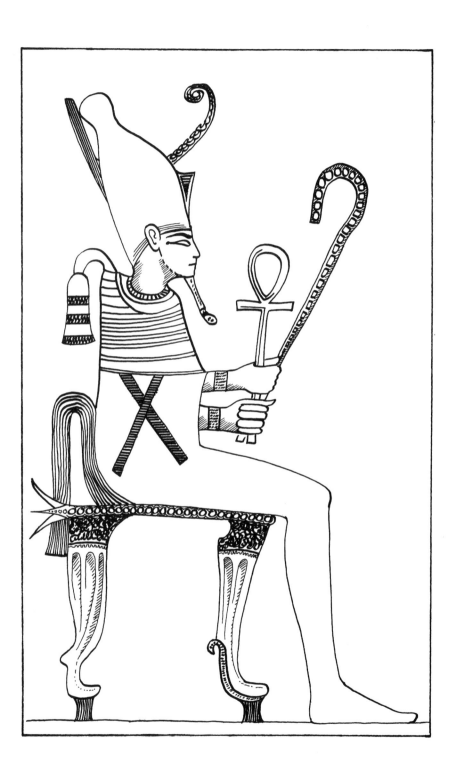

tions would have to be countered; when rest was longed for, we would make people run; when they were thirsty, we would choke them with incense, not out of malice, but in order to break down their cognitive and critical faculties, and allow faith in the miraculous to enter in. This is the purpose of protracted and repetitive ceremonies in all rituals (drumming, dancing, genuflecting) to bring one to the point of exhaustion, intoxication or hypnosis, to prepare one for the change – even a quite slight change. Then the brain cries 'print!' and the transformation is recorded and remembered for life. The exact point at which this change occurs cannot be predicted, for as Jung says, 'rebirth is not a process that we can in any way observe. We can neither measure nor weigh nor photograph it. It is entirely beyond perception.'[1] But that it can be prepared for and that the means of preparation have been understood by the makers of rituals the world over is beyond question. With the help of my co-workers I was trying to locate these nodal points: it was there that I wanted to embed the scenes most calculated to have a lasting effect. I don't know to what extent we succeeded – one never does – but I do know that after the première we had many long and thoughtful letters from initiates who said that *Ra* had changed their lives.

Before any of the composition began, I prepared large graphs on which I structured the contours of activity and repose, and I also read a good deal about the function and formation of initiation rituals in Greek, Middle-Eastern and other cultures. In doing so I became more fully aware of the magnitude of the problem I had set myself: I no longer wished to entertain theatre customers but to induce a radical change in their existential status. Perhaps it was for myself that I was preparing this work which was destined to be so exhausting, both for those who would undertake it and more especially for those who prepared and participated in its performance. 'In philosophical terms,' writes Mircea Eliade in *Rites and Symbols of Initiation*, 'initiation is equivalent to a basic change in existential condition; the novice emerges from his ordeal endowed with a totally different being from that which he possessed before his initiation; he has become *another*.'[2]

Roughly speaking, the form of *Ra* is tripartite, with an introduction leading to the Halls of Preparation, the descent into the Duat (Underworld), culminating in death followed by rebirth and concluding with the ascent towards the rising sun of the new dawn. Since the

---

1   C.G. Jung, *Collected Works*, New York, 1959 etc., vol. 9 (1), p. 116.
2   *Rites and Symbols of Initiation*, New York, 1958, p. xii.

Hierodules will guide the initiates throughout the night, it is essential that they gain their confidence and respect right from the beginning, establishing a kindly but firm relationship with them, and especially one that fills them with a sense of wonder at being allowed to participate in the miraculous. The first sign of this is when they participate in conjuring the Ennead of gods into existence. This mingling of the human and the divine is a matter the Egyptians took for granted and it is one which the Hierophant and Hierodules, as the servants of divinities, must demonstrate by their deportment at all times. They know the sacred script; therefore they can converse with the gods and even participate in their activities by impersonating them. The Egyptians believed 'they were ruled by kings who were themselves gods incarnate; their earliest kings, they asserted, were actually gods, who did not disdain to live upon earth and go about and up and down and through it, and to mingle with men (Budge, *The Gods of the Egyptians*, vol. 1, p. 3).

Before entering the Halls of Preparation, the initiates are given their last chance to withdraw; from this point on we expect them to continue throughout the night and in the twenty-five performances of *Ra* to date almost all of them did so, although occasionally an individual was temporarily overwhelmed and had to be assisted to a 'greenroom' for some reassurance or a cup of tea. Originally, I had thought of including a couple of bouncers in the cast, strong demi-gods who could march off troublesome visitors and shackle them to the walls of deserted corridors until after dawn. The most troublesome characters we have ever encountered in *Ra* have been critics so perhaps this is still a valid idea for future productions. There was also an incident when in Holland a gang of motorcyclists wanted to join the performance at 3 a.m. and began throwing beer bottles when they were refused, but the police eventually cleared them off.

Inside the Halls of Preparation, the initiates are instructed in a number of matters designed to assist them as they pass through the Duat. The stress here is on the haptic, the olfactory and the aural, i.e., the three senses that are especially sensitive in darkness. As in many initiation ceremonies, they are also given a new name (one of the seventy-five magic names of Ra) and are empowered with the secret names of the serpent Apophis in order to help defeat him later in the night. Each of the gods has its own special sound and perfume and the initiates are instructed in these in order to be able to recognize them in the dark. Although all the exercises of the Preparation are simple, their effect on the initiates always proves to be strong. For instance, they are given three 'sacred tones' to hum and are told that the tones have apotropaic powers to ward off evil. It is surprising to observe how frequently groups of initiates will spontaneously recall these tones, and hum them during their ordeals in the Underworld.

Traditionally the Duat consisted of twelve Caverns of the Dead. The ordering varies in different texts and they will also of necessity vary with the production of *Ra* since different kinds of spaces are required, some indoor, some outdoor, and these must be joined with minimal discontinuity. There are two pairs of units that must occur in sequence, however, and these are the slaying of Apophis followed by the Feast and later the Suspension followed by Amente-Nufe's aria. The first pair marks the zenith of physical activity in the entire work, since the initiates participate in the slaying and ensuing celebrations. This should occur at about the mid-point of the work. The second set comes somewhat later and marks the nadir of inactivity since it symbolizes death. It is following this set that rebirth and the ascent to the Hall of the Double Maat will occur. From this point on everything moves in sequence: The King's heart (a metonym for the soul of each initiate) is weighed against the feather of truth in the scales of Maat; Ra arrives and receives the King in his sun barque to rise with him into the dawn sky; the Hierophant leads the initiates out to greet the dawn, the chorus chants joyfully while baboons dance and Khephera (the scarab symbolizing regeneration) slowly mounts the temple wall towards the rising sun.

I reproduce two schemes for the events in the Duat, that of the first Toronto production and that necessitated by the very different setting of the Holland Festival production, which occurred in the centre of the city of Leiden. In the second ordering, the more active and demonic elements occur earlier in the night before the Feast; in the first, the active and passive elements are more equally balanced. I cannot say which I prefer, and in any case, as I mentioned, each production will result in variable arrangements.

| *Toronto Production* | | *Holland Production* | |
|---|---|---|---|
| Editing Unit | Event | Editing Unit | Event |
| 11: | THE DESCENT | 11: | THE DESCENT |
| 12: | ANUBIS | 12: | ANUBIS |
| 13: | THE CORRIDORS | 13: | SEKER |

The actual duration of *Ra* will vary between nine and eleven hours depending on the time of year and the latitude at which it is performed. Units such as the Feast and Suspension are expandable or contractible in order that the conclusion will coincide with sunrise.

Though it may appear at first sight that the music and text of *Ra* could be undertaken by traditionally trained performers, this is certainly not so, for the work requires playing techniques as well as a general attitude no performer will have acquired on a traditional stage or in a traditional performing arts school. For *Ra* to work, everyone involved must believe in it, must believe that if they do not execute the ritual flawlessly the sun may not rise – that an eclipse may take it or clouds cover it, that its warmth may

AT THE HEIGHT OF THE BATTLE, THE HIERODULES GATHER THE INITIATES TOGETHER IN SMALL GROUPS AND THEY ROAR OUT THE NAMES OF APOPHIS AS THEY HAVE BEEN TAUGHT (EDITING UNIT 10) TO THE ACCOMPANIMENT OF FURIOUS DRUMMING.

Ca pō pᵉ

12
4

T QĀ ABU-AL GHAYT

IT IS IMPORTANT THAT THE INITIATES SHOULD BE INCORPORATED INTO THIS S⟨

RA LANDS HIS SPEAR IN APOPHIS. THEN HIS HELPERS GASH HIM WITH THEIR KNIVES AND JAVELINS. THEY CRUSH HIS BONES AND CUT OFF HIS HEAD, LEGS AND TAIL. THEY SCORCH HIS BODY AND FINALLY BURN IT IN A GREAT COMBUSTION OF FIRE.

ĕ mằĉ Rĭĉằ emtē
RA IS JUSTIFIED IN THE UNDERWORLD!

sằhᵉrnằf Ăpŏpᵉ
HE HAS OVERTHROWN APOPHIS!

ĕ nằk hằ⟨
PRAISE HIM!

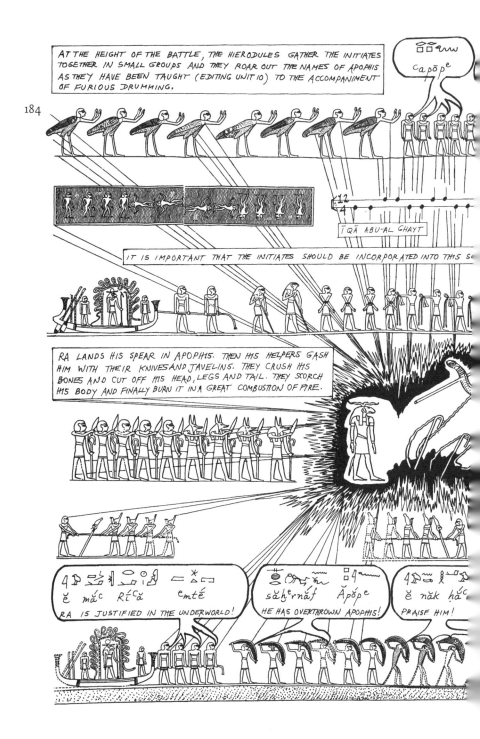

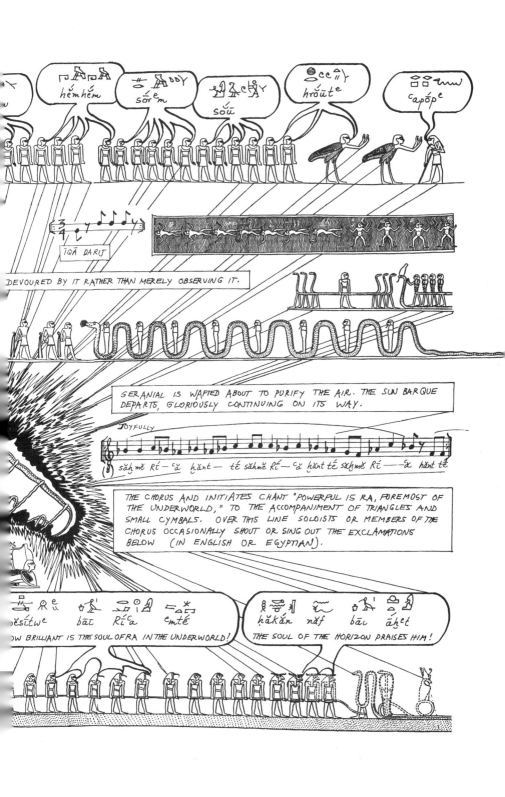

ABOVE, ON THE TEMPLE WALL, THE INITIATES SEE THE
SUN BARQUE, SHINING IN THE LIGHT OF THE NEW
DAY. RA AND THE KING STAND IN THE PROW WITH
ISIS AND NEPHTHYS BEHIND THEM. IN THE STERN, ABDU
AND INET ARE RAISING, AS IF IT WERE AN ANCHOR, A
LARGE REPRESENTATION OF THE SCARAB KHEPHERA.
WHEN IT REACHES THE TOP OF THE TOWER, ISIS
AND NEPHTHYS SLOWLY RAISE THE ORB OF THE SUN
DISC HIGH OVER THE BARQUE. THE BRILLIANT MAT-
ERIAL OF WHICH IT IS MADE CAUSES THE SUN'S RAYS TO
GLINT IN ALL DIRECTIONS AS IF FROM A THOUSAND EYES.

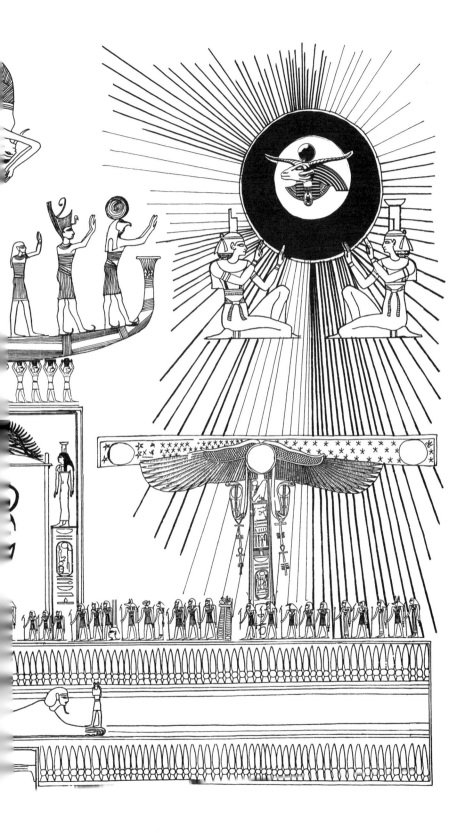

be withdrawn from the earth. This is not an easy attitude to acquire, given the scientific rationalism of modern education; but it can be acquired by degrees as one releases oneself from the fatalism of scientific thinking towards the older philosophy when humans actually believed they possessed powers to affect the external world, instead of merely being knocked about by incontrovertible natural laws. The old philosophy dignifies us with creative gifts: we can act and shape, and rituals are the means of focusing these powers. Certainly the Egyptian priests believed this as did the Pharaoh when he 'walked solemnly round the walls of the temple in order to ensure that the sun should perform his daily journey round the sky without the interruption of an eclipse or other mishap.'[3] During performances of *Ra*, I used to tell the performers that if they performed their parts well during the night, the ensuing day would be brilliant and beautiful, and that if it was dull or stormy, it was because they had made errors, or had become careless in executing their roles. Did they believe it? Certainly I believed it.

In approaching the original Egyptian texts which form the substance of *Ra*, language must be thought of in a different way. These are magic texts; they do not describe or argue; they are certainly not logical. They are hard physical presences and when they are delivered properly they unite themselves with the things of which they speak and literally bring them into existence. It is this striving to find the correct tone of the desired object and to conjure it into being that characterizes all so-called primitive languages; and that is what is required here. My note to the performers reads:

> Do not shy away from the strange sounds of this language. It is a magic language. Deliver its phonetics firmly and with faith that you understand and control its properties. When you repeat the words and phrases try to hit the right resonance that will release their magic powers.
>
> This is not the language of poetry or of fiction, where words 'stand for' objects or ideas. These words are concrete, palpable and complete in themselves. They are themselves the objects and when uttered properly those objects come to life. This is what you must think when you are performing *Ra*: you are creating the world with your mouth.

In posture, and movement too, the performers must believe themselves to

---

3   Sir James Frazer, *The Golden Bough*, London, 1954, p. 78.

be hypostasized divinities and servants of the gods. When the Hierophant puts on the mask of Anubis or of Thoth he *is* Anubis or Thoth, but even when he is the Hierophant his deportment is as precise and undeviating as that of an image in an Egyptian cartouche. Edward Gordon Craig understood the style when he turned to Egyptian art as an inspiration for his famous essay 'The Actor and the *Übermarionette*.'

> Look at any limb ever carved by the Egyptians, search into all those carved eyes, they will deny you until the crack of doom. Their attitude is so silent that it is deathlike. Yet tenderness is there, and charm is there; prettiness is even there side by side with force; and love bathes each single work; but gush, emotion, swaggering personality of the artist?... not one single breath of it. Fierce doubts or hopes?... not one hint of such a thing. Strenuous determination?... not a sign of it has escaped the artist; none of these confessions ... stupidities. Nor pride, nor fear, nor the comic, nor any indication that the artist's mind or hand was for the thousandth part of a moment out of command of the laws which ruled him. How superb![4]

Notice the reluctance of the gods in Egyptian art to lift the sole of the foot from the ground. Treading on both soles, they seem to be standing in their walk and walking in their stance. They seem condemned by rank to a majestic and imperturbable slowness, recalling Nietzsche's definition of nobility as 'slowness in all things – also the slow glance.' A study of modern Middle Eastern mannerisms as well as those evident in Egyptian art would be valuable in determining the right deportment of the gods and the priests in *Ra*. Greetings, for instance, might be performed by crossing the hands at the throat and bending the trunk, surprise by putting the fingers to the corners of the eyes, or readiness to receive someone by touching the brow and the breast before extending the arm. Wrinkles drawn between the eyebrows and hands pinching the throats in numerous hieroglyphic illustrations also indicate nasal or compressed speaking or chanting at high pitch.[5] One of the mortuary texts speaks of the gods (or priests impersonating them) answering Ra 'in a voice which is like that of male cats when they mew.' Far from being affectations, these are thaumaturgical tech-

---

4   Edward Gordon Craig, 'The Actor and the *Übermarionette*," in *Total Theatre*, ed. E.T. Kirby, New York, 1969, p. 53.
5   Cf. Claire C.J. Polin, *Music of the Ancient Near East*, New York, 1932, p. 33.

niques, but if they are to be effective the performer must believe in them totally. Magic, says *The Book of the Dead*, is 'more rapid than the hounds, more quick than the shadows....'

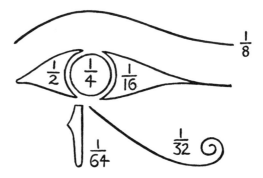

That magic belonged to a higher realm than reason for the ancient Egyptians is evident in their explanation of the Udjat Eye or the Eye of Horus. It is this eye that Ra presents to the King before their ascent. Each part of the eye symbolized a fraction. Added together they produce 63/64ths of the whole. What makes the eye magical is the invisible 64th part. Can one believe this? Without it *Ra* will be a farce.

The incorporation of incense and perfume into *Ra* is intended to create a cradle for the miraculous. Incense has been used in religious ceremonies the world over and it is said that 'the nostrils of the gods delight in it.' In these matters the Egyptians were masters and they also used perfumes in unguents and in their elaborate embalming ceremonies.[7] The best known Egyptian incense was *kuphi* or *kyphil*, a mixture of sixteen ingredients burned at sunset in honour of Ra. The French chemist Loret has suggested that its chief constituents were calamus, cassia, cinnamon, peppermint, citronella, pistacia, *convolvulus scoparius*, juniper, acacia, henna, cypress, 'resin', myrrh and raisins. Plutarch said of *kuphi* that it 'lulled one to sleep, allayed anxieties and brightened dreams.'

All the incenses and perfumes employed in *Ra* come from the Middle East or were known there in ancient times, with one significant exception (see below). Each of the gods exudes a characteristic perfume, and many of the different playing spaces are suffused with incense or aromatic sprays. In the Incense Corridor to the Hall of the Double Maat, many kinds of

---

6  Egyptian perfumery has been researched by the archaeologist Giuseppe Donato, Director of the Institute for Applied Technology for Cultural Artefacts, Rome.

incense are arranged in sequence and various spices and aromatic herbs are also employed to evoke the sensation of moving towards the grand finale in the same way that an architect would prepare one's entry into the grand ballroom by means of a flared corridor, arching stairway or figured balustrade. I never did have the time or opportunity to work out the details of the Incense Walk in order to create this crescendo of aromatic sensations. It needs to be done in the same way lighting or costume design is worked out and with equivalent expertise and attention to detail. Here is an inventory of the incenses, perfumes and spices employed in *Ra*:

*Editing Unit 3: The Inscriptions*
Braziers of *kuphi* and cedarwood burn under images of Ra and Osiris. The Hierodules give incense to the initiates to offer to the gods.

*Editing Unit 10: Preparation*
The hall is lightly scented with benzoin, perhaps with a slight touch of rose. Benzoin, a balsamic resin, has a slight vanilla-like fragrance and I chose it to reinforce the manner in which the preparation exercises are carried out. On entering, the initiates wash their hands in water slightly scented with musk. Later they are given tamarind to chew to purify the breath. Among the Preparation exercises, the initiates are introduced to the perfumes of the various gods. These are passed around in small bowls and are identified by the Hierodules as follows:

1.  'Geraniol is the perfume of Ra....' Geraniol or citral has a bracing fragrance, obtained from the oils of lemon and orange.
2.  'Cedarwood is the perfume of Osiris....'
3.  'Jasmine is the perfume of Isis....'
4.  'Opopanax is the perfume of Nephthys....' The fragrance of opopanax is somewhat like galbanum or myrrh but is fruitier and blends well with jasmine. (Isis and Nephthys are sisters.)
5.  'Turpentine is the perfume of Seker ...' who was the hawk-headed death god at Memphis.
6.  'Musk is the perfume of Anubis....' The jackal-headed god should smell like an animal; musk is obtained from the abdomen of the musk deer or sometimes from muskrats or otters.
7.  'Clove is the perfume of Hasroet....'

**ca. 9'00"**

**E**

RA AND THE ENNEAD RECEDE SLOWLY TOWARDS THE UNDERWORLD. VERY SLOWLY THE LIGHT ON THE DISC FADES. THE CHORUS CHANTS A UNISON ACCLAMATION AS THE WAVES OF SOUND SURGE FORWARD FOR A LONG TIME AND THEN RECEDE.

**JOYFULLY**           Trans: "Thou great God..."
STARTING SLOWLY; THE SPEEDING UP TO MODERATO

CHORUS *f*
SOLOISTS

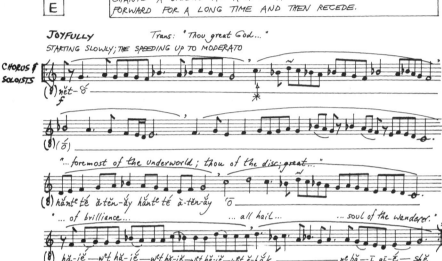

(8) nĕt—ŏ́
*f*

(8)(ŏ́)

"...foremost of the underworld; thou of the disc; great..."

(8) hănt tĕ ă-tĕn-ăy hănt tĕ ă-tĕn-ăy   ŏ

"... of brilliance..."        ... all hail ...        ... soul of the wanderer."

(8) hă-jĕ—wĕt hă-jĕ—wĕt hă-jĕ—wĕt hă-jĕ—wĕt ĕ-hăk   ne bă—ĭ gĭ-ĕ—shĕ

THE CHANTING IS ACCOMPANIED BY TRIANGLE AND SMALL (COPTIC) CYMBALS, BEGINNING AT THE POINT MARKED ✳.

**ca. 10'00"**   THE LIGHTS AND CHANTING GRADUALLY CROSS FADE INTO EDITING UNIT 8.

# Editing Unit 8: THE KING

DURATION : ca. 10 MINUTES
PLACE : OUTDOORS ; AN ALCOVE NEXT TO THE TEMPLE

FROM BEHIND THE INITIATES ANOTHER CHANTING IS HEARD. BY TORCHLIGHT A CHORUS
OF MOURNERS BEARS THE SARCOPHAGUS OF THE KING, CHANTING WITH GREAT
EMOTION. THE PROCESSION IS LED BY SEM, KHERHEB AND AMKHENT. THE HIER-
ODULES SIGNAL THE INITIATES TO FOLLOW THE PROCESSION INTO THE ALCOVE,
WHERE IT PAUSES TEMPORARILY BEFORE THE HIEROPHANT.

8. 'Lotus is the perfume of Mehurt....' Goddess of rebirth, Mehurt is often depicted holding a lotus which she appears to be smelling.

9. 'Sandalwood is the perfume of Amente Nufe....'

10. 'Cade is the perfume of Seth....' The oil of cade, a Mediterranean species of juniper, is not pleasant and is used in the treatment of skin diseases. It seemed appropriate for the murderer of Osiris.

11. 'Civet is the perfume of Apophis....' The most disagreeable odour of all is reserved for Ra's arch-enemy, who also exudes the strong smell of sulphur when he is burned.

12. 'Cinnamon is the perfume of Mates, the murderer. Beware of Mates, who seizes those who pass in the Netherworld, tearing out their hearts. Recognize his smell that you may avoid him.'

Many of these odours are already known and most of the others are emphatic enough to be recalled if encountered again in the Caverns of the Dead as they certainly will be.

*Editing Unit 11: The Descent*
At the end of the Preparation, each initiate is anointed with balm oil and is sent immediately down in the Duat. Nothing is seen during the Descent, but one clearly smells civet, clove and cinnamon.

*Editing Unit 13: Corridors of the Dead*
The Arabian gum resin of myrrh was well known throughout the Middle East and was employed, together with calamus, by the Egyptians in their elaborate embalming ceremonies. The seventy-five mummies of the Corridors of the Dead exude the odour of this heavy antisepsis.

*Editing Unit 16: The Opening of the Eyes and Mouth*
Frankincense, myrrh and cedarwood burn in braziers as the priests prepare the body of the dead King, massaging his hands and feet with perfumed unguents. The atmosphere is very thick and oppressive here.

*Editing Unit 17: Rope-walk*
Olfactory sensations are especially important in this blindfolded walk which begins indoors and ends outdoors. Many of the perfumes of the gods are apprehended along the route together with strange unaccountable odours such as hair or skin burning.

*Editing Unit 18: Apophis*
The burning changes to sulphur for the outdoor battle with Apophis.

*Editing Unit 19: Feast*
Sulphur is replaced by the bracing scent of geraniol to celebrate Ra's victory.

*Editing Unit 20: Hasroet*
The entire area reeks of burnt clove as Hasroet attempts to lure the initiates into her necropolis.

*Editing Unit 22: Osiris*
Cedarwood is burned in Osiris's sanctum.

*Editing Unit 23: Suspension*
This is where the initiates lie down on individual mats to rest and one idea I had (though we have never tried it) was to cover their faces with light scarves, faintly touched with perfumes of the more attractive gods.

*Editing Unit 24: Amente-Nufe*
Sticks of sandalwood are lit as Amente-Nufe sings her aria.

*Editing Unit 26: Dark Messengers*
The smell here is one of miasma and putrefaction. We had a chemist manufacture something called 'slum city' for this scene in which the initiates are forced to run past frightening giants who attempt to catch them in nets.

*Editing Unit 28: Rebirth*
The cow goddess, Mehurt, goddess of rebirth, is saturated with lotus perfume as she embraces the initiates and then passes them to the Hierodules, who wash their faces and anoint them with geraniol, lotus and cedarwood unguents on the forehead, cheeks and throat.

*Editing Unit 29: Mysteries*
As the Hierophant explains the mysteries, the Tet of Osiris and the Scarab of Ra are passed around the circle of initiates. The Tet is perfumed with ankham flowers and the Scarab is scented with the leathery odour of styrax.

*Editing Unit 30: The Incense Walk, etc.*
As mentioned, this is the culmination of the olfactory dimension of *Ra* and the themes need to be drawn together and orchestrated as carefully as those of any musical composition. I can only suggest some of the ingredients here. As the initiates pass down long corridors, various incenses are identified for them: 'The corridor of galbanum ... the corridor of labdanum ... the corridor of olibanum (frankincense) ... the corridor of styrax ... the corridor of *kuphi* ...' etc. Somewhere along the corridors they are also beckoned aside by figures holding trays or bowls of Middle Eastern spices: cumin, coriander, fennel (anise), fenugreek, oregano (marjoram), rosemary, saffron, sage, tarragon (estragon), thyme, benzoin, meloit, oakmoss, orris, etc. Each of these might be given an artificial name suggestive of a divinity or legend, somewhat in the manner that the Japanese incense ceremony (*ko wo kiku*) dilates the odoriferous sensation by means of poetical titles to achieve synaesthesia.

Reaching the Hall of the Double Maat, the initiate is surprised to experience the light fragrance of camphor, an alien incense from the Far East. I chose it for two reasons: first because I wanted the Hall to be in every way a displacement from the ordeals of the Underworld, an elevation to the assembly place of all the gods; secondly, for the purely practical reason that camphor is a light incense and therefore less likely to disturb singers, who have much work to do in this large and rather operatic scene.

Leaving the Hall for the pure air of dawn is perhaps the strongest sensory stimulation in the whole of *Ra* and has to be experienced to be believed; but the preparation for it began the night before when the initiate dropped those first pellets of incense on the braziers below the images of Ra and Osiris.

I will not say I have been satisfied with the olfactory dimension of *Ra* in the performances to date and I have spent time on it here as an affirmation of the importance I accord it. There is a tendency for producers to slough off those aspects of *Ra* that are not in conformity with traditional theatrical operations. The Feast is another example of a vital element that can too easily be neglected. What is needed is a *Lebens-Speise*, a Feast of Life, in which each morsel is placed in the initiate's bowl with reverence and joy and is consumed as if it were ambrosia. A great deal is known about the foods of ancient Egypt and many of the recipes linger on in the delicacies of Middle Eastern cuisine today: baked quails, pine nuts, stuffed vine leaves, zucchini, lentils, fava beans flavoured with lemon juice, rosewater, baklava, basboussa, ma'amoola, etc.

Ra is an experience for all the senses and just as the curves of activity and relaxation need to be carefully shaped with regard to the music, dances and texts of the work, so too they need to be shaped for the other senses, sometimes enhancing, sometimes counterpointing one another. When this is fully understood, Ra will be adequately performed.

Afternote: Is Ariadne present in Ra? Of course she is always present as song, the energy that leads us out of the maze. It has been suggested that she might have taken the form of Amente-Nufe, the Beautiful West, who directs the soul after death. Without thinking about this consciously, I gave Amente-Nufe the all-interval Patria tone row to sing, the only instance of its appearance in Ra. It is the same row that was sung by the Princess of the Stars after her descent to earth and again during her ascent into the heavens – though treated quite differently during her Egyptian transfiguration.

BIBLIOGRAPHY

Allen, T.G. *The Book of the Dead or Going Forth by Day.* Chicago, 1974.
Borghouts, J.F. *Ancient Egyptian Magical Texts.* Leiden, 1978.
Budge, E.A. Wallis. *The Book of the Dead.* New York, 1967.
———. *The Gods of the Egyptians* (2 volumes). New York, 1969.
Fairman, H.W. trans. *The Triumph of Horus.* London, 1974.
Faulkner, R.O. *The Ancient Egyptian Coffin Texts.* Warminster, 1973.
———. *Ancient Egyptian Pyramid Texts*, Oxford, 1969.
Frankfort, Henri. *Ancient Egyptian Religion.* New York, 1961.
Hornung, Erik. *Conceptions of God in Ancient Egypt.* Ithaca, N.Y., 1982.
———. *Das Amduat, die Schrift des verborgenen Raumes* (3 volumes). Wiesbaden, 1963-67.
Piankoff, Alexandre. ed. *The Litany of Re.* Bollingen Books, Series XL-4. New York, 1964.
———. ed. *The Tomb of Ramesses VI.* Bollingen Books, Series XL-1. New York, 1954.
Saurenon, Serge. *The Priests of Ancient Egypt.* New York, 1960.

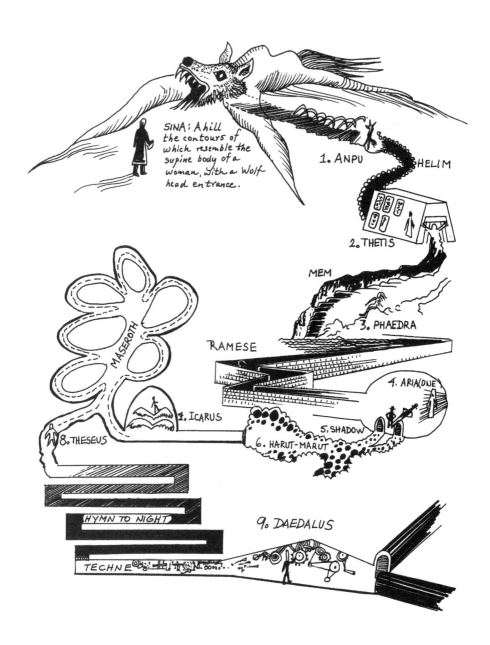

SINA: A hill the contours of which resemble the supine body of a woman, with a Wolf-head entrance.

1. ANPU

HELIM

2. THETIS

MEM

3. PHAEDRA

RAMESE

MASEROTH

4. ARIADNE

7. ICARUS

5. SHADOW

8. THESEUS

6. HARUT-MARUT

HYMN TO NIGHT

9. DAEDALUS

TECHNE

# Patria 7: *Asterion*
## A *Pataphysical Hierophany*

What lies beyond is full of marvels and unrealities, a land of poets and fabulists, of doubts and uncertainties.

> PLUTARCH, *Life of Theseus*

If we wish to outline an architecture which conforms to the structure of our soul..., it would have to be conceived in the image of a labyrinth.

> NIETZSCHE, *Aurore*

As the eye to the sun, so the soul corresponds to God.

> JUNG, *The Religious and Psychological Problems of Alchemy*

## 1. *Labyrinthos*

A LECTURE is about to be given on Cretan mythology at a university. It does not matter where, nor does it matter who the lecturer is. Whether many people have gathered to hear the lecture, or few, or none at all, is also unimportant. The lights in the hall are dimmed as the lecturer bends over his notes and begins. At this moment a person standing by the open door at the back of the hall becomes intrigued and, entering, takes a seat at the back. This is what is heard.

It is rare in drama for an artifact to figure more prominently than the leading characters of the story, but such is the case with the labyrinth at Knossos in Crete, the site of a drama concerning Theseus, Ariadne and the Minotaur, later to be immortalized in Greek mythology. The labyrinth Daedalus built for Minos to house the Minotaur is not merely the scenery to the drama: it *is* the drama. And the image of the labyrinth still holds, transposed to countless baffling contemporary structures and situations, each seemingly controlled by an invisible force at the centre, dark and malignant. All ancient accounts agreed that anyone entering the labyrinth would never return. Either they would become lost among the endlessly forking paths, or they would be devoured by the Minotaur who prowled there. Theseus was the only person who ever returned, and he did so by means of a thread given to him by Ariadne. Somewhere in the labyrinth he met the Minotaur, killed it, and escaped, taking Ariadne with him, then later abandoned her. The myth, it is said, was invented to explain the destruction of the Minoan empire by the Greeks, sometime after 1400 B.C.

It took over three thousand years before Sir Arthur Evans was to excavate the palace at Knossos, but he failed to discover any convincing archaeological evidence of a labyrinth there.[1] In a later study, the paleontologist Hans Georg Wunderlich has suggested that the palace itself, far from being a habitation for living kings and queens, was actually a huge necropolis where embalming rituals were carried out.[2]

The Minoan labyrinth was not the only one known. Many existed in ancient times, and Pliny (in his *Natural History*) called them 'the most stupendous works on which man has expended his labours.' The Egyptians had one that the historian Herodotus considered more fascinating than the pyramids.

It has twelve covered courts – six in a row facing north, six south – the gates of one range exactly fronting the gates of the other, with a continuous wall around the outside of the whole. Inside, the building is of two stories and contains three thousand rooms, of which half are underground, and the other half directly above them.

Herodotus was allowed to visit only the upper rooms, those below being reserved for the tombs of the kings who built the labyrinth, and also the tombs of the sacred crocodiles.

The upper rooms, on the contrary, I did actually see, and it is hard to believe that they are the work of men; the baffling and intricate passages from room to room and from court to court were an endless wonder to me, as we passed from a courtyard into rooms, from rooms into galleries, from galleries into more rooms, and thence into yet more courtyards. The roof of every chamber, courtyard, and gallery is, like the walls, of stone. The walls are covered with carved figures, and each is exquisitely built of white marble and surrounded by a colonnade. Near the corner where the labyrinth ends there is a pyramid, two hundred and forty feet

1   Sir Arthur Evans, *The Palace of Minos*, 7 vols., New York, 1964.
2   Hans Georg Wunderlich, *The Secret of Crete*, New York, 1974.

in height, with great carved figures of animals on it and an underground passage by which it can be entered.[3]

We do not know what rituals were associated with the Egyptian labyrinth, if any. Evidently it was not an administrative centre; the Egyptians did not build airtight office blocks for their slaves. Nothing of the Egyptian labyrinth remains and no myths have been preserved concerning it. The Cretan labyrinth alone provided the spectacular drama, or rather vestigial drama, celebrated in mythology. I say vestigial because no details of what transpired within its walls were ever made known; the sole survivor never spoke of his experience there.

Though many myths and legends were associated with his name, Theseus was not a god. He is believed to have been a historical person, the founder of Athens, and it is as such that Plutarch treats him in his *Lives of the Noble Grecians and Romans*; but Theseus associated freely with divine figures, notably Ariadne. As the eldest daughter of the moon queen Pasiphae, Ariadne was destined one day to inherit the queendom in that matriocentric society, had not love intervened. In aiding Theseus to escape the labyrinth she abandoned her country for love, only to be abandoned in turn. Mythology provides two conclusions to her story; either she died of sorrow on the isle of Naxos, or she was discovered by the wine god Dionysus, who raised her up as the queen of a cult of love. Certainly she had none of the hubristic cunning of her sister Phaedra, whom Theseus eventually married, and who sought to bring down her husband by falsely accusing her stepson, Hippolytus, of violating her.

The legends concerning Theseus, as preserved by Plutarch, adequately provided him with superhuman powers. Believing they were descended from the gods, not ascended from the apes, ancient heroes set themselves elevated tasks and aspired to extraordinary goals. Odin and Osiris, probably historical figures like Theseus, actually became gods. Aeneas was divinely protected in the execution of his mission. Such faith kept the back straight and the eye firm throughout life's adventures and adversities.

Heroic myths are not popular today because there is no room in them for mediocrity. The aspiring hero either wins or loses. And winning is not to win the lottery or inherit a tax-free fortune. Losing was more frequent. Even in the days before republicanism dwarfed everyone, society was conspicuous for its losers, the victims, whose only claim to memory was that they provided Minotaur with his dinner.

3   Herodotus, *The Histories*, Book 2, Penguin Books, 1954, pp. 188-94.

I doubt if much has changed. There is still massive subjection, and the world is full of contrivances to prevent us from achieving illumination, even though the classrooms of all our educational institutions are packed full of citizens desperately cramming techniques for personal advancement. The modern megalopolis advertises conviviality and produces loneliness, exploitation and an environment increasingly unhealthy and dangerous. Many of the victims of these streets are unwilling, but an equal number destroy themselves willingly. There is as much meanness, vulgarity and determined ignorance as there is poverty or lack of opportunity. One might say that an unwritten article in the republic's constitution is the right to remain ignorant.

What *has* changed is the approach to solving these problems. The victims are treated as invalids, requiring crutches and social workers rather than the inspiration of heroes and heroines. The artist is not a social worker, but can serve a valuable social function if art is allowed to inspire even a few people to raise themselves up and move forward with dignity, confidence or a new-found sense of purpose. It is strange, then, that even during eras when the arts were expected to provide inspirational leadership, the Theseus-Ariadne story did not attract the attention we might expect. There are few plays and fewer operas (Monteverdi, Strauss), but none present the heroic aspect of the drama effectively. Like Wagner's Siegfried, Theseus seems to be a very simple hero, without doubts, sufferings, reflections or conflicts of conscience; he was totally unconscious of his actions, driven by instinct rather than premeditation. We know nothing of what he thought while he groped his way through the labyrinth, nothing of the dialogue of words or eyes that took place between himself and Minotaur. Nor do we know how he felt about Ariadne, whether he loved her or why he abandoned her.

If heroism becomes chronic, says Jung, it ends in a cramp. The problem with Theseus is that he is never *not* a hero. It is the same problem Virgil had with Aeneas and what makes him a cardboard figure despite the poet's genius. If a work celebrating the Cretan myth was to become capable of firing the modern imagination, Theseus would need to be provided with a more subtle character, Ariadne's role would require expansion, and the Minotaur would need special treatment, either by giving him the intellectual cunning of a Nietzsche or the physical prowess of a Nijinsky. But how would that be possible within the cramped space of a labyrinth, where the corridors are so narrow that two people can scarcely pass? Clearly, the execution of such a work would require something quite unlike the traditional theatre as a performance space. I know some people believe that the newer technologies are creating formats for intense one-to-one confrontations; but what is missing is terror – the smell of the beast and its roaring in the darkness everywhere. You cannot produce darkness on the light medium of the computer.

A few years ago a ritual drama called *Ra* was produced in which the participants were initiated into the cult of the Egyptian sun god. All participants were robed. Priests instructed them as they passed through the underworld. They died with the god after sunset and were reborn with him in the rising sun of the next morning. But the experience for the most part was collective. Any drama in a labyrinth would have to be experienced individually, one on one; and that is why traditional theatre or opera couldn't deal with it.

That Crete was a matriocentric civilization has been mentioned by many researchers. Though classics scholars of the past (mostly male) developed this theme less ambitiously than modern feminists, the theory is that Cretan religious and civic life was dominated by the worship of an Earth Goddess or Mother Goddess from earliest times up until the destruction of Knossos. Certainly women are very much in evidence in Cretan iconography, appearing as boxers, acrobats, charioteers, potters and hunters. As priestesses they often dwarf their male companions. Animals associated with the Mother Goddess were snakes and bulls; the emblem was the two-headed axe or *labrys*, depicted everywhere, and presumably employed as a sacrificial instrument. Robert Graves has pointed out that the two crescents of *labrys* symbolized the waxing and waning of the moon,[4] the planet most often associated with woman since it measures the rhythms of fertility. In Crete the moon goddess takes helios as her spouse; Pasiphae ('the one who shines for all') rules with her consort Minos 'the moon's creature,' according to Graves's suggested etymology. If all this sounds convincing, would it be too far-fetched to equate the labyrinth with the feminine body? A body of dark passages anticipating penetration by the male, absorbing him, devouring him, exulting over his demise.

A series of consorts having failed her, Pasiphae resorted to copulating with Poseidon's bull. The result disturbed the classical Greek mind, but might not the Minotaur once have been a more incandescent figure to the bull worshipers of Crete, than the blood-thirsty beast the Greeks made him out to be? Might we dare to call him Asterion, acknowledging the celestial light he inherited from his mother? At any rate, he retains the

4    Robert Graves, *The Greek Myths*, New York, 1955, p. 297.

mystery of everything we do not know or cannot know, and as such he may be said to prowl in the unconsciousness of each of us.

His presence is revealed long before he is encountered in the intangible worlds of smell and of sound. The labyrinth is an odour: a miasma, a sewer, an abattoir of rotting human corpses, overlaid perhaps with rich perfumes and incenses to beguile the visitor. Its odorous leitmotif is the tawny smell of the Prince of Darkness, whose identity is also made known by the clattering of his hooves and his bellowing roar. We hear him throughout the labyrinth, now near, now echoing further away. At times he may howl or whine or mewl or growl. At times his voice reaches our ears as deceptively enchanting music.

None of the characters in the Cretan myth are real people. They neither talk like real people nor develop like characters in realistic drama or even hyper-realistic opera. They are archetypes, symbols of the psyche, paradigms of exemplary behaviour, drawn from both the light and dark sides of our nature and presented for inspection in order that we may know ourselves better. There is nothing new in this; it is the function of all mythology and folklore to turn the dimly perceived intuitions of the unconscious towards consciousness so that they can be interpreted and integrated. When an idea is clear and straightforward, there is no reason for more than one name for it. But when it is little known or can be envisioned from many angles, then a multiplicity of forms is needed to express its mysterious or unsettled nature. When society was homogeneous and accepted more uniform dogma, these figures were clearer and were more easily accepted, but in today's shifting and unrooted society their function is cloudy and their forms less easy to identify or name. Joseph Campbell put it this way:

> There can be no question: the psychological dangers through
> which earlier generations were guided by the symbols and spiri-
> tual exercises of their mythological and religious inheritance, we
> today (in so far as we are unbelievers, or, if believers, in so far as
> our inherited beliefs fail to represent the real problems of
> contemporary life) must face alone, or, at best, with only a tenta-
> tive, impromptu, and not very effective guidance. This is our
> problem as modern "enlightened" individuals, for whom all gods
> and devils have been rationalized out of existence.[5]

oseph Campbell, *The Hero with a Thousand Faces*, New York, 1949, p. 104.

If a straight line is the shortest distance between two points, digressions will lengthen it so that the eternal digression of the labyrinth, one might say, is the flight from death. Death might be endlessly avoided if we could go on inventing increasingly complex diversions and imaginary stratagems to escape it. This is not the way of Theseus. He would move by the most direct route to confront the enemy without delay.

But the nature of the hero has changed in our day. No longer is he a warrior with a sword, ready to gore everything in sight. No longer is his aptitude merely that of the swashbuckling youth. No longer is he necessarily masculine. There are heroes of faith, heroes of perseverance, heroes capable of realizing the most fragile dreams without any visible weaponry at all. These are the heroes of a different order, I don't say higher, but certainly in possession of talents badly needed in the modern world. And so let us allow Theseus to dissolve back into the mists of Greek mythology and preserve only the vehicle by which anyone, male or female, young or old, might test whatever heroic strengths they possess or aspire to.

The crucible in which this perilous, puzzling, profound and illuminating experience takes place is the labyrinth. For ancient man, their meandering paths, imitated in initiation dances, ceremonies and complex ritual objects, represented the archetypal endeavour to merge into the world, or to be born anew. This reincarnation theme interested the romantics also. For them, one must descend into darkness, confront the adversary, some sort of evil *Doppelgänger* or Mephistopheles, triumph over him, and emerge transfigured into the light of higher reality.

But the experience of a quest amid diversions is not merely a romantic notion. It fans out into life itself and is replicated in the plans of all civilized communities. The labyrinth is in the alleys of the Middle Eastern bazaars, as well as in the intricate plotting of the thousand and one tales of Shahrazad. It is in the twisted passageways of catacombs, strewn with the bones of martyrs; and it is in the plan of the city with its endless network of streets and shopping malls. The palace is a labyrinth to anyone but a king. Government administrations adopt the labyrinth as their model, and all institutions have followed their example. The hospital may be a labyrinth, and also a school or office building. The mazes of the library are equally inexhaustible to anyone who fails to understand the cataloguing system. And books themselves can be labyrinthine, especially those in which endless digression becomes the theme: Sterne, Diderot, Musil.

Then there is the map. How baffling are the towns and cities with unpronounceable names. Then the victim is anyone who gets lost in the unknown metropolis, with its dangers of traffic, hooligans and muggers. Does one ever find a destination, or is one condemned to eternal wandering? Does one want to find a destination? Isn't it easier to remain a *flâneur*, wandering about town like a visitor with plenty of time and money in one's pocket? Ah yes, it would be a mistake to think that the labyrinth's victims are all killed off at the entrance. Some wander amazed and contented for years without realizing their predicament, for the labyrinth serves opiates of all varieties to the gullible. The Minotaur will find them eventually in whatever trough they slurp, ramming his horns into their flabby bodies, no matter which Ariadne they cry out to in mortification.

And there are the labyrinths of the telephone system, in which the enquirer, seeking perhaps some elusive information, is shunted from dead ends to busy signals, endlessly ringing phones, answering services, decoys, changed numbers, operators who refer the caller to further sequences of new numbers, recorded messages and so on. And there are labyrinths beneath the streets, in the waterworks and sewer systems, or above the streets in the coursing of electrical pulses and the wave forms of broadcasting, amplifying and cancelling each other in turn. Here is the real labyrinth of modern life, from which one seeks release in weekend visits to the country.

But there, too, stands another labyrinth, the densely productive labyrinth of nature, the jungle, the forest, the swamp with its myriad forms of life, even the tall grass and weeds that crowd in on the garden and ploughed field, erupting from nowhere to choke out all botanical designing.

And finally there is the labyrinth of your own body: of the ear, of the stomach, of veins and arteries, neurons and synapses leading to the brain with its millions of tiny charges, memories and traces of half-comprehended or half-forgotten thoughts.

What the child or youth found and finds outside himself, the mature adult finds within. Thus the labyrinth is an invertible figure, both exotopic (outward facing as in the life of the adventurer) and endotopic (inward facing as in meditation). Both processes are necessary in the search for individuation. But how could anyone presume to arrange a series of experiences suitable for everyone? The folly of the labyrinth is the folly of life: experiences rarely arrive at the moment when they could be most useful, that is, to stimulate existential change. Any arrangement of experiences in a linear sequence is bound to seem contrived, like an unrelieved exercise in religious dogma or an educational curriculum. The means of breaking it is the forking path, and the insertion of a sufficient number of these into the labyrinth immeasurably increases its complexity.

Like no other construction on earth, the labyrinth seeks to create maximal complexity and tension within minimal space. To be so near and yet so far from victory or from death, just a wall away: that is its appeal. One wrong turn and one could be lost forever; but by some miraculous accident of correct turns one might equally well find the treasure. In all elementary constructs of labyrinths and mazes the goal is always depicted as the centre. But as Borges once observed, 'Nothing is so frightening as a labyrinth with no centre.'

The original Cretan labyrinth was unicursal, with a single path leading from the rim to the centre; or at least this is how it is presented in the innumerable motifs on Cretan seals and coins.

This has led some researchers to believe that such diagrams do not replicate the real labyrinth but suggest, by means of the number of turns to the left or right, the solution to the puzzle. This can be appreciated by removing the key. If, for instance, we take out a single straight line on the left side, the figure is at once exceedingly difficult to solve.

The Minoan labyrinth is usually depicted as being round, though the same network of passageways was sometimes presented in rectangular form. In all cases it was a very concentrated use of space, in fact a maximal use of space. Of course, building codes would prohibit the construction of such a labyrinth today. Fire regulations would make that impossible. To circumvent these problems the circularity of the structure could be topographically altered into a snake-like construction spread over a wider area, perhaps even incorporating some open areas with topiary or other natural features.

The planning of any ritual space would invariably involve the magic of numbers, particularly as they might affect the volumes and shapes of the structure. There are countless studies of number mysticism as it affected the building of temples, cathedrals and shrines. The Golden Section, or some proportional series equivalent to it, has appeared repeatedly in architecture as has the Fibonacci series (1,2,3,5, etc.), which, as a matter of fact, has been shown to be the design principle of the palace at Knossos, where it evidently extended beyond architecture to govern even the shapes of artifacts such as gaming tables.[6]

Seven is a restless number, the number of 'Chance.' Iamblichus calls it an 'unwed virgin' because it is born neither of mother (of even number) nor of father (odd number). Nevertheless, seven has always had special significance in both Eastern and Western cultures because of its relationship with many natural phenomena. There are seven days of the week, seven colours in the spectrum, and seven tones in the scale. There are seven vowels (alpha, epsilon, eta, iota, omicron, upsilon and omega) and seven alterations in pronouncing them: with an acute, grave or circumflex accent; aspirated or unaspirated; short or long.[7] Ancient Hindu, Persian, Chaldean and Egyptian scriptures made numerous references to 'seven worlds.' The Phoenix was thought to have been reborn seven times.

Seven is said to be the number of primary concord (4:3) when presented as four numbers connected by three intervals. Multiples of seven are also significant. Four times seven is the duration of the lunar cycle. The conjunction of seven with four is particularly significant since it unites energetic instability with balance and order. Starting with the monad and doubling (1,2,4,8,16,32,64), the seventh number, sixty-four, brings us to the double quaternity of eight squared, a number of rich significance. Seven multiplied by itself (forty-nine) is the number of days the soul must remain in the *Bardo* state after death in Tibetan Buddhism.

6 Donald A. Preziosi, "Harmonic Design in Minoan Architecture," *Fibonacci Quarterly*, VI, vi, 1968, pp. 370-85.

7 Iamblichus, *The Theory of Arithmetic*, trans. Robin Waterhouse, Grand Rapids, Michigan, 1988, p. 87ff.

The audacity of constructing or reconstructing with mathematical precision such an experience as I have been describing is obvious; and yet such an attempt has been made, perhaps an impossible attempt, but an attempt nevertheless. The formula, in so far as we can understand it, is based on the number 49, the square of the numeral 7, divided in the following manner: 4 is the number of preparatory episodes before the labyrinth can be entered, of which this lecture, with all its faults and omissions, is evidently the first, to be followed by three others. Then it would appear that the labyrinth itself consists of a diminishing cycle of events as follows: an Ennead of Encounters, an Ogdoad of Trials, a Heptad of Experiences, a Hexad of Perceptions, a Pentad of Contemplations, a Tetrad of Arcana, a Trio of Deceptions, a Duet of Divinities and a Finale. In what order these events manifest themselves we cannot be certain. In fact the entire arrangement is conjectural since no one knows the actual makeup of the labyrinth except Daedalus, who built it, and Asterion, who inhabits it. But if we are correct in our assumptions, the following pattern emerges:

7 times 7 equals 49
4 plus 45 equals 49
4 plus 5 equals 9
9 plus 4 equals 13
1 plus 3 equals 4 (the Quaternity)
4 minus 3 equals 1 (the Monad: Asterion)

Those who think our calculations immoderately simple we respectfully refer to Plato's comment that 'Daedalus would look a fool if he were to be born now and produce the kind of works that gave him his reputation.'[8] Despite changes of circumstance or fashion, each artificer labours with his futile genius. And that is all that is possible in this imperfect world.

In conclusion, I apologize if these opening remarks have seemed confusing or mystifying. As Plutarch has said: 'What lies beyond is full of marvels and unrealities...' For those wishing to undertake the journey from darkness to light, application forms have been left on the table.

The lecturer packs up his notes).

---

Plato, *Greater Hippias*, trans. B. Jowett, Oxford, 1953, p. 282a.

## 2. Minotaur-Asterion

Suddenly there is darkness. Then slowly, in a dull spotlight, the contours of a head appear. Who can say what it looks like? There is nothing frightening in its demeanour. No mask. A neutral face, mature, sexless, but strange, owing to the protuberance of three small horns on the brow.

ASTERION:  One of us is a phantom. We do not both exist. For us both to exist, there would have to be two worlds, yours and mine , which is unacceptable. Let us say we are merely embodiments of one another on different planes, giving us each an illusion of independence. In reality we are the same. Hearing together, seeing together, moving together, knowing together.

All your life you have feared facing me. Suddenly I am here, your deliverer. Would you kill me then? Cut me in half and I am two: Minotaur and Asterion. But the killer and the killed are one. and the knife that kills is also that which is killed.

Minotaur. Asterion. Darkness. Light. Two forces united in one deity. To know the light you must seek the darkness; for a known god is no god. I am the light in the darkness. I am the darkness in the light. Neither is vanquished by force; only by acceptance and submission.

The death of the god is also the birth of god. And know this also: there are no gods on earth if you are not yourself a god.

I am the thought you are thinking. If you would know yourself, die before you die; dare to enter the darkness before you and within you. Trace the labyrinth of your days.

I will be with you even unto death, pouring light into your life until the great extinguisher fractures your spirit and sends it hurtling throughout the universe.

The figure withdraws. Eventually the light returns. Those who wish may pick up copies of the application form for a visit to the labyrinth, mentioned by the professor.

The person at the back of the hall picks up a copy and departs.

## 3. *Application*

Name _____

Address _____

Telephone _____

Date of birth _____

Sex _____

Education _____

_____

Religious affiliation _____

Allergies or medical problems _____

_____

Answer the following questions in as much detail as possible.

1. Why do I wish to experience Asterion?
2. What do I bring to offer to the experience?
3. What does fear mean to me?
4. What does courage mean to me?
5. What does pain mean to me? What are its positive
   and what are its negative qualities?
6. What am I prepared to sacrifice in my life?
7. How does the thought of death affect my life?

The questions are answered, and the application is mailed to an address provided.

## 4. *The Meeting*

Those whose applications are accepted (which does not mean everyone) are informed by return mail. A date, time and meeting place are given. Applicants are also provided with a general outline of what to expect and how to prepare themselves.

At the appointed time the participants are met, blindfolded and transported to the site of the labyrinth, the exact location of which they should never know. When they arrive there the blindfold is removed, and also their shoes. Perhaps there is also an appropriate change of clothing. The entrance is indicated without speech and each neophyte enters the labyrinth alone.

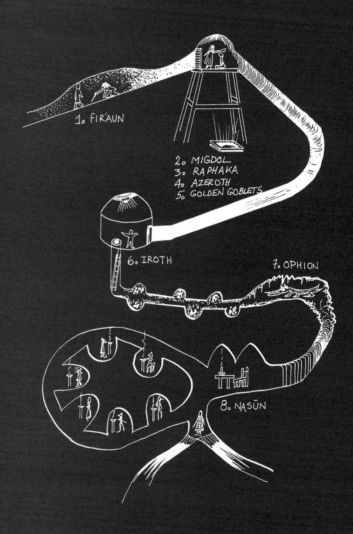

# Patria 8:
## The Palace of the Cinnabar Phoenix

*Composed*: 1999-2000, Indian River, Ontario.

*Cast*: Actor, 5 singers, choir (SSAA), puppets, t'ai chi quartet, archers, dragons and waterbirds (swimmers).

*Orchestra*: Erhu, pipa (Zheng), violin, viola, cello, flute (piccolo, exotic flutes), clarinet (bass clarinet), trumpet (Flügelhorn), trombone, accordion (Sheng), 2 percussionists.

*Duration*: 2 hours

*First Performance*: Wolverton Hills, Ontario, September 2001.

THE CHALLENGE OF *Asterion* may be beyond human endurance. Certainly this is the most intense experience of the entire *Patria* cycle – the confrontation with the Self. To follow this I wanted to create a series of fabulous worlds where everything resonates with the miraculous. We have come out on the other side of ourselves and can understand the languages of birds and animals, fairies and magicians. Like children, we take them seriously. The simplicity of the next three works contrasts vividly with the complexity of much that came before.

The first of these, *The Palace of the Cinnabar Phoenix*, was actually the last to be composed. Many years ago I had a dream in which I saw a miraculous castle slowly rising out of a lake. It was multi-coloured, and seemed to be vibrating as it hovered above the water. That was all. Later, I connected this dream with my desire to send Wolf (in some form or other) to the Orient to seek enlightenment, just as I have frequently sought it myself in Oriental art and philosophy. I imagined a lake or a large pond at night with a castle of Chinese lanterns in the centre. Let the light that knows no glare illuminate and transform us.

Later, in 1988, I gave the projected work a name, *The Floating Kingdom of Wei Lu*, and attempted to find a group of people interested in developing it for presentation on Little Lake in Peterborough. But it was premature. Over the years, however, I continued to fashion the text. An unexpected incentive came from the well-known sinologist Edward H. Schafer, who wrote me from the University of California wondering whether we might be distantly related. He had heard a concert of my choral music and sent some of his publications as a gift. In the communications that followed I was able to refine the text of what I was now to call *The Palace of the Cinnabar Phoenix*, clearing it of at least the worst social and historical blunders. For instance, the word 'phoenix' is a misnomer. The Chinese word is *feng*. It was a magic bird that ruled the southern quarter of the sky just as the dragon did the east. But 'phoenix' sounds better than 'bird,' and my new-found cousin agreed, so I let it stand. Cinnabar is a red sulphide of mercury and was virtually sacred to the Taoists of ancient China. It yielded the pigment vermilion, the colour of life and blood and eternity. It was applied to all sorts of holy objects and was also used as a drug in the treatment of serious diseases.[1] The Cinnabar Phoenix (or Vermilion Bird) was the south-facing gate of the Great Luminous Palace at Ch'ang-an during the T'ang Dynasty (A.D. 618-907). So I decided to position my story in the time of T'ang. The story is original, but I checked it out with my 'cousin' to ensure that it was not too wildly anachronous or implausible.

Long ago, the gods placed a palace on earth as a symbol of celestial harmony and sent down a phoenix to live in it. But when the Warring States attempted to capture the palace and imprison the phoenix, both vanished and were replaced by a Lake of Dragons. Each year the Emperor Wei Lu comes to the site to mourn the disappearance of the palace and the sacred bird. The evening opens with the arrival of the court in the Pagoda Boat. As the aging Emperor surveys the Lake, his son Wei Li chases women. According to his philosophy, women are *yin*, and *yin* is rain, and since China is experiencing a drought, the more women he seduces the greater the chance of rain – so he takes a new one every night. The Prime Minister is his procurer, much against his will, since the women are costing the court a great deal of jade and silver.

The Philosophers of the Right and Left engage in a debate on the merits of *yin* versus *yang*. Lavish cascades of trashy music accompany preparations for the debate; the Philosopher of the Right can only philosophize when opulently dressed, while the Philosopher of the Left can only philosophize when completely naked. When the debate becomes absurd, the Emperor interrupts it:

---

1    Edward H. Schafer, *The Vermilion Bird*, University of California Press, 1967, 156-57.

The honourable philosophers argue with words. But words are not the best means for expressing harmony and equilibrium. Music is a better means, and in the motions of t'ai chi ch'uan balance can also be suggested.

A quartet of t'ai chi performers entertains the Emperor, accompanied by Schafer's Sixth String Quartet (Parting Wild Horse's Mane),[2] when an alchemist unexpectedly appears.

> I was quietly working at the forge
> when I heard a flock of cockatoos.
> That's not cockatoos, I thought,
> that's Schafer's music at the court of T'ang!

The Alchemist is followed by his daughter whose face has been disfigured by an accident at the athanor. In describing his work, there is a hint that he may have discovered gold, though when asked directly by the Prime Minister he gives evasive answers. The Prime Minister orders a torture machine to be brought in to pull his ears, which are already long and red from previous applications. His daughter, Shen Nü, begs the court to show mercy, explaining that the gold is not ordinary gold but is intended to restore harmony to the world. The Emperor asks if he may see this gold, and the Alchemist, clapping his hands, produces a golden ring in mid-air. The Emperor takes it and sings for the Lake of Dragons to be dried up and the Palace to be restored. Nothing happens. The gold is powerless. Not powerless, says the Alchemist, but incomplete. 'To be efficient the ring must meet its silver mate.' 'What price for the silver mate?' 'No price, for it is missing.' In despair Wei Lu throws the ring into the lake. Immediately the lake is full of dragons laughing and mocking the Court of T'ang. End of act 1.

As *The Palace of the Cinnabar Phoenix* begins at twilight, it is now dark. The Court Censor brings a lantern to the Emperor, who sits alone and disconsolate. They converse about the difficulties of ruling well, citing the wise proverbs of Confucius. In the distance a pale blue light appears and seems to be moving across the water. A voice is heard chanting. The court is assembled and is astonished when a Blue Man steps ashore. The Blue Man confesses he doesn't know why he has come, only that a silver ring he

---

2   The structure of this quartet parallels the movements of t'ai chi.

found deep in a cave in his native land has drawn him to the Court of the Emperor of China. Now it seems to want to rest, and hovers in the air before the Emperor.



Wei Lu: 'This seems like a miracle. Who can explain it?' 'I can,' proclaims Shen Nü, who now confesses how, fearing that the gold and silver rings might be used for evil purposes, she resolved to rob them of their power by separating them; she swam, like Melusina, 'to a land where water turns to stone,' and there buried the silver ring. The Emperor: 'Woman, the ring belongs to you. Do with it as you please.' Shen Nü approaches the silver ring. As she does, the scales fall from her face.

> Fair, fair, O she is fair,
> this girl of the silver ring,
> lovely the woman of water,
> bride for a king.

Shen Nü takes the ring and throws it into the lake.

The Grand Astrologer announces that the stars have reached the right configuration for celebrating the Feast of Celestial Harmony, in which both the court and the audience will partake.

As the feast draws to a close, the longed-for miracle occurs. We recall from *Patria 4* that if the alchemist succeeds in producing gold and silver and blends them together, the *filius sapientiae* will appear. The encircling of the gold and silver rings in the Lake of Dragons is about to produce a similar miracle to the appearance of the Divine Child in *Patria 4*. The lake begins to glow and slowly the Palace and the Phoenix rise up from its depths, the Phoenix singing –

> I am the source of all inspiration,
> of intelligence and understanding,
> of becoming, being and departure,
> mortality and immortality.
>
> I am the secret of permanence and motion,
> of change and equilibrium,
> of destruction and creation,
> the potency of life.

*Patria 8: The Palace of the Cinnabar Phoenix*, as performed at Wolverton Hills, Ontario, September 2001. Stage design: Jerrard Smith; puppets by Puppetmongers.

Wei Li steps forward to ask the Emperor for his permission to marry the courageous Shen Nü. But the Emperor has turned to stone. The gates of the Palace open and Illuminated Water Birds move forward to gather his soul for eternal life in the Palace. The gates close and slowly the lights flicker to darkness as the Phoenix sings:

> changing, unchanging,
> passing, returning,
> presence eternal...

My original plan for *Patria 8* called for enormous forces. How could one present one of the great eras of China with anything less? But even with a substantial millennium grant from the Canadian government and a mounting interest in *chinoiserie* in Canada, the budget we drew up seemed totally unattainable. So I went in the opposite direction. The exotic grandeur of T'ang would be presented as puppet theatre. All history is to some extent miniaturized, but this change of scale can also transform a grand court into a fabulous one. All fairy tales are small scale. A pond would do for the Lake of Dragons, and I would put real swimmers in it. Contrasted with the puppet court would be the Blue Man, a giant from another world. The t'ai chi performers would also be live, but placed in the distance to diminish their size.

How would the audience take all this? I wondered one night while eating in Peter's Chung King restaurant in Toronto's Chinatown. An interpreter would be helpful. Well, why not Peter Chung King himself?

You will find the customs here
a little strange and artificial.
I must confess that I do too,
that's why I came to Canada
and open restaurant on College Street.

But I remember the tradition
from life on other side of ocean.
So if you don't know what to do,
watch Peter Chung King and I show you.

So Peter Chung King would be our master of ceremonies for the evening. Although performed outdoors, like several other *Patria* pieces, *The Palace of the Cinnabar Phoenix* calls for a traditionally seated audience. But I wanted them to engage in some form of participation, and so each time the Emperor speaks I would have Peter Chung King call the audience to its feet to repeat: 'The Son of Heaven has spoken.' And during the Feast of Celestial Harmony the audience would eat three or four Chinese delicacies in ritual order, with each bite orchestrated by Chinese music. These little "correspondences" would lighten the formality of the evening.

According to an ancient tradition, Chinese law was delivered to the world in the form of the following diagram, brought up out of a river in the mouth of a dragon-horse.

The correspondence between seasons, colours and materials could be illustrated by the performers in an introductory procession. The South group could be dressed in red or could carry red cloud-banners and could be accompanied by fiery instruments such as *cheng-cheng* or cymbals. The East group could enter dressed in green or carry green cloud-banners and be accompanied by wood blocks or claves. The North group could be dressed in black or carry black cloud-banners and be accompanied by water-phones. And the West group could be dressed in white or carry white cloud-banners and be accompanied by temple bells or crotales. Certainly there must be formality in a work set in the ancient court of

China – in the arrangement and motions of the characters, in the colours and shapes of their clothing, in their manner of speech. It is said that in ancient China the Emperor faced away from the other members of the court to emphasize his superiority. It is also said that the upper members of the court had their own manner of speech. We know that in ancient China certain poets sought to arrange their poems with a balanced number of inflections (up, down, level) in order to emphasize the equilibrium of all things in a well-governed state.[3] The theme of *Patria 8* is the secret of balance as expressed in Confucian philosophy. It is the essence of all the Emperor's speeches and actions. Accordingly, in the melodic line of his singing, the number of ascending, descending and level or oscillating phonemes is equally distributed, and I believe one can sense this in his various declarations.

The voices of all the puppet characters are impersonated by four solo singers: soprano, alto, tenor, baritone. The Blue Man is a bass. For the voice of the Phoenix, I decided on a children's choir, hidden from view on the other side of the pond. This replaced an earlier plan for an adult choir with a soprano and tenor soloist – much too ostentatious. The text sung by the Phoenix at the end of the work comes from the Upanishads, the Bhagavad Gita, and I know not where. I've always been intrigued by the idea of having children sing texts of profound wisdom, not that they possess wisdom – they don't – but because, if by some miracle, they did, the world would truly be a better place.

---

3  In music also, *p'ing*, or level, unmodulating pitch, with its attributes of smoothness and repose, was said to evoke *yin*, while *tsê*, oblique movement with its attributes of activity and aggression, was said to evoke *yang*. A piece of classical Chinese music could be analysed in terms of its steady and active moments. John Hazedel Levis does this for a number of compositions in his *Foundations of Chinese Musical Art*, Henri Vetch, Peiping, 1936.

PATRIA 9:

THE ENCHANTED FOREST

R. Murray Schafer

# Patria 9:
## *The Enchanted Forest*

*Composed:* 1993, Indian River, Ontario

*Cast:* Solo soprano, mezzo-soprano, tenor and bass, 3 baritones, 9 actors, girls' choir, children's choir, about 20 dancers and movers

*Orchestra:* 2 flutes, 2 clarinets, several recorders and penny whistles, 2 French horns, 4 trombones, 4 tubas, 4 didgeridoos, guitar, 10-16 drummers

*Duration:* Two hours

*First Performance:* Winslow Farm, Millbrook, Ontario, September 15, 1994

A Canadian settler hates a tree....
MRS. JAMESON, *Winter Studies and Summer Rambles in Canada,* 1838

THE THEME OF *The Enchanted Forest* is nature, and its ideal is that the human beings participating in it as performers or audience may discover bonds with the natural environment they had not sensed before or had forgotten. While the environment is a topical problem and has even begun to concern some artists, it seems strange that many of the expressions of concern take forms contradictory to the cause; like photographs of vanishing animals on glossy paper torn from their forest homes.

*The Enchanted Forest* is intended for performance in a forest, or more correctly, in a forested area adjacent to a meadow or fields. In writing the text I was not imagining an abstract territory, but one that begins at my study window and across which some of the animals and birds described in the text can at times be seen or heard. The scene begins with a sloping hill; beneath it lie two broad hayfields, separated by a wide ditch, occasionally containing water. At times I have seen deer grazing in these fields, and foxes, coyotes and the occasional wolf will cross them too. At the extreme end of the second field, about a quarter mile from my window, there is a wall of evergreen trees. Moving through these, one enters a third field, unploughed for perhaps ten years, covered with wild flowers and quickly growing in with small cedar trees. There is a beaver pond at the side of this field and one crosses it by the beaver dam to arrive in a glade of evergreens leading back to a more open area with a hill on the right and a small but beautiful forest of mature maple and beech trees on the left. In the top of one of the trees is the capacious nest of a pair of hawks. I mention this landscape only to show that much of what follows could take place in this setting and actually occurred to me as I have walked through or sat observing and listening to it.[1]

*The Enchanted Forest* begins at sunset. The audience arrives at the edge of the forest where they observe Earth Mother, surrounded by Flower Spirits (dancers). Their evening reverie is interrupted by a group of Children coming out of the forest, lamenting that one of their number, Ariane, has become lost. Earth Mother explains that 'everything lost exists to be found again' and sends the Flower Spirits with the Children to try to find Ariane, requesting the audience to accompany and protect them.

All enter the forest and the first scene they witness is the death of the White Stag, who has evidently been shot. The Still Earth Spirits arrive to cover him with branches and carry off his soul to the Great Gate of Light. Passing into a meadow, we are confronted by Marsh Hawk, who declares that he has carried off Ariane on orders from Murdeth the Wizard 'for one of his experiments,' but refuses to say anything more.[2]

Passing deeper into the forest, the Children meet Stump, a head poking out of a real tree stump, who explains that Murdeth's agents cut him down. Murdeth intends to cut down the entire forest and sell it to builders and developers. The only impediment to his plan is Fenris the Wolf[3] who is fighting to keep the forest as a wilderness habitat. Stump gives the Children a magic branch to light the path, for by now it is quite dark. The branch leads us to the sleepers, a group of singers and instrumentalists hidden along the sides of the path, who warn us that we are entering the territory of Murdeth. Our intrusion is signalled ahead by a group of xylophones playing in Morse code. The magic branch draws us forward to the centre of the forest where we discover Murdeth, surrounded by fire pots,

---

1   The idea of a work celebrating the forest seems to have first occurred to me in 1973. In a diary entry, dated June 10, I read: "Idea for a work to be entitled The Enchanted Forest to be performed outdoors in a forest at night in which a magician-musician creates an enchantment to protect the trees and prevent their being cut down."
2   In an early draft of the text Murdeth was called Odin, after the Norse god. Later I changed it to Murdeth (murderer?), which is more appropriate for the role he was ultimately to play; but his assistant, Mimir, as well as his missing eye and the two prophetic ravens who advise him, are relics of the earlier version.
3   In Norse mythology Odin attempted to chain Fenris the Wolf unsuccessfully. He broke all chains and brought about the destruction of the world by devouring the sun. In the Epilogue to *Patria* Wolf is redeemed and will inherit the moon.

logging equipment, drummers and four tuba players in business suits and dark glasses, playing the 'Loggers' and Developers' Riff.' Murdeth orders us to leave the forest, but the Children insist they have come to find out what has happened to Ariane. Murdeth calls on Mimir ('Eye of night, my second sight'), who sees everything that happens in the forest. Mimir appears in a tree and scans the horizon with his ominous red eye, then reports back: 'Master, I see her. She is alive and well.' The Children demand to know more and Murdeth placates them by asking the two ravens, Anvir and Emor, to provide some details. Anvir sees into the future and Emor sees into the past, but the birds only scream cryptic messages we cannot understand, which Murdeth interprets to mean that Ariane intends to remain in the forest 'where all the birds and animals will come to love her.' He then orders us again to leave, throwing something into the fire that sparks up as Fireflies.

The Fireflies conduct us away and eventually we come to the hut of an old woman who calls herself Hatempka. Hatempka knows everything that goes on in the Enchanted Forest and tells us that Murdeth plans to use Ariane as a hostage to trap Fenris the Wolf in a grove of birch trees, where he will kill him with the Arrow of Thunderstone. The Children implore her to help them to free both Ariane and Fenris, and Hatempka agrees to take them to the home of Shapeshifter, a strange three-horned caterpillar who lives at the bottom of a deserted well, the only creature in the forest with

Ray Crossman as Fenris the Wolf in *Patria 9: The Enchanted Forest*, Fourth Line Theatre, Millbrook, Ontario, September, 1994.

magic strong enough to thwart Murdeth's plan. Although she appears sinister, Shapeshifter listens to the Children's plea, then, transforming herself into a moth, she flies off to the birch grove where Ariane is being held captive, while the Children and audience are made invisible by jewel stones from Hatempka's medicine bundle so that Mimir won't see them. They then sneak into the grove where they see Ariane, flanked by the Still Earth Spirits.

Fenris arrives singing a war chant, but the sight of Ariane incarnate in the birch tree melts his heart and he goes to sleep beneath the tree. This is Murdeth's cue to light the Arrow of Thunderstone, but Shapeshifter flies about him, ruining his aim, so that the arrow explodes. Fenris escapes and Murdeth limps away, tangled in the chains of his two ravens. But Shapeshifter has used up all her magic powers. Ariane has been transformed into a birch tree and no one can bring her back.

The White Stag now appears reborn and leads us to the Circle of Life, where Earth Mother welcomes us back and explains that because we have left our soul in the Enchanted Forest in the form of Ariane, we must never allow the forest to be cut down. The work ends with a candlelight procession back to the meadow from which we began.

Everyone knows that fairy tales have always been the receptacle for moral wisdom. *The Enchanted Forest* belongs to this genre and its message is ecological. It contradicts the arrogance that humans are God's supreme invention. It substitutes the notion that everything is equal, interdependent and in a constant state of transformation. Shapeshifter's metamorphosis exemplifies this; White Stag's rebirth is another instance, as is Ariane's transfiguration into a birch tree.[4]

Transfiguration is a theme that grows stronger in the later *Patria* works. In *Patria 10: The Spirit Garden*, Ariane reappears as the Spring Child of the renascent garden metamorphosing into the Corn Goddess of autumn, then assumes human shape in the Epilogue, *And Wolf Shall Inherit the Moon*, before her divinity is restored and she returns to the heavens, from which she fell at the beginning of the cycle. It is also in the Epilogue that Wolf discovers the anima within himself, and inherits the moon, a symbol normally designated as feminine.

---

4  Even Ariane's name is a mutant form of Ariadne, just as previously we had metathesis in La Testa d'Adriane (*Patria 3*). These are like wardrobe changes, necessitated by varying social situations, through which the same characters pass in the different *Patria* works, though as archetypes they remain constant. But Adrienne the hairdresser, also in *Patria 3*, is a corruption intended only for the gaping multitudes that the show seeks to attract.

## Community

Obviously, the territory where *The Enchanted Forest* is played is as important as the selection of performers. There are a lot of places in the world where performances *will never take place*. Civic parks will not do, no matter how large. The work needs quiet and rather wild countryside.[5] Each scene requires its own special site, sheltered or open, on a hill or in a ravine. Entrances will be from grottos or groves, across streams or down rock faces. Once the sites have been chosen, paths will have to be cut to connect them. Then secondary trails will have to be cut so that performers and stage crew can move to their positions undetected by the audience. Any production of *The Enchanted Forest* will take a great deal of on-site organization by people who know the territory. For the first production, we chose Rob Winslow's one-hundred-acre farm, more or less central to four towns (Port Hope, Peterborough, Cobourg and Campbellford), from which our performers and crew were drawn.

Like many of my other works, *The Enchanted Forest* is intended to unite the talents of both professionals and amateurs, adults and young people. Children are at the centre of *The Enchanted Forest*. And I wanted them to sing because nothing is so enchanting as the voices of children singing. The younger children would accompany the audience through the performance, and the older would be the Still Earth Spirits and would also accompany Ariane in her final aria.

The program lists 115 members in the cast, including child dancers as Flower Spirits and Fireflies, with young musicians playing penny whistles (in imitation of bird calls), drums and didgeridoos. The rest of the cast was made up of adult performers, including several members of the Wolf Project, who knew the theme well since in many ways it prefigures *And Wolf Shall Inherit the Moon*. The program also lists about sixty helpers behind the scenes, most of whom volunteered their talents and time.

A word needs to be said about the relationship between the Children and the audience. The Children lead the audience through the experience, but also need their companionship and protection. The small hand of a child in yours is an irresistible invitation to enter a world of fantasy, so we encouraged the Children to speak and sing directly to individual audience members and to take their hands between scenes.

5   I am reminded here that when asked what stopped the Saracen invasion of France in the Middle Ages, André Malraux answered with one word: 'Trees.' Desert warriors didn't know how to fight in the forest. The same could be said for urban 'warriors' today, but their anxiety could be used to advantage in the production.

To a certain extent, the audience participates in the performance merely by walking from scene to scene. But I also gave them a modest role to play: at one point the Children teach them a song which they sing together; later Hatempka teaches them how to roar and howl in order to help Shapeshifter abort the Arrow of Thunderstone.[6] A thesis or two could be written on the various levels and types of audience participation in *Patria* works. That required for *The Enchanted Forest* is modest; nothing has to be learned in advance and no one is made to stand out self-consciously.

I will not dwell on the desirability of works like this in improving the cultural life of smaller communities. They have suffered the drain of talent to the big cities for over a century now and desperately need to be reinvested with cultural enterprises that help reverse this trend. We live in a centre-margin society, where culture products are manufactured in the centres and the rest of the country is expected to suck them up like a ditch sucks water.

Entertainment imperialism has been made possible by electricity and plastic. That every village or gas station in the country has a video outlet pumping foreign films is a disgrace desperately needing rivalry in every way possible. In this sense, *The Enchanted Forest* is civil defence against media fallout.

By candlelight, the newborn White Stag kneels before Earth Mother at the conclusion of *Patria 9: The Enchanted Forest*, 1994 production.

---

6   This is similar to the chanting of the magic names of Apophis in *Patria 6: Ra* (editing unit 18). To know the secret names of your enemy can be a weapon in his defeat. In the present case, however, the roaring and howling is merely a supplementary noise, adding confusion to the scene.

## Forest

Today we are used to having our interests in forest devastation deflected to distant places. Everyone in Canada knows about the destruction of the Amazon rain forests. But to cross Canada by air is a more painful experi- ence. Northern Ontario and Québec appear (anno 1998) to be about eighty per cent denuded. Everywhere are the worm lines of logging tracks.

Passengers in the aircraft assuage whatever concerns they may feel for what they see beneath them by watching the movie. We are even asked to lower the window shades to improve the viewing. One's pride of country reaches its nadir at this altitude. Every day our leaders preach loyalty to our country, to its institutions, to its ideals, to its flag. But to its forests? We claw at them. We mutilate them. We murder them. And I think: as the forests of the world decrease, wisdom will decline, because it seems to me that wisdom consists of remaining still while foolishness is rushing about.

When you wound the earth you wound yourself. When others wound the earth they wound you. The only way to revoke the staggering destruction taking place today is to remythologize the land. This is what I tried to do in *The Princess of the Stars*. If the Princess is imprisoned at the bottom of a known lake, you won't pollute that lake. If Ariane is transformed into a tree numen in a known forest, who would wish to cut that forest down?

## Music

In a footnote to a youthful poem of Edgar Allan Poe's entitled *Al Aaraaf*, the following line is found:

> The verie essence and, as it were, springe-heade and origine of all musiche is the verie pleasaunte sounde which the trees of the forest do make when they growe.

Poe says he found it in an old English tale but forgot the source. It is a phrase I have often recalled while writing music, but for no other work is it a more appropriate motto.

Most of the music for *The Enchanted Forest* was sketched during a three-week period in June and July 1993. It is simpler and more tuneful than any of the other *Patria* works, with a couple of borrowings from the Elizabethan period. The all-interval *Patria* tone row is present only tangentially. In composing the music, I tried to find a medium that would not thwart the avowed purpose of creating a fairy tale with a simple moral.

Some critics declared the music was derivative. They missed the point. I have said it before, but since no one listened, I'll say it again: the great revolutions in art history are not changes of style, but changes of context. Had the antecedents mentioned by the critics (Wagner, Debussy, Gustav Holst[!]) ever conceived anything for a moving audience out-of-doors, I might have learned something from them. As it is, any imaginative somersaults the score possesses are *not in the notes*, but in the territorial disposition and groupings of the singers and instrumentalists in order to achieve grades of *depth*, from the very near all the way back to an acoustic horizon of such ineffable identity that the listener may not be sure whether real sound is present at all, or only a presentiment of it.[7]

The forest is always an acoustic environment because it discriminates against vision, and forest dwellers cultivated clairaudience to an extent no longer known today. The medieval Schoolmen inherited something of this aural awareness when they defined God as 'an intelligible sphere whose centre is everywhere and whose circumference is nowhere,'[8] for this is equally a definition of an acoustic universe, as McLuhan realized when he used the quotation to invoke the aural world that preceded the world of print and, he believed, would replace it again.

A clairaudient listener knows how to listen at all depths and distances. In the crowded life of the city, distant listening is no longer possible and the skill is lost. It is totally absent from the concert hall and recording studio, and contemporary listeners have forgotten how sound can be 'sweetened by distance' or can become unfocused by the drift of air currents or the blur of rain. Their CD players don't produce this kind of impressionism. But such sound is central to *The Enchanted Forest*, right from the opening scene where flutes and clarinets, concealed from the audience at varying distances up to several hundred metres and over a wide area, imitate bird calls at dusk, like them, gradually modulating to stillness.

The Children call Ariane's name and it is echoed three times from different places in the gathering dusk. Ariane replies from the heart of the forest. One night, perhaps, her voice is crystal clear, another night it is only partially present. If the singers knew how to read the environment, they

---

7    One critic, Robert Everett-Green, got the point: 'In one early scene in an open area, he spreads his concealed musicians around so that their twittering pipes sound from close-up and also from places so remote, you have to strain to hear them. In two later scenes, the shouts of Murdeth and his minions echo off the hills with astonishing force.' *The Globe and Mail*, September 26, 1994, p.C4.

8    Cf. St. Bonaventure, *Itinerarium mentis in Deum* (The Soul's Journey into God), Paulist Press, New York, 1978, p.100.

would be able to position themselves to take advantage of wind currents, rather than waiting for the director to tell them where to stand. I am convinced that outdoor performers of the past knew these secrets; performers of environmental music dramas today need to relearn them. Reflection and refraction might also play a role in achieving the desired effect. There is no point in always facing an audience who cannot see you.

Let me speak a moment about what I call *phantom sounds* – sounds that seem to linger after the singer or instrumentalist has performed them so that it is impossible for the listener to decide whether they are present in reality or only in the imagination. Of course, the phenomenon only works in places of great stillness. You won't find phantom sounds in New York or Paris, but Canadian mythology is full of them. The Qu'Appelle Valley in Saskatchewan harbours one such myth. An Indian brave, paddling up the river, thinks he hears his beloved calling his name. 'Who calls?' he cries, 'Qu'appelle?' The voice is heard again. 'Katapaywie sepe? Who calls?' he cries again. When he reaches the camp, the girl is dead. Lake Minnewanka in the Rocky Mountains means 'Water of the Spirits,' because the spirits of ghosts are heard there. Often in the Wolf Project, after the nocturne across a deserted lake, I have heard the music lingering moments or hours after I know the performer has ceased. You won't find any discussion of phantom sounds in music theory books; they were all written in cities, but Jean-Jacques Rousseau, who used to take long solitary walks in the countryside, probably heard them. 'Il faut que la musique se rapproche de la nature,' he wrote in his *Lettre sur la musique française*. Canada is probably one of the few countries left in the world where human music can carry over imperceptibly into the breathing of nature; and there are places in *The Enchanted Forest* where this could and should be allowed to happen.

## Weather

Ideally, environmental works should only be performed on halcyon days, but we live in an imperfect world, where natural works such as *The Enchanted Forest* are forced to respect an agenda set by producers, patrons, unions, and other votaries of mercantile entertainments. Like *Princess of the Stars*, *The Enchanted Forest* is timed to the sun. When Earth Mother says, 'Look, the sun is setting,' it *is* setting; or, if hidden behind clouds, she will change the line. By the time we reach the glen where the White Stag dies, the light is very murky and it will be dark when we reach Murdeth. Changing weather conditions made every night a première, and the audience picked up on it. 'I couldn't believe it when the Wolf howled at the moon and the moon suddenly emerged from behind the clouds,' said one audience member. We resolved to run the show rain or shine and managed to do so without cancellation. Everyone became a weather fore-

caster, reading the sky and wind shifts with astute interest. I think by the end of the month, people were just beginning to trust their senses more than the radio weather reports. It was a new kind of sensation and a healthy one.

For years I have wondered why society continues to employ meteorologists and provide them with vast amounts of public money when their predictions are so often wrong. What other worker or entrepreneur could afford to be wrong 50 percent or even 20 percent of the time and still hold a job or sustain a business? Yet here is a massive and unquestioned subsidization of an activity serving.....whom? I am asking a serious question.

So far as I can tell, the only people who might benefit from advance information about the weather are fishermen and the captains of ships and aircraft in storm-prone areas of the world. A few lives might thereby be saved. But what does our history and mythology consist of if not exciting and unpredicted natural disasters and miracles that changed things? If Odysseus had not been blown off course – no *Odyssey*. Without a storm, Aeneas would never have met Dido, and Jonah would never have become a prophet. Snowstorms, windstorms, fog, floods, drought – the military annals are full of them; and artists, poets and musicians have captured them in thrilling and memorable representations.

Myth-makers have never feared natural catastrophes. They are the vibrations that give life new meaning. If forecasters could *change* the weather, there might be a serious point to funding them. That is what our ancestors tried to do when they danced and drummed the rain chant. As nature's creatures, they *believed they had the power* to influence environmental changes. If you set your goal at creating a storm or ensuring a sunrise, you may have a chance of achieving it. If your goal is merely to take a lot of wind and temperature readings, then joggle them together in a computer and cough up a pattern, that is all you get. I've argued this matter with intelligent people and they laugh at me. But what a colossal waste of money. If I had the influence, I'd divert a good chunk of the public purse into a celebration of nature's surprises instead of wasting it on flummy forecasting. While we were performing *The Enchanted Forest*, facing the elements, forecasters were zapping away imprecisely at their computers and satellites to tell us whether we'd be able to perform it or not.

Item: In 1994-95, the federal government appropriation for meteorological and hydrological warning systems was 151 million dollars with another 98 million to operate related services. Item: If you call the Environment Canada weather office in Peterborough, your weather report will be preluded by an ad from Dominique's Pizza – 'this week's special, a meatza-pizza feast for $10.95.' Item: In 1994-95, the federal government appropriation to the Canada Council for Canadian cultural enterprises was 98 million dollars. Item: From the Canada Council we received zero dollars to assist in the presentation of *The Enchanted Forest*. Dominique's Pizza made no contribution either.

## The Media

Another serious question: sooner or later it is bound to be asked, Are you videotaping or filming *The Enchanted Forest*? People who ask such questions – and they do daily, hourly – can't see the contradiction. Even those who can appreciate it still hope the work will be preserved for future viewing. It seems that works only achieve veracity when cast into such a medium. Such is the success of the media *douche*. But can't you understand that *The Enchanted Forest* is conceived the way it is in order to be independent of the microphone and camera? The only time I fought with the producers and participants of the production was when a national TV program wanted to shoot the show for a news documentary. I was astounded at the craving people had for media attention, even when it served no purpose. The entire series of eight performances was sold out weeks in advance. We didn't need the media to sell tickets. We didn't need them to inform a public who would never be able to attend a performance of what they were missing, and couldn't in any way be replaced by their interventions.

I can see some of the *Patria* works in film form as an extension of their life on stage – I say *extension*, not *replacement*. *Patria 1: Wolfman* and *Patria 2: Requiems for the Party Girl* are containable within the camera frame and might even gain in intensity with closeups of the protagonists and their tormentors. I permitted a film company to make a film of *Patria 3: The Greatest Show*. As the whole work is full of brouhaha, it didn't seem inappropriate that film people should be there pushing other people out of the way to add to the cynicism. I only regretted that they made such a bad film, rescripting the text to 'clarify' what they considered incoherent mystification. I refused them the right to call their work *The Greatest Show*, so they retitled it *Carnival of Shadows*, and sold it to European television, from which I received no royalties. One day in a book shop in England, I happened to see a new encyclopedia of music where, under my own name, I was informed that Schafer is the author of a number of music dramas of which the best known is *Carnival of Shadows*.

This is media's biggest accomplishment: to spread misinformation, prejudice and hypocrisy throughout the world. Voltaire once said of academics that they serve only the dead and themselves. When it comes to the media, subtract the dead. One Gawd-awful image, repeated almost daily, ought to haunt the TV viewer: that of the smartly dressed, well-fed and perky TV *vedette* before a multitude of crippled, paralysed or starving human beings, spouting about their plight without offering a single hint as to what should be done about it.

The real question is: Who precisely do the media serve? Who are their masters and mistresses? What do they or does anyone think is the purpose of their mission? The German philosopher, Peter Sloterdijk[9] asks this question and quotes Kafka's parable about the king and the couriers to try to pull it into focus:

> They were offered the choice between becoming kings or the couriers of kings. The way children would, they all wanted to be couriers. Therefore, there are only couriers who hurry about the world, shouting to each other – since there are no kings – messages that have become meaningless. They would like to put an end to this miserable life of theirs, but they dare not because of their oaths of service.

I would also like to put an end to this miserable life of theirs. *The Enchanted Forest* is such an attempt. It is addressed to a community and its message is simple. Those who understand it could become kings and queens in their own area of the planet, rendering it healthier and richer for everyone who lives there.

---

9   In "Das soziale Band und die Audiophonie: Anmerkungen zur Anthropologie im digitalen Zeitalter," manuscript text for the German radio (1994).

# Patria 10:
## *The Spirit Garden*

*Composed*: Spring Section 1995-96; Harvest Section 1997; Strasbourg, France; Indian River, Ontario.

*Cast*: About 150 actors, singers, dancers, musicians and gardeners; children's choir and mixed choir.

*Duration*: Spring Section 1 1/2 hours; Harvest Section 40 minutes, followed by banquet.

THE ORIGINAL PLAN for *The Spirit Garden* came to me in a dream in 1985, the night of my arrival in Banff to begin work on a production of *The Princess of the Stars*. This is what I wrote in my diary:

> A ritual in which a garden is prepared and planted. The participants arrive at the designated place and together they dig up a garden plot, breaking up the soil and removing the weeds. As they work they accompany themselves with a slow, rhythmic chant. The planters arrive, richly costumed and accompanied with joyful music. I imagine each dressed like the vegetable or fruit he or she will be planting, somewhat like the Hopi Kachina dolls. There is a special dance and a special kind of music for the planting of each type of seed. Then the planters water the soil, singing a special watering song. Birds (dancers) arrive and try to peck at the seeds but they are frightened off by a shaman with a bull roarer. A scarecrow is erected to protect the garden, but he is more of a vegetable spirit than a mere scarecrow – more like Adonis or Dumuzi, and his costume is beautifully designed and has been previously stitched together by the participants themselves. The work closes with songs to the sun and the rain to make the seeds grow and the garden prosper.

I had been looking for some time for a simple activity I could infuse with special values in the way the Japanese have invested so much significance in the drinking of a cup of tea. Simple, repetitive activities can be dignified, sacralized even, by ritualizing them. Thus the Japanese tea ceremony became a profound formality after it was influenced by Zen in the fifteenth century.

The thought of a ritualized planting ceremony occurred to me again in 1991 while I was planting my own garden. My notebook tells me that on April 25 I put in three rows of Little Marvel peas, two rows of Boston lettuce, two rows of radishes, one row of escarole and two rows of mustard greens. This information is followed by a reflection:

> The Spirit Garden would have to be a work in stages, corresponding to the planting times of each type of vegetable. Maybe they could be gathered into two or three groups. Each stage would comprise the following activities:
>
> 1. Raking the garden. Raking song.
> 2. Preparation of the rows; making the seed beds by hand or with a trowel. Invocation to the planters to prepare the bed carefully.
> 3. Arrival of the Seed Spirits in costume with music.
> 4. Dance of the Seed Spirits.
> 5. Distribution of the seeds to the planters.
> 6. Planting the seeds and covering them.
> 7. The watering ceremony.
> 8. Invocation to the sun to make the garden prosper.

I mention this entry to show that The Spirit Garden came into existence through the activity of gardening. It was never a rationalized construction. Other diary entries record my research into the subject. This, from March 1993:

> In between lectures and work of all kinds, I've been researching The Spirit Garden, a work I want to begin to develop seriously. My aim, to be naively conscious (rather than consciously naive) has taken me back to the vegetation rituals discussed in Frazer and Eliade, where nature's sexuality is revealed, admired and personified in myths of divine lovers: Adonis and Aphrodite, Tamuz (Dumuzi) and Ishtar, Attis and Cybele, etc.

These parallel stories dominated mythologies and religions from Babylon to Rome. In all cases it is the male lover who dies to be mourned and resurrected by his female partner. When Tamuz died and went to 'the house of darkness,' Ishtar, the great Babylonian Mother Goddess, went in search of him. While she was absent, passion, love and all the reproductive energies of nature ceased on earth. Adonis died a violent death, killed by a wild boar the legend says, which may be understood as a subrogation for the violent destruction of corn by the sickle in late summer, the rime of his festival in Western Asia. Attis was a shepherd or herdsman who was loved by Cybele, goddess of fertility in Phrygia. There were two legends concerning his death: in one he was killed by a boar, like Adonis; in the other he castrated himself under a pine tree, into which he changed after he bled to death. In imitation of the deity, the priests of Attis castrated themselves in Roman times. To an extent, all vegetation myths hint at emasculation. Even the killing of the hunter by the hunted animal contains a suggestion of this.

It would be too simple to characterize the killing of animals as masculine and the raising of crops as feminine, even though in many societies men are the hunters and women are the gardeners. Where I live in rural Ontario, the men still attend to the animals (now domesticated) while the women weed the vegetables. But has anyone suggested that a carnivorous society is a masculine society whereas the swing towards vegetarian diets might be considered a shift towards a female-dominant, earth-centred society? All these thoughts circulated in my mind as I prepared to write *The Spirit Garden*.

*The Spirit Garden* celebrates the cycle of planting and harvesting – birth, maturing, death and rebirth. The cycle is recurrent but not progressive. No point in this cycle is beginning or middle or end in an absolute sense. Everything is in motion towards another state. As with water, never dying but progressing through endless transformations, the garden sustains the notion of reincarnation and to every gardener this is both evident and inspiring, perhaps especially now since humanity has traded or is trading its identification with nature's biorhythms for faith in a mechanical world, where life pulses with a different rhythm energy, a relentless future-mad acceleration in search of money and productivity. It is largely an urban attitude, for it is in cities that the triumphs of human engineering are most conspicuous. In the centre of the city almost everything you look at is man-made. The lines are straight and the angles perpendicular, unlike anything in nature, and the only things growing there are the profits or the debts.

But what happens if we lose our appetite for this kind of progress? Can nature's biorhythms be rediscovered? It goes without saying that if sufficient numbers of people could be persuaded to rediscover them and celebrate them, the quality and taste of the food we eat would be vastly improved. Nature is not a series of agronometric calculations or agrobusiness strategies; it is the result of forces we will never completely understand that can work for or against us. Plants live or die as a result of these forces and not by so many kilos of potash flung at them by the passing tractor, or by trucks carting them to customers half a continent away.

To redeem the garden as a philosophy of life it is not enough merely to go about attacking weeds with a hoe. We have to believe in the garden with the faith of ancient myths, with the faith of a child who believes that the doll to whom she speaks is real and must accompany her to bed or at mealtime in order for the world to be sustained. That is, we must believe in order to prevent disbelief.

*The Spirit Garden* is propaganda for nature by putting the audience back into a natural setting, a garden, which they must prepare, plant, care for and harvest over a season, encouraged by two rituals: the first during the planting season, and the second after the harvest. The work is consciously naive, a pageant of colour, costume, movement, music and speechifying to illustrate the perdurable myth of the birth, death and rebirth of plant life — the so called Corn Goddess myth. It is an antitoxin against the plastic doll, against video games, against packaged entertainment and all the other filth of our surrogate civilization.

## The Garden

The stage for *The Spirit Garden* is a real garden and it has to be planned with care. To harmonize with references in this and other *Patria* works, a garden respecting the double quaternity symbol (either embracing eight sides or eight points) is obligatory. The space also needs to be divided into a playing area and a planting area, since both are equally important. Opposite is Ann Schau's design for the Ottawa garden (1996).

Here we see eight planting areas on the perimeter and eight smaller areas between the stone pathways at the centre. To correspond with this the audience will be divided into eight Seed Groups. The selection of the eight seeds to be planted will depend on the soil and the length of the growing season.

All the aisles, as well as the stone pathways, will be used by the actors and musicians at various times, and may also be used by the Gardeners and members of the Seed Groups during the Raking, Planting and Watering Ceremonies. At other times the audience and performers will stand or sit on the perimeter of the garden area.

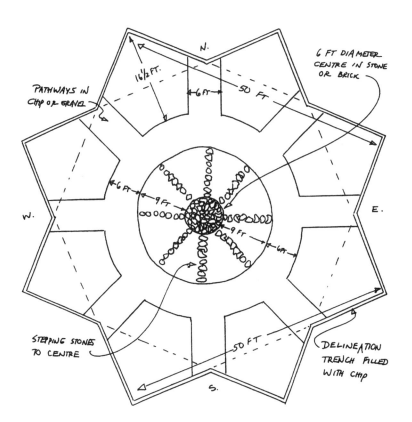

N.

6 FT DIA METER
CENTRE IN STONE
OR BRICK

16½ FT.

PATHWAYS IN
CHIP OR GRAVEL

6 FT

50 FT

6 FT

9 FT

W.

E.

9 FT

6 FT

STEPPING STONES
TO CENTRE

50 FT

DELINEATION
TRENCH FILLED
WITH CHIP

S.

Rohahes (Iain Phillips) entreats the gardeners to be kind to the land, at the opening of *Patria 10: The Spirit Garden.*

## Preparation

The real work of preparing the garden is done long before the date of the performance by the Gardeners. The Gardeners may also be responsible for the induction of the Seed Groups, though this could also be the responsibility of others in the cast. The idea is that the audience, or at least some members of the audience, may become involved with *The Spirit Garden* before the planting date just as the Gardeners and performers are. For one thing they could make costumes representing the flowers and vegetables they will be personifying. Other visual indicators such as head bands, necklaces or decals, to be worn by all members of each Seed Group, could be made in advance. Each Seed Group will also require a large emblem, mounted on a pole, to serve as a rallying point for their 'clan.' They could also construct one or several scarecrows, since scarecrows are actually mounted in the Spirit Garden during the performance to frighten away the birds. Each Seed Group also requires a Spirit House to protect their seeds while they grow. These are also ceremoniously brought in and placed in the garden during the performance.[1]

---

1  Just as temples and churches are protected by lions, griffins and gargoyles, our garden requires similar treatment, but I wanted children to create these Spirit Houses, filling them with poems and drawings to frighten away potential robbers of the seeds and plants. This wish has been followed in each production of the work to date.

Of course all these things could be designed and executed by professionals, just as the garden could have been prepared by engineers and could be planted by tractor...

The leaders of each Seed Group are also required to prepare a song, a dance or a story (or a combination of all three) illustrating the history, mythology or botanical peculiarities of their chosen plant. After the audience assembles and is divided into Seed Groups they will be given fifteen or twenty minutes to listen to the story and learn the song, which may be sung again during the actual planting.

Example of a story, told by the zucchini Seed Group:

> One day a young woman was abducted and murdered in the forest. Her body sank into the earth and was reborn as a beautiful tree. A logger was sent out to cut the tree down, but as he raised his chainsaw he heard a voice in the tree cry: 'Stop! Don't rape me again!' But the logger only laughed and he cut down the tree. The wood was of exceptional quality, and eventually it fell into the hands of an instrument maker, who used it to make a beautiful oboe. He sold it to a musician and whenever he played it he heard the woman's voice deep within the wood of the instrument. One day the woman came out of the instrument and married the oboist. They were very happy together but they never had children because the woman could not conceive. That is when I appeared selling zucchini seeds. Nine months later the woman had twins, a boy and a girl. Now the whole family makes music together and here they are to do just that as a demonstration of the effectiveness of the zucchini in bringing joy and productivity into the world.[2]

Much could be made of folk customs relating to different seeds. For instance, before planting carrot seed, a handful of camphor should be sprinkled over the soil to protect the seed from the carrot fly. Beans are sown in mats of hair and a story could be invented to explain why. Garlic should be bruised before planting: 'Bruise me, abuse me, I am used to it!' Olive stones are set around each plant to stimulate its growth. Flowers

---

2   Adapted from a Santali folk tale, see: Mircea Eliade, *Patterns in Comparative Religion*, New York, 1963. 'A human life which has been abruptly cut off is carried on in a plant; the latter, in its turn, if it is cut or burnt, gives birth to an animal or another plant which eventually finds human form once more.' (p. 301 ff)

such as delphiniums, hollyhocks and sunflowers should be doused with beer after planting, and should be given weekly infusions afterwards.

Old books on garden lore are full of such tips and traditions as are anthropological studies of vegetation rituals from around the world. The point is not to encourage thoughtless planting, but to stimulate a recognition of the magical and spiritual powers of seeds and plants and to encourage each Seed Group to discover and celebrate this potential.[3]

## *The Performance of the Spring Section*

Following the preparation, the Seed Group audience is welcomed by the Hierophant (a carryover from *Ra*) and the King (the same impotent King from the alchemists' experiments in *Hermes Trismegistos*). The King commends the participants for having discovered agriculture because unlike other cultural endeavours it doesn't cost him anything. He even promises to attend a banquet at which the garden produce will be consumed in the fall. In fact, his barren Queen will become pregnant as a result of his introduction to the fertility rituals of nature, a fact that will be made evident at the banquet.

The Hierophant leads everyone joyfully towards the garden, near which they meet the Corn Mothers, just aroused from their winter sleep by the Mistress of the Planting. The Corn Mothers distribute the seeds to the appropriate groups and all process into the garden to the sound of an orchestral fanfare.

The Mistress of the Planting calls for the Spring Child to appear, but it is too soon, for the sun has not yet warmed the earth; so the Hierophant invokes the sun in a text derived in part from the beautiful Hymn to the Sun (Aton) from the time of Akhenaten (1379-62 B.C.).[4] This is followed by the raking of the garden in which the audience participates while a choir of children sing a Raking Song: 'Earth, feel our moving feet and be fruitful!'

Simple as the song may be, its origins are profound. In both Latin and Chinese, the sole of the foot is semantically related to the word 'planting' – later becoming 'season.' Thus we have an earth's-eye view of the planting ritual. The earth hears and feels the moving feet above it and knows that soon it will be called on to be productive.

---

3   Two books I have found especially helpful are Sir James Frazer's *The Golden Bough*, London, 1954; and Mircea Eliade's *Patterns in Comparative Religion*, New York, 1963. Both have extensive sections on vegetation rituals.

4   My source was 'The Hymn to Aton' in *The Ancient New East (An Anthology of Texts)*, ed. James B. Pritchard, Princeton University Press, New Jersey, 1958, p. 369 ff.

The soil is raked by the audience during a performance of *Patria 10: The Spirit Garden* at St. Norbert Arts and Culture Centre, Winnipeg, May, 2001.

I follow this with the appearance of a vulgar figure called Baloom. The prototype of Baloom is Baal (or Moloch) the ancient Semitic god of fertility to whom children were sometimes sacrificed. Flaubert has described this infanticide vividly in *Salammbô*, and I once stayed in a hotel owned by a Jehovah's Witness in rural Sweden who quoted me chapter and verse where the atrocity is described in the Bible, but I was never able to locate it. The general tendency for history's most vulgar heroes is to become comic, and Baloom is no exception. I make him a carnivore: 'Meat eater, devourer of children! … big beefy man with big fat feet, the enemy of gardens!'

Baloom is chased away by the Gardeners to be followed by Doktor Humus, a more equivocal character, who emerges from a dung heap to pontificate on the virtues of fertilizers, both ancient and modern. The ancient world used dung, and while there may sometimes have been a choice, frequently there was not; while today's fertilizer recipes are so varied that like everything else in our society the whole subject has degenerated into a fashion industry. Now, of course, we live in the era of genetically engineered food, and Dr. Humus is all for it. In the end he is chased away.

The children's choir calls the Spring Child a second time and now she appears. The text of her aria is derived in part from a hymn to Inanna

(Ishtar), who was goddess of both fertility and warfare.[5] It is the vibrant earth the child will soon become who sings; and the part is therefore performed by an adult.

I am the child of spring.
Awakened by your singing,
I have arrived to sing my own song for you,
the song of my victorious ascension!

My mother gives me the earth.
Queenship she gives me.
She sets the green sandals on my feet,
and wraps a green robe about my body.
Food she gives me from the soil,
and water from rain.
She promises to prolong the summer
so that I may grow strong.
My father gives me the heavens.
He sets the crown of stars on my head
as a sign of my authority.
He gives me all living things,
all creatures of earth and all birds of the sky.
He gives me the passion of the wind,
and the violent motion of the storm
to embrace me as a lover.

I am the child of spring!
Growing in the fields.
Let me be seeded now,
let me be caressed to my bliss
in the moist earth of the new year!

The Spring Child's aria is followed immediately by a 'Rites of Spring' dance, chanted and performed by the adult choir of Spring Bringers.

Now the Seed Groups step forward to plant their seeds, perhaps singing their own songs, as mentioned before. When the planting is finished, the Spirit Houses are ceremoniously brought in and placed at the top of each garden bed.

---

5   See: Thorkild Jacobsen, *The Treasures of Darkness* (*A History of Mesopotamian Religion*), Yale University Press, New Haven, 1976, p. 138.

After the performance, the gardeners will tend *The Spirit Garden* all summer to provide food for the banquet during the harvest section of the work.

The Mistress of the Planting invokes the rain to come and germinate the seeds.

Thunder men descend!
Beat your skittles to bring the rain!
Let the dancing feet begin!

The Thunder Men enter and dance to rhythmic drumming while the members of the audience are invited to water the seed beds.

Bird dancers arrive. At first the mood is happy but soon becomes rowdy as the birds begin to peck the seeds out of the garden. At this point the King offers a prize for the best scarecrow to frighten away the birds. Two of the scarecrows are alive and engage in conversation, making an amusing case for themselves as philosophers. 'How would it be possible to live here and not reflect on life!' In fact, they give a very sensible account of the joys of meditation in a natural environment.

The garden is now handed over to the Gardeners to care for it all summer and the first part of *The Spirit Garden* closes with a Hoop Dance in which the full cast and audience participate, leaping to show how high they want the plants to grow.

# Harvest

When I was young, Thanksgiving was a prayer and a gobble. Today it's just a gobble. Probably it's impossible for anyone who does not live with the agrarian calendar to appreciate the miracle of food; and the consumption of food without the work of producing it will always be a stolen pleasure. In wealthy countries, where food is stockpiled, overconsumed, or goes to waste, food production is scarcely appreciated. Only the gardener knows that tomatoes or apples produced a thousand miles away in another bioregion never taste as good as those freshly picked at home. When the naturopath says, eat only organically produced food grown in your own region, the intention is nutritional; but uncalculated benefits accrue on other fronts as well. Local employment is stimulated and with it a mistrust of foreign imports of all kinds – including culture.

*The Spirit Garden* is a celebration of local culture in both food and art. The few hundred people who ceremoniously planted and tended the garden during the first production of *The Spirit Garden* in Ottawa gained, or should have gained, a greater self-respect by doing so. Perhaps some of them even sensed a sacredness in celebration.

Thanksgiving Day in Canada is held on or around October 12. (In the generally warmer USA it is held on or around November 26.) By this time the produce has been stored or preserved for the winter. Actually there is no single date when the garden is emptied, so any date chosen to celebrate Nature's gift is arbitrary.

For the Harvest Section I chose Allhallowmas Eve, better known as Hallowe'en, October 31. The Celtic new year, from which this celebration is derived, began on November 1, and was a fire festival.[6] Then all fires were extinguished and the Hallow fires were kindled from consecrated wood and carried to the homes and farms. 'Down to about the middle of the nineteenth century, the Braemar highlanders made a circuit of the fields with lighted torches at Halloween, to ward off all evil spirits and to ensure fertility during the coming year ... By this fire ritual, the fields were both purified and fertilized.'[7]

I immediately realized that this Celtic practice could be applied to *The Spirit Garden*. The Garden could be razed to the ground; the ashes would purify and fertilize it for next spring. The ceremony need not be long, less than half the duration of the Spring Section. It would be conducted at night and followed by the banquet promised by the King.

6   See: F. Marian McNeill, The Silver Bough, Glasgow, 1957, 4 vols., vol.1, p. 15.
7   J.M. McPherson, Primitive Beliefs in the North-East of Scotland, London, 1929, p. 8.

## The Performance of the Harvest Section

The audience is led to the garden in a solemn procession by torchlight, bearing the effigy of the Corn Goddess, in whose womb lies the Green Doll, next year's Spring Child. While the Fire Keepers mark out the eight points of the garden with their torches, the Hierophant recalls the glorious days of spring and summer. The chorus replies: 'From her highest glory she descended wailing ... into death.'[8]

The Master of the Fires, a dark and swarthy figure, carrying the three-pronged stick of Shapeshifter, whose substance is fire, informs the King that all is prepared for the ritual burning. A birch log, smeared with wolf blood, has been placed on the pyre at the centre of the garden. This allusion to *Patria 9: The Enchanted Forest* is amplified by a significant detail when the Master of the Fires tells us that following her incarnation as a birch tree, Ariane has been restored to womanhood and has returned from the forest with a child.[9] The ritual log celebrates the miraculous meeting of Ariana and Wolf in the forest long ago.

The King responds with an ancient memory of his own, a dream in which he was being burned alive by alchemists but is miraculously saved by the cool, moist body of a woman. The King then is the same as in *Patria 4: The Black Theatre*. There follows almost a repeat of the Scarlet Mass scene from that work at the climax of which the fire is ignited.

The Corn Mothers rush forward to save the Green Doll from the womb of the Corn Goddess effigy before it catches fire, proclaiming 'The Spring begins!'

Now effigies of devils and evil spirits representing the sins of the old year (made by members of the audience) are thrown into the fire to the beating of drums, while the whole audience performs a snake dance around the garden, circulating clockwise then counterclockwise and chanting:

> Around the fire we twist and turn!
> Devils burn! Devils burn!

---

8 The text of the chant is partly derived from a Mesopotamian hymn to Innana (Ishtar), who descended each fall into hell in search of Dumuzi.
9 Ariane's metamorphosis from tree numen to Corn Goddess to Spring Child to Earth Mother constitutes her final and most significant cycle of transformations on earth, prior to her departure to the heavens from which she originally descended.

The dancing is interrupted by the arrival of Winter, accompanied by the Four Winds. In his company are also the Poorlings, dressed in ragged clothes and carrying tin cups. While Winter proclaims his authority, the Poorlings move through the audience, plucking at them and shaking their cups. On signals from Winter the Four Winds will hurl clods of earth on the embers of the fire, extinguishing it.

The King acknowledges the authority of Winter and invites everyone, including the Poorlings, to the promised banquet. All exit to a solemn fanfare leaving the Master of the Fires who rakes the ashes into the earth.

## The Banquet

For the banquet I want to create a work combining culinary delights with exquisite performance vignettes. In the article on *Patria 1* I described a banquet celebrating the marriage of Philip the Good to Isabella of Portugal in 1454. I attach a sketch I made from the description of that banquet, showing an incredible array of musical and theatrical events, some originating at various points in the hall, some itinerant between the tables of the seated guests, which I've not shown. (see page 247.)

It's something like this that I have in mind, perhaps reintroducing some of the more memorable *Patria* characters: Sam Galuppi as Master of Ceremonies, the White Stag singing Machaut's 'Mon fin est mon commencement,' Zip the Idiot in a cookie jar, Beauty riding the Beast who cries out against cruelty to animals, Mimi Mippopolous the bearded soprano singing the Barber of Seville, Melusina swinging her tail from a castle tower, Nobert Pivnik and his brethren singing hymns in a giant pastry, and so on, and so on.

No, not so disorganized as that. Even disorders need recipes. Perhaps the meal should be prepared according to the tetrad of opposites: dry, moist, hot, cold; or sweet, salty, sour, bitter (approximately speaking) with a sequence of performance events paralleling or counterpointing the same sensations.

Years ago I asked a class of graduate music students to imagine a banquet in which each course was to be accompanied by a specific piece of music and to explain why the recipe and the music belonged together. I was trying to get them to relate music laterally to other subjects, something music students rarely do. We chose the most inspired suggestions and created an elaborate menu. The final assignment was to prepare and serve the dinner while the music was played live. Silence was observed while eating and listening; but when the music was over and the plates were collected, the guests relaxed and talked until a little bell signalled the beginning of the next course.

Naturally you don't get three hundred people to engage in a routine like that, but there must be some curve irrefutably relating attention to relaxation: moments of surprise; moments when we all bite into some delicacy together (as we did at the Celestial Harmony banquet in *Patria 8*) or lift our glasses in unison, as well as unctuously magnificent moments when the Queen's pregnancy is announced or the Hierophant is suddenly heard to sing like Nat King Cole.

A. CITY GATES

CHOIR

120 SILVER TRUMPETS

B. BANQUET HALL

① ① ⓐ CHURCH BELL

ⓒ PISSING BOY

② ③ ④ ⓑ 4 SINGERS & ORGAN

⑰ GIANT, ELEPHANT & SINGING NUN

⑯ CHURCH GROUP & PIE GROUP ALTERNATE

ⓓ TROPICAL FOREST & ANIMALS

⑬ DUET BETWEEN CHILD & STAG. "JE NE VIS ONCQUES LA PAROLLE"

⑫ CHURCH GROUP & PIE GROUP ALTERNATE 4 TIMES

ⓓ PIE WITH 28 MUSICIANS
③ BAGPIPE
⑥ GERMAN CORNET
DOUCAINE (2 INSTRUMENTS)
② 2 HURDY-GURDYS
3 SINGERS - "SAUVEGARDE DE MA VIE"
⑤ LUTE & 2 SINGERS

ⓕ WINDMILL

④ HORSE & 2 TRUMPETERS

⑨ TIGER, SERPENT & CAMEL

ⓔ CASTLE WITH MELUSINA THE SERPENT & FOUNTAINS

⑧ 4 TRUMPETS, JASON & THE DRAGON

# Patria: *Epilogue*
# *And Wolf Shall Inherit the Moon*

*Composed:* 1983 ...

*Cast:* 64 adult members (plus several young people and children).

*Duration:* 7 days.

*Performance:* Annually since 1988.

> Humanity is not the supreme triumph of nature
> but rather an element in a supreme activity called life.

A WEEK-LONG RITUAL-DRAMA, *And Wolf Shall Inherit the Moon* is performed annually in the forest by a group of people who camp there. Its purpose is to reunite Wolf and the Princess of the Stars and thus save the world from destruction.

We read that Charles Fourier, the French social theorist who believed that society would be improved if reconstructed according to communal aspirations, announced to the public that he would be at home at noon each day, to discuss his projects with anyone interested in helping him to realize them, but that while he observed his promise for ten years, no one appeared. He died in 1837, still firm in faith but deeply disappointed.[1] His ideas survived to influence some notable experiments, among them Brook Farm (1841-47), with Nathaniel Hawthorne and Ralph Waldo Emerson among its original shareholders; and his ideas left an indelible impression on Karl Marx as he struggled towards his own definition of the ideal state.

In 1988, in the *Patriotic News Chronicle*, the ghoulish newspaper programme that accompanied performances of *Patria 3: The Greatest Show*, there was an announcement of a free workshop celebrating a new adventure in communal art "which will be conducted at a remote location." It invited anyone interested to contact me in writing, giving a brief outline of their interests and accomplishments and to await further instructions.

Five people replied and we had our first meeting shortly afterwards at Indian River to begin work on the scenario I had sketched out a few years earlier entitled *And Wolf Shall Inherit the Moon*. I wanted this work to be

---

1 As reported in *To the Finland Station*, Edmund Wilson, New York, 1940, p. 91.

created communally by a group of industrious and committed individuals who shared, or could be persuaded to share, my concern that something profoundly unhealthy had happened to art during our time and who wished to set out on a new course to try to cure it.

My dissatisfaction had been made clear in the Theatre of Confluence articles, and in *The Greatest Show*, where the illusions and self-deceptions of contemporary society were smashed into fragments and dust. Out of this dissatisfaction, which had a parallel in my personal life at the time, I wanted to begin work on a nobler theme, the reconfiguration and apotheosis of the *Patria* cycle. The title *And Wolf Shall Inherit the Moon* was derived from Teutonic mythology, where the giant wolf Fenris devours the sun, bringing about the end of the world. But my Wolf was to be instrumental in initiating a new world, though at the time I had only a vague notion of what form this would take.

During our first two-day meeting in 1989 we fumbled with many ideas. Everyone had read books on mythology and was anxious to talk about them. We also talked about the relationship between art and ritual. We built a medicine wheel out of stones and a corn goddess from corn stalks. We told stories and sang songs and agreed to meet again in a year, somewhere more isolated than my farm. During the year we corresponded regularly and a few new people became interested so that by the summer of 1990, sixteen people camped for five days at Gunn Lake in south-central Ontario.

A few things evolved that year that have remained more or less unchanged since then. We built a prototype of Hatempka's hut and acted out the scene with her (see below), this becoming the first of eight Forest Encounters. We also established the rituals of silence on rising and at the end of the day, though this came about in an unusual way. Some people had stayed up at the campfire rather late one night, drinking beer and disturbing others who had gone to bed. The next day two things were decided: first that we should have silent periods in the Wolf Project and second, that alcohol should be restricted to dinnertime (beer and wine only). This has been the situation ever since.

The silent times frame the day and they are identified by an aubade and nocturne. The aubade is the wake-up call, sung or played at sunrise usually across the lake. We rise and assemble in silence, then greet the sun and the four directions with a simple ritual. The nocturne signals the end of the day, and occurs when the campfire dies to embers. When the notes of the nocturne begin, talking ceases. Then we sit at the campfire silently, departing one by one to go to bed.

This very beautiful experience has introduced me to something I can only refer to as phantom sounds. Sometimes the music of the nocturne seems to remain present long after I know the musician performing it has ceased playing or singing. The sound refuses to disappear, hovers over the lake and is wafted into the forest. It's as if the music belongs to the place, and our playing or singing has released it. Anyone can perform the aubades and nocturnes. Some of them are written and some are improvised. I have written quite a few over the years but have always regarded them as revelations of place rather than personal property.

In 1991 we made the acquaintance of Dr. Peter Schleifenbaum, an ecologically minded forester and owner of the Haliburton Forest and Wild Life Reserve, a 50,000-acre forest spotted with lakes. At the northern extremity of this property, away from all roads and habitation, we began the serious development of *And Wolf Shall Inherit the Moon*. With a permanent home we were able to create campsites, clear trails and situate the Forest Encounters at appropriate sites, more or less along the lines I had first envisioned. The map shows the layout of the project.

I'm not going to say anything more about the history of the Wolf Project (as it has come to be known).[2] As I write it is twelve years old and has evolved to a point where it is completely operational, though in continuous evolution. More to the point would be a description of how the work is structured to show how it differs from a conventional work of theatre or art – and equally from a conventional ritual. Let's assume you are seeking membership in the Wolf Project. Here is the outline guide for new members.

*Equality*

All members of the Wolf Project are equal. No one is encouraged to think his or her contribution is more important than another's. It doesn't matter whether you are a trail-maker, a cook, a musician or dancer. We could not survive without all the various skills and interests of our combined membership. All tasks are shared equally and all are expected to do their part.

---

2  This has been done quite satisfactorily by others. In particular see: Ellen Waterman, *A Documentation and Analysis of Patria, the Epilogue: And Wolf Shall Inherit the Moon*, Ph.D. diss., University of California, San Diego, 1997; and Marisa Trench Oliveira Fonterrada, *O Lobo No Labirinto: uma incursão à obra de Murray Schafer*, Ph.D. diss., Pontificia Universidade Católica de São Paulo, 1996.

## Elders

We attempt to arrive at all major decisions by consensus. When this is not possible or practical, a Council of Elders, consisting of a minimum of five members who have been in the project at least three years, will make deci- sions. The meetings of the Council of Elders are private and their decisions are final.

## Finding Your Place

When you are accepted into the project, you will be assigned to a clan. We encourage clan members to keep in contact with one another throughout the year in order to prepare for the summer. This helps in general orientation and in finding your identity in the project. The more preparation you do throughout the year in anticipation of our summer get-together, the more satisfying the experience will be for you and for all of us.

## Meetings

General meetings will be scheduled each year in different locations in Canada so that all members in the area can meet. These are usually followed by a potluck dinner. There will be a two-day meeting every June in the Peterborough area, Ontario, at which final plans will be drawn up for the summer. The project will always take place during the third week of August: we move in on the Friday before and move out eight days later, on Saturday. As the campsites are remote, an entire day will be required for the move in and another for the move out.

## Equipment

We provide all food, cooking utensils, canoes, etc., though we strongly encourage members to bring a canoe if they have one. You will be expected to have your own camping equipment: tent, sleeping bag, etc.

## Finance

The Wolf Project is self-sustaining. We do not receive grants and we do not seek them. All costs for the summer are divided equally. At the present time (2002), this amounts to $200 per adult, and $50 per child under thirteen.

We are able to keep the costs low because of the extensive donations of time, energy and money of some members. On becoming a member you will also receive our newsletter, *The Wolfcall*, to help you keep in touch with fellow members.

## Commitment

The Wolf Project is a continuous evolution. Those who have been members for some years know how the project has affected their lives, changed and enriched them, taught them new skills and expanded their horizons as to what art can be and can become (you should talk to them about this). We are looking for members who believe this project can help them to grow as human beings, to become more sensitive to others, to discover the true potentiality of their lives. We are not seeking members who think the project would be a smart career move.

When you join the project, we will assume you are making a commitment to *remain* with us and to grow with us. Of course, no one can be certain how their life will develop, but we want you to know that the role you discover for yourself in the Wolf Project will be *your* role, and no one will take it from you. We will come to depend on you and we want you to depend on us. This means that *any* vacated role puts a hole in the project. After all, if the Wheel of Life and the ritual we perform every day within it has any meaning, it is about sharing and caring for one another and for everything about us. We regard our August meetings as absolutely vital for the success of *And Wolf Shall Inherit the Moon*. This is why we will suspend any member not present during August. Suspended members may re-apply in writing and their requests will be considered by the Council of Elders.

## Ecology and Spiritualism

The Wolf Project is both active and spiritual. To be living in unspoiled nature is very important to us and is a key to understanding the work itself. We respect the environment and try not to damage it. We try to bring in as little foreign material as possible, seeking ways to blend with the environment itself. We also collect trash left by hunters and snowmobilers and remove it. That, too, is part of our commitment.

## Rituals

The spiritual nature of the undertaking has given rise, over the years, to a number of rituals that have been incorporated into the project. When a ritual is satisfying to the majority of the membership, it is incorporated; if it ceases to have significance, it is discarded. These rituals may have a varying intensity of significance for individual members. We do *not* expect every member to participate in every ritual, but we *do* expect every member to know all rituals and to respect those times and places where the rituals occur. We encourage private contemplation of nature as much as any shared expression in the unique environment in which we find ourselves.

## Recreation

All this may sound terribly disciplined to new members, but we want you to know that there are also recreational times (generally after lunch) for swimming, canoeing, contemplating and napping, as well as our working periods together. Once you have understood what is expected of you, you will be free to enjoy a very beautiful and healthy environment.

## How to Become a Member

Anyone seeking membership in the Wolf Project must be sponsored by at least two existing members. They will explain the work to you and answer any questions. They will also be responsible for providing you with the outline and any back copies of *The Wolfcall* you may require. Once you have discussed matters thoroughly with your sponsors, you should write a short letter to our membership secretary. The letter need not be long, but should tell us something of your background and interests. Your application will be considered by the Council of Elders and you will be informed of the outcome as soon as possible. As the full complement of participants in the Wolf Project may not exceed 64 adult members, preference may be given to individuals possessing needed skills. Other applications may be delayed or denied. The Wolf Project does not aim to be exclusive, but our work takes place in a total wilderness area where all trails, campsites and infrastructure must be operated by us and this forces us to be selective in choosing new members likely to make the kind of contribution the project requires.

The limit of sixty-four adult members in eight clans at four campsites conforms to the principle of the double quaternity of all later *Patria* works; but it is also practical because the campsites could not be expanded without severe damage to the environment. A few children and young people attend each year with their parents and are enthusiastic and appreciated participants.

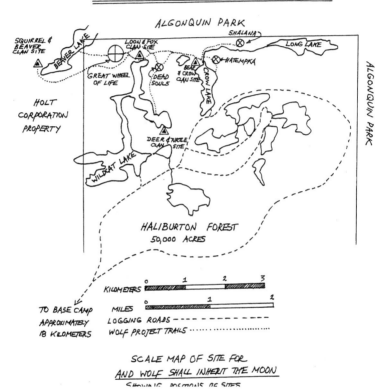

An early idea that an audience would be invited to attend the Great Wheel performance on the final day was abandoned because of the remote location and the difficulty of getting there (logging roads, canoe portages, etc.). Also it could rain; and while we have performed the Great Wheel ritual in pouring rain on more than one occasion, it would be hard to imagine an audience tolerating this or any of the other trials nature occasionally throws up. In this rather fortuitous way, we have solved one of the great problems of artistic performance today: the split between performers and customers. In the Wolf Project everyone is a performer at one time or another and at other times an observer.

The accusation that *And Wolf Shall Inherit the Moon* is private needs no apology. All art is restrictive in one way or another. Sometimes it is restricted by taste and education, more often by money or social status. It is the location of the Wolf Project that limits its membership and therefore the appreciation of its artistic achievements. On the other hand, the privacy of the project has strengthened the sensation, real or illusory, that something profoundly important is being revealed to us through our sustained efforts each summer.

"What is the social significance," asks T.W. Adorno, "of a phenomenon that in fact cannot get through to the public at all?"[3] Of course the answer is that it depends on what you take away with you from the experience. If you have been changed by the experience, your modified attitudes will affect your social encounters. The fact that the Wolf Project has grown to full membership without any attempt to advertise or sell it confirms this. Could "another" Wolf Project be mounted somewhere else? I don't see why not, if there was commitment. It would be different, of course.

A note now about finances. I have always resented the fact that artists in Western society are forced to behave like beggars. The humiliation of chasing patrons, private or public, sustained over a lifetime, ought to be unpardonable, yet few artists stop to consider what flunkies they've made of themselves, unless of course they've got out of the profession or contorted themselves so perversely that they've become fashionably successful. Encouraged by rave reviews of their talent while mere children, many artists decided to remain in that state. Others, wishing for something more, allowed themselves to be trained in our art schools and conservatories for jobs that only marginally exist. The result is that we have many exceptionally well-trained artists in all disciplines, some approaching middle age, with evaporating prospects of employment. The Wolf Project includes several members who have indulged in an *examen de conscience* and have discovered a new outlet for their talents without feeling the necessity of being paid to reveal them.

In fact we all *pay* to be members. We take the expenses as they come and divide them evenly to arrive at the fee. We even have a small fund to help members from great distances with their travel costs. Where else in the world would you have a wilderness lake to yourself with food and companionship for a week at the rates we pay? Of course Haliburton Forest isn't Butlin's Holiday Camp!

---

3  *Introduction to the Sociology of Music*, Theodor W. Adorno, New York, 1976, p. 39. Adorno is talking about "Das Problem des Publikums" since the advent of atonal music in the early twentieth century.

Somewhere Ortega y Gasset spoke of a shipwrecked person flinging his arms about in order not to drown and equated the desperate motion with culture. ART SHOULD BE DANGEROUS! We are talking about transforming lives here, not enchanting boobies. That *ought* to be the difference between art and entertainment, but the two activities have slithered together, or to be more precise, the word *art* has been stolen by the entertainment industry in an attempt to hoist itself into the empyrean. True art aspires to project something not contained in the immediate surroundings, or, at any rate, not immediately perceptible to us. In this sense art is always anti-environment. Entertainment can never be art, because it makes no attempt to make anything perceptible except itself.

The Wolf Project is a heteroclite of irrational forces drawn together because they have been neglected by the great computer. First of all there is the 'problem' of nature, which today is being avoided because it cannot be controlled or tamed. The Wolf symbolizes that irrational force, and the Wolf Project puts us back as miniaturized humans in the great sweep of a nature beyond our control. To the extent that some of us still have an atavistic respect for nature as the all-powerful force that has created and continues to shape us, the work can and will succeed.

I am constantly amazed at the inability of Canadians to prize the one distinguishing feature they still possess in this crazed world, and that is pristine wilderness. At one time they were forced to face it, whether they liked it or not. Susanna Moodie did not like it, as she makes plain in *Roughing It in the Bush,* and eventually deserted the 'dictates of nature' by moving back to town. But others remained, like the Indians before them; the bush got into their genes and was passed on to their children.[4] Somewhere in the head of these descendants you'll still find a thousand acres of wilderness.

You have to see the native Canadian alone against the environment to know what I am talking about here. That original inhabitant lived in isolation; in social settings they appear awkward, ill-fitted, even absurd. The whole that those people were part of was a landscape and a soundscape of forest and prairies, winds and storms, not a bustling metropolis. They appear best when viewed in a special light, at a given moment of the day or year. There is always green or white under foot. They are muscular, these people, but their isolation gives them time for reflection, time to meditate

---

4   My own family (on my mother's side) came to Canada about the same time as Susanna Moodie (circa 1830) and homesteaded in the same area.

on the wonders of the world that spreads around them. Above all, that original Canadian is not talking; conversation seems superfluous and alien. They speak slowly, choosing their words carefully.

Somewhere Marshall McLuhan says that the native Canadian goes out to be alone and comes home to be with others, while the European goes out to be with others and comes home to be alone. Perhaps this explains why most of our members have two or three generations of Canada behind them, though no attempt has been made to recruit or exclude anyone.

What Canada still possesses used to be known in Europe, too, as the mythologies of Russia, Scandinavia, Germany or Britain testify, so that the true spirit of the Kalevala, the Mabinogion or the Eddas can today probably best be experienced in the woodlands of Ontario, and we feel no guilt in borrowing from these mythologies as well as from native Indian myths in amplifying the structure of *And Wolf Shall Inherit the Moon*. Tapio, guardian of the forest in the Kalevala, is an example of one spirit who has migrated to become an important figure in the Wolf Project. Hatempka and Shalana could be of Indian provenance, while the White Stag comes out of the Arthurian tradition, as narrated by Chrétien de Troyes.

In his remarkable book *Mechanization Takes Command*,[5] Siegfried Giedion discusses how people in the Middle Ages used to sit closely packed together on benches, partly, one imagines, to keep warm in winter. At any rate, touching was more common in medieval life, before the individual chair separated humans and privatized existence.[6] When conversations were at a close range and at night, where illumination was feeble, we may assume they developed both a more intimate, confessional character while at the same time they were populated with the mysterious and frightening figures of ghosts and phantoms.

The evening campfires are an important feature of the Wolf Project, stimulating both intimacy and the imagination. Some logs or flat stones, enough for sixteen or twenty people, are arranged around a large firepit, in which a teepee of sticks and birch bark has been arranged. When it is almost dark, the fire ritual is danced and the fire lit. We move close to keep

---

5  *Mechanization Takes Command*, Siegfried Giedion, New York, 1948, p. 262 ff.
6  It is worth remarking that tactile societies tend to emphasize three-dimensional art forms over painting, drawing or printed texts. Architecture, sculpture, masks, costumes, and of course, dance, are the primary means of expression. Similarly, while *And Wolf Shall Inherit the Moon* does exist as a printed text, it is rarely consulted *in situ* nor have its rituals ever been photographed.

warm. The Talking Stick is passed around the circle and each person holding it speaks, tells a story or sings a song.[7]

All the songs sung in the Wolf Project and all the stories told have been created (or plundered) by the members, and all, in one way or another, are emanations of the theme of the project itself. Each clan has its Clan Song and there are rain chants, courage chants, healing chants and even a birthday chant. I wrote some of these in the early years of the project, but numerous other people added copiously to the collection, and most of them are sung at one time or another every night. A statement by a North American Indian, which I have often quoted, is most appropriate here. He said: 'No one in our tribe sings a wrong note.' He didn't mean that everyone had a great voice but that everyone was encouraged to sing without censure.[8]

Stories are told, and are repeated. At first this was difficult to encourage. People who are used to seeing a new movie every day have forgotten the value of repetition, but the child who asks to hear the fairy tale over and over, knowing full well how it will end, instinctively appreciates this value. Surviving the perils of a good story together binds us in a timeless unity.

The campfire is only one place in the Wolf Project where creativity is encouraged. People who never wrote or composed or danced or acted before discover this potential in themselves. The open nature of the Project encourages creativity without in the least abrogating imitation, even theft. Who cares where it comes from; it will become yours eventually. In this sense we are creating a kind of cultural container for all sorts of material, borrowed, original, transduced or stolen. The mature phases of all folk cultures were like this. Then every home prized its own creations: in clothing, in artifacts, in cuisine. All contributions were valued. No one would call these inventions great works of art, but as a cultural force they provided a container in which significant works of art could incubate. So it is with the Wolf Project, and time will be the critic and the editor.[9]

---

7 A Talking Stick is a short, carved stick that can easily be held in the hand and ceremoniously passed. Traditionally only the person holding the Talking Stick is allowed to speak or initiate an activity. One may also just hold it silently.

8 You could call this a form of music therapy, and in fact, one anthropologist has insightfully done so. 'I would hope that music therapy could come to define itself beyond the realm of correcting distortions in individual lives and concern itself with promoting the essential restorative experience of coming to know a musical culture as one's own.' The quote is from Robin Ridington but I have lost the source.

Dear Marisa:

How nice to hear your voice last Sunday at the Wolf meeting. Everyone was delighted to know that you had called to greet us from Brazil!

You ask so many questions. Yes, *Patria* is a quest in search of enlightenment. I am not sure one can use the word *development* here. It sounds too reasonable. This is why I speak of transformation – something beyond the abilities of the mind to manage by itself. It's more like a conversion. This can never be managed by reason. At some point you have to take a *leap of faith*, which is quite absurd but absolutely necessary.

I've often said that the principal characters in *Patria* do *not* develop as might be expected in an ordinary sequence of dramas. As archetypes, they do not change. Ariadne is Ariadne forever; she doesn't evolve into Aphrodite or Athene. And whether he assumes human or animal form Theseus can't change either. He's a heroic beast fighting for survival with a dream of something that might be his reward if he lives long enough. This is why Shapeshifter (Mercurius, Minotaur, Three-Horned Enemy) is so necessary. (S)he is the force of change, stimulating transformation from one state to another.

The hero of every fairy tale is not the protagonist but the fairy. The rats and pumpkin that are transformed into horses and coach precede and are altogether more miraculous than the elevation of a dreaming girl to princess-hood in 'Cinderella.' In *Patria* the fairy is Shapeshifter, the one creature resisting the boredom of habit, constantly twisting and turning to transfigure and renew life, regardless of the consequences.

Mythology provides us with a set of existential proposals in which each position is personified by a god or hero, made large and clear for our benefit. We are ourselves a combination of many of these forces, usually rather muddled together. The

---

9  Need I stress again that not all the members of the Wolf Project would consider themselves artists. And here I am reminded that when Basho wrote the famous collective *renki* 'A Winter Shower' his companion authors were a rice dealer, a lumber merchant, a textile retailer, a physician and a man named Koiki Shohei, of no known profession.

hierophany is enacted so that we can see the consequences of various actions. If the hero kills the dragon, this will happen; if the dragon kills the hero, that will happen. And so the myth lives on in our lives as a kind of instructional paradigm. No myth is dispelled if it teaches us something, and to the extent that we can learn from it, we develop. But the gods and heroes do not develop. They live their exemplary lives, constantly repeating themselves. If they were really alive, they'd die of a cramp. Therefore Wolf and Ariadne are really immune to change, and I'm still not sure whether Wolf's discovery of compassion at the end of the cycle is good or not. Maybe he should just go on ripping up the world until Sun Father, in exasperation at the continual unrest on earth, sends him to the moon to get him out of the way.

Shalana and Hatempka were introduced in an attempt to provide psychological depth to Wolf and Ariadne without altering them. Shalana and Hatempka are human; they have a life history and a repertoire of remembered adventures – but even they are touched by magic – restoring youth to one another with their caresses.

I have always intended the *Patria* cosmology to be a balanced system. Wherever there is a displacement of energy there must be a compensation somewhere. This is why everything potentially can be transformed into everything else. The law of the Conservation of Energy states that in a closed system the amount of energy remains constant but the laws of thermodynamics show how it can be transformed. Of course we would like everything to be transformed for the better so that in the end we'll have a nice tidy system of harmonious forces and happy people. But I'm not sure that the end of *And Wolf Shall Inherit the Moon*, where everything is harmonized for the better, is as effective as the end of *The Greatest Show*, where everything is smashed. That's why I don't see *Patria* as a series but rather as a cycle – a circle in which all segments are simultaneously beginning and ending.

Jung's law of enantiodromia is also important. Everything, when pushed to its extreme, turns into its opposite: courage runs to bestiality, cleverness to craftiness, faith to sophistry, etc. And death runs to life as summer follows winter. The Hunter tries to kill Wolf, but kills himself. Shapeshifter turns him into the White

Stag, who dies to be born as Shalana. Shalana, the wise leader of his people, was once a wild man or a wild animal. At the close of *And Wolf Shall Inherit the Moon* everything is transformed. It is an endorsement of what we are witnessing just by being there in nature. The old Latin text, sung by the White Stag in *The Enchanted Forest*, is the theme here: *cinis sum, cinis terra est; terra dea est; ergo mortuus non sum* (I'm recalling from memory so it may not be quite accurate). "I am ash. Ashes are earth. Earth is the goddess. Therefore I am not dead." That this can be felt much more strongly in nature than in the human-made environment is obvious. Sometimes I've thought that the Wolf Project will only become real when the ashes of a few departed members are scattered at the centre of the Great Wheel of Life. I'm sure you know what I mean...

I've mentioned Shalana, Hatempka, Shapeshifter and the White Stag. Each of these characters will be encountered during the week in Forest Encounters acted out by the different clans, and they will be drawn together on Great Wheel Day, the only day in which all the clans assemble together for the final apotheosis in the Great Wheel of Life.[10]

During the week each clan will undertake several excursions through the forest to special sites where they encounter the above-mentioned and other characters and are given more precise background information about them and how they fit into the total drama. Some of the sites for these encounters are themselves quite dramatic and that of Shalana is actually dangerous. (I'll say it again: Art *should* be dangerous!) Shalana's home is a steep, rocky gorge down which a stream cascades. On entering the precinct of Shalana the visitors are met by Utanda, guardian of the precinct, to whom they must prove their worthiness. Utanda then tells the story of Shalana and his relationship to Hatempka – how they were once the leaders of the human clan, but how Shalana grew angry at the greedy behaviour of the humans and deserted them to live in the forest, where eventually he died. On his death Hatempka took his soul and put it in her medicine bundle to keep until the time when Shalana would be called back by his people; but she raised up the body and left Shalana's voice in it

---

10  While each campsite has its own Wheel of Life, the Great Wheel of Life where all the clans eventually meet is situated in a beaver meadow west of Moose Rock at the north end of Wildcat Lake (see map).

to counsel any visitors seeking advice from the Shining One. With Utanda, the visitors climb the walls of the gorge to the top where a giant stone stands in the centre of what is sometimes a meadow and sometimes a lake (depending on rainfall). The stone speaks and reveals the story of Shalana's journey to Sun Father and the wisdom imparted to him there. The rugged nature of the Shalana encounter is appropriately handled by the Bear Clan.

The Encounter with Hatempka is managed by the Crow Clan. Hatempka lives all alone in a little hut in the centre of the forest. Like Shalana she possesses spirit powers. She is a kind old woman and willingly passes on the advice she receives from the spirit world, but she can be devious if she suspects mischief.

The journey to Hatempka is undertaken alone. Those wishing to visit her are paddled across Crow Lake by canoe to the head of a trail where they are left to find their own way. If they succeed in following the trail and overcoming the challenges or surprises it presents, they will eventually find themselves at her hut where they will be invited in and (some of) the secrets of her Medicine Bundle will be revealed.

Dead Souls is enacted by the Loon Clan in a valley darkened by a dramatic rock escarpment pockmarked with shadows that could be entrances to caves. Here we meet Anubis, guardian of the dead (the alter ego of Wolf from *Patria 6: Ra*); he introduces numerous characters from other *Patria* works (Melusina, the Party Girl, Minos and Pasiphae, etc.) who move about somnambulistically reciting fragments of former speeches from the dark coulisses in which all *Patria* characters reside, waiting to make their reappearance.[11]

We move deeper down the valley, knowing that our next confrontation will be with Shapeshifter, the amoral force of all activity in *Patria*, whose ability to harm or help is symbolized by fire. Shapeshifter is also androgynous and impervious to both passions and remorse. (S)he has no heart. It has been left hidden in the forest, where it is jealously guarded by the Fox Clan. Anyone venturing too close could be burned or wounded, for Shapeshifter needs energy and occasionally returns, accompanied by loud drumming, for infusions from the hidden heart.[12]

---

11  I've often wondered where the characters go at the end of a drama. Dead Souls is a response to that question.

12  My original idea of drawing blood from all members failed with the outbreak of AIDS. Nor have I been successful in pursuading members to accept a small three-pronged burn as a token of the encounter with Shapeshifter, the scrapes, bruises and burns normally accumulated during a week in the wilderness being sufficient reminders for most people of what they have endured. Tiens!

Before the Star Princess's departure to the heavens at the end of the Great Wheel Day ceremony, she gives us one of the eight stars of her crown to keep on earth as an inspiration for the newly born human clan. Henceforth the Corona Borealis (Ariadne's Crown, according to the ancient Greeks) will contain only seven stars, as may be clearly seen shining above Arcturus on clear summer nights.[13] She gives the star to a member of the Turtle Clan, who swims out to receive it from her departing canoe. The Turtle Clan thus becomes the custodian of the sacred rock and our encounter with them focuses on the beauty and wisdom to be derived from stones.[14]

I could go on to describe the other Forest Encounters but enough has been said to indicate the flavour of these very distinctive events, all preparing us in various ways for the Great Wheel Day ceremony on the final day. And what of that? But something holds me back from divulging it. Let me only say that by midafternoon all the clans have assembled in their costumes and masks for the procession over Moose Rock to the decorated Great Wheel of Life for a celebration somewhere between music-drama and ritual lasting until dinner time; then recommencing around the Wildcat Lake campfire and continuing until late into the night when Wolf and the Princess finally depart down the lake to begin their heavenly journey. Then we are left alone for another year.

Of course some people will accuse me of being secretive but 'what one cannot speak about we must pass over in silence.'[15] We live in an era in which withholding anything from the public, whether they are inquisitive about it or not, is almost considered a crime. Yet many things are withheld

---

13  According to ancient Greek tradition, the garland Ariadne wore at her wedding with Dionysus (Bacchus) was transformed at her death into the Corona Borealis, known as the Crown of Ariadne. Dante alludes to the tradition in Canto 13 of *Paradiso*.

14  The rock presented to the swimming turtle is actually a piece of tektite, donated by Mikkel Schau, a geologist and member of the Project. "Tektites are bits of glass with an unusual composition. The favoured explanation of their formation is that they are parts of glass droplets formed when an asteroid hit the earth and melted part of the target rock in the resulting impact. The glass then moved along a parabolic path from the earth into outer space and back to earth again, falling in what are called strew fields" (Schau). The actual tektite piece possessed by the Turtles is not, however, from Haliburton but was found in the Philippines.

15  The final sentence of Ludwig Wittgenstein's *Tractatus Logico-Philosophicus*, London, 1921, p. 151. As far as the drama goes, Ellen Waterman has accurately described it in her thesis (see footnote 2) but there is so much more that cannot be communicated.

and with good reason. The average person is not permitted into the operating room of a hospital during a heart transplant; nor permitted to sit next to the pilot landing a passenger jet; nor is he given a free hour on television to tell us what he thinks of himself or the world.

As a matter of fact a few fugitive attempts have been made to take portions of the Wolf Project and present them in more accessible locations, theatres or urban parks, but none successfully, in my opinion. The work was intended to be site-specific and the locations for Forest Encounters and the Great Wheel ceremony were hunted out over several years so that the activities they contain are partly or largely evoked by their settings, thus rendering them essentially non-transferable.[16]

There is, or used to be, a custom of sending a native Indian boy into the forest at the age of twelve for several weeks or months to live alone. Perhaps he took a few tools. He would have to learn how to live with the elements, learn how to use water, the barks of different trees, as well as plants and roots in order to survive in isolation. The animals would feed and clothe him. He would learn to converse with them. An animal would present himself to the boy but only if he had developed sufficient peace within himself and had got rid of all panic. The animal became his spiritual power. The longer he stayed and learned the animal's language, the more power would be gained. If he stayed long enough, the animal would teach him a song. Each time an animal came and taught him a song the young man was said to have received a *snam*, a degree of harmony with nature. When he came back, the youth would sing the song or songs at festivals and ceremonies. Nobody else could ever sing it unless he willed it to them when his strength was waning in later years. But while it was a great honour to inherit a song, it was no substitute for power personally gained.

Such a strenuous experience would not be possible for the cosmopolitan population of today, but the Wolf Project offers a collective outing that helps make it possible for us to appreciate its value – and within our membership there have been individuals who have experimented with passing at least one night camping alone in the wilderness without food or tent. We can never really know what psychological value an experience of

---

16 While no deliberate attempt has been made to create "secret" music, some of the Wolf Project pieces are so site-specific that they could never work elsewhere (for instance, Shalana's music in the gorge). All ritual music in any culture has its specific time and place of performance, so I think it best to leave all Wolf music where it originated until it is required again.

this kind has for the individual because, as Jung says, we can't weigh or measure it.

For the remainder, or at least those who have remained with the Project over several years, we are trying to set the conditions that might be favourable to personal growth and transformation. This in itself is difficult enough during a time of novophilia when new experiences are so numerous and appealing. Loyalty to a cause without the imposition of penalty is difficult to maintain. When services are voluntary it is impossible to get tough with cavalier behaviour, and the work must evolve at its own pace in whatever ways the faithful think are possible.

'To assist Wolf on his way,' says a note in my diary from 1980, 'we will perform the ritual annually and without fail, lest without our prayers and assistance he lose his way and fail in his mission.'

If there is an end to the Wolf Project for me, it will come when I can no longer manage the experience physically. And what then? Will others carry on or will the entire work pass into oblivion?

They say that the deserted fields of Elysium celebrate themselves. In the shadow world of *And Wolf Shall Inherit the Moon*, the Princess will still sing across the water while Wolf prowls the forest... They will meet, unite and rise into the night sky as they have always done.

# Appendix 1: *Some Character Relationships in* Patria

THE FOLLOWING DIAGRAM presents some of the character relationships in the *Patria* cycle. The principal figures returning in the various works are archetypal; like all mythological figures they would repeat their roles without change if left alone. The agent of change goes by various names but it is only by this intervention that transformation and the ultimate resolution of the cycle can occur. The number after each name indicates the principal work in which the character can be found.

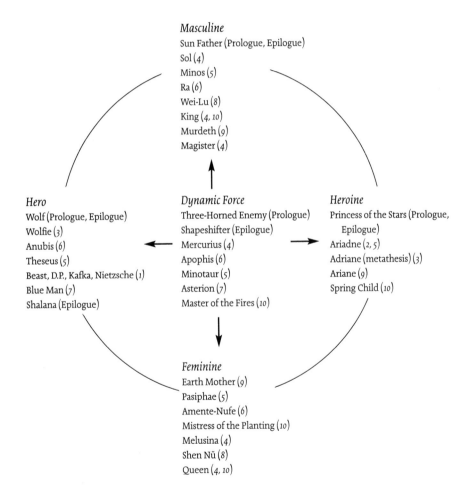

*Masculine*
Sun Father (Prologue, Epilogue)
Sol (4)
Minos (5)
Ra (6)
Wei-Lu (8)
King (4, 10)
Murdeth (9)
Magister (4)

*Hero*
Wolf (Prologue, Epilogue)
Wolfie (3)
Anubis (6)
Theseus (5)
Beast, D.P., Kafka, Nietzsche (1)
Blue Man (7)
Shalana (Epilogue)

*Dynamic Force*
Three-Horned Enemy (Prologue)
Shapeshifter (Epilogue)
Mercurius (4)
Apophis (6)
Minotaur (5)
Asterion (7)
Master of the Fires (10)

*Heroine*
Princess of the Stars (Prologue, Epilogue)
Ariadne (2, 5)
Adriane (metathesis) (3)
Ariane (9)
Spring Child (10)

*Feminine*
Earth Mother (9)
Pasiphae (5)
Amente-Nufe (6)
Mistress of the Planting (10)
Melusina (4)
Shen Nü (8)
Queen (4, 10)

# Appendix II: *Brief Synopsis of the Patria Works*

WHILE THE TWELVE WORKS in the *Patria* cycle are each independent and are not intended for consecutive performance, there is a continuous progression among them so that something like the following structure occurs:

| | |
|---|---|
| *Prologue: Princess of the Stars* | North American wilderness |
| 1. *Wolfman* | Twentieth-century |
| 2. *Requiems for the Party Girl* | urban |
| 3. *The Greatest Show* | North America |
| 4. *The Black Theatre* | Exotic lands, |
| 5. *The Crown of Ariadne* | travelling |
| 6. *Ra* | back in time |
| 7. *Asterion* | Interior voyage, search for self |
| 8. *Cinnabar Phoenix* | Mythical times, |
| 9. *Enchanted Forest* | natural |
| 10. *Spirit Garden* | settings |
| 11. *Epilogue: And Wolf Shall Inherit the Moon* | Return to North American wilderness |

There are many cross-references between works and many of the same characters reappear. The following thumbnail sketch of each work in the cycle may be helpful.

*Prologue:* The Princess of the Stars

In this dawn ritual, the Princess of the Stars falls to earth in a blaze of light before Wolf who lashes out in fear, wounding the Princess. Running to a lake, the Princess is dragged to the bottom by Three-Horned Enemy. Wolf tries unsuccessfully to find and release her. At sunrise the Sun Disc arrives to settle the trouble on earth. He tells Three-Horned Enemy to return the crown of stars to the heavens; but the Princess must remain on earth, assuming the name of Ariadne. Wolf will search for her in order to discover enlightenment. His travels will take him to many lands and will take many centuries to complete. The Dawn Birds are then told to cover the lake with ice and snow until this is achieved.

*Patria 1*: Wolfman

In his first incarnation, we find Wolf in human form as a refugee in a modern country of no name, understanding neither the language nor the social customs. The main interest in this country seems to be earning money, buying consumer products and watching sex films. While other immigrants are able to integrate into the new society, Wolf is not, with the result that he is abused and alienated. Finally, at a party, he sees Ariadne, but she is torn from him before they can meet. Broken and disillusioned, Wolf reverts to animal behaviour by holding a child hostage at knife-point before finally plunging the knife into his own stomach.

*Patria 2*: Requiems for the Party Girl

Here we find Ariadne in a lunatic asylum surrounded by doctors and nurses ostensibly trying to help her, but totally failing to read the secrets of her mind. Ironically, Ariadne is the most intelligible of all the characters, speaking the *lingua materna*, while the doctors speak foreign languages and the inmates speak nonsense. Reference is made to Ariadne's having been held hostage at knife-point as a child; also to encounters with Nietzsche, Mozart, Theseus (all fantasy-transformations of Wolf). Ariadne, in her first earthly transformation, is still a prisoner and in the end she desperately proposes and perhaps commits suicide.

*Patria 3*: The Greatest Show

*The Greatest Show*, as its name implies, is a carnival or fair, performed outdoors at night, consisting of dozens of attractions in various tents and booths. Wolf and Ariadne appear as spectators but the Showman, Sam Galuppi, compels them to volunteer for two magic acts in which Ariadne is chopped into pieces and Wolf is made to disappear. While the police stalk the grounds hunting for Wolf (who is suspected of some unspecified crime) pieces of Ariadne's anatomy begin to appear in some of the side shows. From a burlesque beginning, the show becomes more macabre until the magicians, attempting to reconstitute the hero and heroine, bungle the job and produce Three-Horned Enemy, who destroys the entire fairgrounds.

*Patria 4*: The Black Theatre of Hermes Trismegistos

The theme of *Patria 4* is medieval alchemy. Around the crucible alchemists are attempting to transmute the base metals into their higher, more purified forms of gold and silver. The guiding spirit of the alchemists is Hermes Trismegistos, the father of Hermetic philosophy. The elements are personified as characters and the drama consists of their interaction during the processes of smelting and distillation. Wolf is present as antimony and Ariadne as a volunteer catalyst in the process of the Chymical Marriage, the wedding of Sol and Luna, gold and silver.

 *The Black Theatre* is in a way complementary to *The Greatest Show* but it takes us further, for here the hero and heroine, after a dark ordeal, are given a hint of the perfection to come in the form of the Chymical Marriage.

*Patria 5*: The Crown of Ariadne

*The Crown of Ariadne* takes us back to Crete for a re-enactment of the myth of Theseus (Wolf), Ariadne and Minotaur (Three-Horned Enemy). We are introduced to the brilliant, but declining, matriarchal culture of the Minoans, the legend of the Moon Queen Pasiphae coupling with the bull to produce Minotaur, and the labyrinth Daedalus created for him to live in. Was the Minotaur human, animal or divinity? The Minoans regard him as a new sun, an Asterion, and on the death of Pasiphae prepare the new Moon Queen Ariadne to marry him. But Ariadne falls in love with Theseus, who has been brought as a prisoner to feed the Minotaur, and she gives him the thread by which he may escape the labyrinth. Ariadne also enters the labyrinth to assist her lover. One of the three is killed and two hooded figures escape, set fire to the Palace of Knossos and flee in a ship. We may assume that Theseus and Ariadne have finally been united as lovers, but the work is deliberately inconclusive since the world has not been transformed by their actions but merely destroyed.

*Patria 6*: Ra

This is the story of the death and rebirth of the sun god. The setting is ancient Egypt and the work is based on an Egyptian mortuary text, dating from 1500 B.C. Darkness and light, death and life are the themes of *Ra*, as they are in many of the other *Patria* pieces. The underworld is a dangerous necropolis which even the gods must visit in order to be reborn.

In form, *Ra* is a hierophany or sacred drama lasting ten hours in which the audience, clothed as initiates, are prepared by the priests and then taken to the underworld where Anubis (Wolf) guides them through the corridors of the night. Like Ra, the initiates also pass through darkness to be reborn in the light of the rising sun.

*Patria 7:* Asterion

The set for *Asterion* is a real labyrinth and the initiate undertakes the passage through it alone, meeting various well-known *Patria* figures in its various tunnels and chambers. The passages are arranged in a diminishing series and consist of nine encounters, eight trials, seven experiences, six perceptions, five contemplations, four arcana, three deceptions, a meeting with Theseus and Ariadne, and a final encounter with Minotaur–Asterion.

*Patria 8:* The Palace of the Cinnabar Phoenix

The first of three fabulous works, this one is set in the time of the T'ang Dynasty in China (A.D. 618-907). Each year the Emperor Wei Lu comes to the Lake of Dragons to mourn the loss of the Palace and the Cinnabar Phoenix, sent down by the gods to ensure harmony on earth. But the Warring States, fighting for its possession, caused it to disappear. An Alchemist and his daughter have succeeded in producing a miraculous pair of gold and silver rings that may be useful in recovering the Palace and the Phoenix, but the silver ring has gone missing. A strange Blue Man (Shalana) discovers it on the other side of the world and returns it to the court of T'ang. Together the rings succeed in restoring the Palace and the Phoenix from the depths of the Lake of Dragons. The work is a puppet opera performed by and on and under the water of a large pond.

*Patria 9:* The Enchanted Forest

The audience arrives at sunset at the edge of a forest. They are met by a
group of children who lament the loss of their abducted companion
Ariane. Earth Mother asks the audience to accompany the children into
the forest to search for her. After numerous strange adventures, they eventually meet Murdeth the Wizard, who is keeping Ariane captive, intending
to use her to lure Fenris the Wolf into a trap. Fenris protects the forest, but
Murdeth wants to have it cut down and sold as lumber. With the help of
some fairy spirits, the children manage to foil Murdeth's plan, but in the
course of the action Ariane is transformed into a birch tree. Earth Mother
explains to the children that their soul mate must remain in the forest as a
protection against trees being needlessly destroyed.

*Patria 10:* The Spirit Garden

*The Spirit Garden* is in two parts: Spring and Harvest. The work takes the
form of a ritual planting of a communal garden by the audience. After
ceremonial invocations to the Sun, the Thunder Men and the Seed Spirits,
each member of the audience plants a seed. The spirit of vegetation,
Spring Child (Ariadne), arrives to bless the project.

 The Harvest Section is performed after the garden has fruited. It begins
with a torchlight procession at night, followed by a ritual burning of the
Corn Goddess, but not before the Green Doll of the New Year is saved, and
concludes with the passing of the garden over to Winter and his Four
Winds. The audience then moves indoors for a banquet featuring the
garden produce.

*Epilogue:* And Wolf Shall Inherit the Moon

For the Epilogue of *Patria* we return to the forest where the cycle began.
The production takes the form of an eight-day pilgrimage and ritual celebration by a group of sixty-four people who are simultaneously the
creators, performers and audience. During the final ritual-performance on
the last day, Wolf and Ariadne are apotheosized by Sun Father, Ariadne as
the Princess of the Stars, returning to the heavens to regain her crown
(Corona Borealis), and Wolf departing to inherit the moon.

## In Appreciation

It would be impossible to thank all the people who have contributed to *Patria* productions over the years. The list is long, but I may mention a few people whose involvement has been intense and extensive.

Joe Macerollo and Michael Cumberland have performed in several works and are now also members of the board of Patria Music Theatre Productions. Jerrard and Diana Smith have repeatedly produced wonderful designs and unlike many designers, have stayed around to see them realized. Thom Sokoloski directed and produced many of the early works: *Requiems for the Party Girl*, *The Greatest Show*, *The Black Theatre* and *Ra*. Barry Karp directed *The Enchanted Forest*, *The Spirit Garden*, and is a longstanding member of *And Wolf Shall Inherit the Moon*. Chris Clifford's lighting designs for *Ra*, *Princess of the Stars* and *The Palace of the Cinnabar Phoenix* made audiences gasp.

Among singers, two in particular have captivated audiences over the years. Both Eleanor James and Wendy Humphries have performed the role of Princess in *The Princess of the Stars*, and Wendy has performed the part of the Princess a dozen times in the Patria epilogue, *And Wolf Shall Inherit the Moon*. Eleanor created the roles of Hasroet in *Ra* and Melusina in *The Black Theatre*. And there have been others – Ray Crossman, Tilly Kooyman, Alec Tebbutt, Doug Brown, Don and Bea Quarrie, Marisa Fonterrada, Claire Heistek – and so many others, to whom I will simply say that without your faith and help, the realization of *Patria* would have been impossible.

Set in Cartier Book, a typeface designed by Rod McDonald.
Printed and bound at the Coach House on bpNichol Lane, August, 2002

Edited for the press by Doris Cowan
Cover design by Stan Bevington

Read the online version of this text on our website: www.chbooks.com
Send a request to be included on our e-mailing list: mail@chbooks.com
Call us toll-free: 1 800 367 6360

 Coach House Books
401 Huron Street on bpNichol Lane, Toronto Ontario M5S 2G5